T0354974

PRINCIPLES
OF HUMAN RESOURCE
MANAGEMENT

—————— SECOND EDITION ——————

Rebecca Dei Mensah

authorHOUSE

AuthorHouse™
1663 Liberty Drive
Bloomington, IN 47403
www.authorhouse.com
Phone: 833-262-8899

Published by AuthorHouse 12/30/2020

ISBN: 978-1-6655-0749-3 (sc)
ISBN: 978-1-6655-0748-6 (e)

Print information available on the last page.

This book is printed on acid-free paper.

CONTENTS

Part Four

Methods of Attracting Human Resources

Part Five

Employee Selection and Interviews

Part Six

Rewarding and Retaining Human Resources

Part Seven

Assessing and Developing Adroit Human Resources

Part Eight
Enhancing Employee Relations in Organisations

Part Nine

Improving Employee Health, Safety and Well-being

Part Ten

Employee Retention Strategies

Part Eleven

Importance of Leadership, Teamwork, and Communication in Contemporary Organisations

LIST OF TABLES

LIST OF FIGURES

PREFACE

Globally, organisations today are faced with many Human Resource Management (HRM) challenges. Dramatic changes in both the internal and external environment of companies during the past years has resulted in Human Resource (HR) managers being faced with new and more difficult people management issues such as retention, managing change, health safety and well-being, work-life balance and containing cost. Hence, increasing pressure is being exerted on them, to make a more significant contribution to the success of their companies. Indeed, globalisation and the significance of properly managing employees throughout the world is no doubt becoming challenging.

The changing work environment in the knowledge economy has made human resource management very essential for the attainment of competitive advantage by organisations. As the pace of socio-economic changes continues to accelerate, effective human resource management has become even more critical to the success of organisations. Managing human resources is a very important function in any organisation. This is due to the fact that irrespective of the size or type of business, people are the most important asset of any organisation and there is no doubt that successful management of people with emphasis on their well-being, enhances an organisation's chances of success. Due to its relevance, the effects of HRM practices on employees and organisations have been extensively studied in the recent times.

Organisations today face a lot of competitive challenges, and it is how human resource issues such as recruitment, training. career development, engagement and work-life balance are addressed that will give an organisation a competitive edge. Though it is important to be abreast with issues in one's own country, globalisation and the creation of regional economic blocs requires HR practitioners who are knowledgeable about HR issues worldwide. Accordingly, this book provides the principles of HRM practices from both Ghanaian and international perspectives.

This second edition of the Principles of Human Resource Management which is based on the successful first edition, is practical and very interactive. The overall objective of this edition is to build upon the first edition by adding some useful information to almost all the previous chapters. Also, five new chapters have been added. These are;

- Analysing job requirements
- Job design and the changing nature of work
- Industrial relations in organisations
- Occupational health, safety and employee well-being
- Work-life balance: a retention strategy

This new edition is organised into eleven parts and twenty chapters as outlined below:

- Part one gives an overview of the human resource management environment
- Part two deals with the legal environment of human resource management
- Part three looks at work analysis and job design
- Part four deals with the methods of attracting human resources
- Part five discusses employee selection and interviews
- Part six deals with rewarding human resources
- Part seven focuses on assessing and developing adroit human resources
- Part eight identifies ways of enhancing employee relations in organisations
- Part nine concentrates on ways of improving employee health, safety and well-being

- Part ten deals with employee retention strategies
- Part eleven focuses on the importance of leadership, teamwork, and communication in organisations

This book aims at providing students and other readers with the principles of HRM. It will also make interesting reading to people who are not HR professionals but are interested in the subject. It is expected that readers will understand the historical development of HRM, identify the contemporary challenges of HRM, comprehend the concept and development of equal employment opportunity, plan, develop and manage their careers, analyse the roles and responsibilities of employers and employees on issues relating to sexual harassment in the workplace, understand the importance of leadership, teamwork and communication in organisations, and examine other HR issues such as occupational health safety and well-being, as well as employee work-life balance.

I thank all students and other readers for accepting this book and contributing to its success. I have no doubt that they will appreciate this revised edition even better.

Rebecca Dei Mensah (PhD)
October 2020

ACKNOWLEDGEMENTS

This book would not have been complete without the assistance of others. First of all, I am most grateful to the Almighty God who I draw on every minute of my life and by whose providence I have been able to write this book.

I am also grateful to Prof. Dora Francisca Edu-Buandoh, Prof. Edward Marfo-Yiadom, Prof. Francis Enu-Kwesi, Prof. John Gartchie Gatsi, Prof. (Mrs.) Rosemond Boohene, Prof. Francis Boachie-Mensah, Prof. Siaw Frimpong and Mrs. Mildred Asmah for their support in diverse ways.

I am thankful to all my colleagues especially Dr. (Mrs.) Regina Amoaka-Sakyi, Dr. (Mrs.) Mavis Benneh Mensah, Dr. Dominic Owusu, Mrs. Dorothy Amfo-Antiri, Mrs. Edna Naa Amerley Okorley, and Ms. Gladys Attah-Gyamfi.

To my distinct and teaching assistants, Mr. Jonathan Frank Amoah, Mr, Richard Kofi Boateng, Miss Dorcas Ochil and Miss Justine Eyram Nyadanu I say thank you for your selfless efforts over the years.

My sincerest appreciation to Mr. Anthony Ross, Ms. Rose Sheldon, Ms. Leigh Allen, the editor and all the staff at AuthorHouse Publishing Company for helping me to publish this book.

I also wish to express my profound gratitude to my husband Prof. Ishmael Mensah for his love, encouragement and support throughout the writing of the book. To my children Colin, Carol and Mandy, I say thank you for understanding me when I had so little time to spend with you.

I also owe a debt of gratitude to my parents, Mrs. Mary Dei and my Late Father, Mr. Daniel Dei and all my siblings, Victoria, Christiana, Emmanuel, Mary, Elizabeth and Samuel for helping me in diverse ways to get this far.

Finally, I wish to extend my sincerest gratitude to all the students I have taught over the years.

PART ONE

HUMAN RESOURCE MANAGEMENT ENVIRONMENT

1 AN OVERVIEW OF HUMAN RESOURCE MANAGEMENT

Learning Objectives

After reading this chapter, you should be able to

- Understand the historical development of human resource management
- Define human resource management
- Describe the functions of human resource management
- Know the competencies and responsibilities of human resource managers
- Recognise the consequences of poor management of human resources
- Identify the contemporary challenges of human resource management

Introduction

Human Resource Management (HRM) is very different from personnel management that was prevalent decades ago. The personnel function has undergone a significant change both locally and internationally. Indeed, the management of people have evolved from the crafts system, the scientific management era, the human relations period to the personnel management; at present, what is popularly known as human resource management era has emerged.

Today, HRM is often described as the major factor differentiating successful organisation from unsuccessful ones. People or employees are the most important resource in any organisation. Employees are central to the organisation, and they play a very important role in building a firm's competitive advantage. In today's knowledge-based and competitive business environment, the way in which human resources are managed is seen as an increasingly crucial component in achieving the organisation's goals and objectives.

The effective resourcing of employees and managing them in contemporary organisation has become a critical factor of an organisation's survival as well as its success. In spite of this, research has shown that there is no single prescription or formula in securing employee commitment towards organisational goal. Therefore, to retain committed employees, the resourcing process must be thorough, their performance must be managed, and the right motivation must be given to them. Thus, range of policies must be adopted for recruiting, developing, and rewarding employees. Employees are dynamic; hence, several factors influence different employees. Human Resource (HR) managers must therefore be aware of what positively affects human behaviour at the workplace and adopt such in managing individuals, teams, and the organisation as a whole.

Thus, the success of organisations depends hugely on the knowledge, skills, and abilities of its employees. No matter what strategies an organisation has, it is only its adroit human resources that can help them realise these goals. It is therefore very important that organisations find unique ways of unlocking the potentials of their employees. When the potential and talents of employees are valued and leveraged in the organisation, it is likely that such organisation can have competitive advantage over its competitors. It can also achieve its aim in terms of product quality, high performance, increased productivity, and profitability.

HRM is an indispensable function that focuses on satisfying the needs of individuals at work as well as meeting organisational objectives and goals. When performed effectively, HRM can make the crucial difference between successful and unsuccessful organisations. HRM is currently faced with several challenges including globalisation. HR managers must therefore be competent, impartial, knowledgeable, and trustworthy to conduct their business effectively. Employees are valuable assets of any organisation, and they make tremendous positive impact on organisations. According to Lewis Platt, CEO of Hewlett-Packard, 'Successful companies of the twenty-first century will be those who do the best jobs of capturing, storing and leveraging what their employees know.'

1.1 Historical Development of Human Resource Management

The history of HRM can be traced from 1600, from the crafts system, scientific management age, the period of human relations through to the personnel management era.

1.1.1 Crafts system

People who worked during the 1600s to 1700s were guided by a craft system. These craftsmen included carpenters, masons, and leather workers. Under this system, the production of goods and services were generated by small groups of workers in relatively small workplaces, sometimes in their homes. Work was customised and supervised by a master craftsman. Each master craftsman had several apprentices and journeymen who actually performed the work. Whenever the craftsman retired, the most senior journeyman would normally replace that person. Due to this procedure, there was no confusion about career path and no disputes over wages.

As demand for products increased, the craft system could not keep up. Craftsmen had to hire much more apprentices and journeymen, and their small workplaces became more like small factories. Among other things, both space and speed to produce the needed product gradually became an issue. Just about that same time, machines that could be used to help produce high-quality products much faster than could experience craftsmen were being introduced. These changes led to a new era – the Industrial Revolution.

1.1.2 Scientific management

In the early 1900s, there came about many changes in the workplace. Machines and factory methods were introduced, and this increased production. However, with this increased production came several associated problems. Due to the introduction of machines, several people were required to operate it, and this led to the increase of the number of workers. This new development also forced managers to develop procedures, rules, and regulations in order to control the workers. Some of these regulations required an increase in job specialisation, which led to boredom and monotony. The change was radical; constant supervision and the threat of losing one's job was the order of the day. Specialisation also allowed managers the ability to replace quickly and economically any worker who demanded too much wage or created any other problem. One of the most significant developments which arose during this time was the scientific management process.

The premise of scientific management is that there is one best way to do a job. This one best way will be the cheapest, fastest, and most efficient way to perform the task. While the process may not be the safest or the most humane, it will allow the company to make the most profit. Frederick Taylor, the father of scientific management, spent his career collecting data and analysing the specific motions required to perform various jobs. He would then break the job into specific tasks and refine motions needed to complete the task until it could be refined no more. He would then select, train, and closely monitor workers who performed the tasks. Those workers who were successful – that is, those who followed the orders of management exactly and by doing so significantly increased their production – earned a great deal of money. Those who were not successful had their appointment terminated.

While scientific management did prove to be an effective management tool that increased the productivity of workers, it was criticised for treating the worker like a tool and not like a person. To compensate for this tendency to depersonalise the work environment, welfare secretaries were hired. People in these positions oversaw programmes for the welfare of the employees, such as the installation of libraries and recreational facilities, financial assistance programmes, or medical and health programmes. The welfare programmes were the forerunner of modern-day benefit packages, and the welfare secretary position was the forerunner of the current-day HR manager.

1.1.3 Human relations

The next significant step in the development of human resource occurred in the late 1920s and early 1930s. This period produced the classic Hawthorne studies. Elton Mayo and Fritz Roethlisberger were asked by the Western Electric to determine what could be done to increase the productivity of workers at the Hawthorne Works plant in Chicago. While the researchers were specifically examining the effect lighting had on productivity, their results really had nothing to do with the lighting level. What they concluded was that the human interaction and attention paid to the workers by the researchers caused their productivity to increase. This finding was the first one to indicate that the social factors in the work environment could have a significant effect on the productivity of workers.

Fuelled by the findings of the Hawthorne studies, further research on social factors and how individuals respond to them was undertaken. Results from these studies indicated that the needs of employees must be understood and acted upon by management in order for a worker to be satisfied and productive. Communication between the worker and his or her superior was stressed as was the need for a more participative workplace atmosphere. More often than not, however, these tactics did little to increase a worker's productivity. The idea that a happy worker is a productive worker failed to be proven, and many of the concepts were abandoned.

It is worth noting that the shift to human relations approach was also influenced by the growth of unions the world over. The approach was undoubtedly instrumental in improving the work environment of many workers, but it was unsuccessful in increasing the output of the worker and their job satisfaction. Management fell out of favour with the approach during the 1950s and 1960s.

The human relations approach failed because among other things, it did not consider the fact that individual workers are unique and complex and thus have different wants and values. Another reason why the concept failed was it did not recognise that a human relation is just one of many conditions needed to sustain a high level of employee motivation. Other important issues such as performance management, career development, and job enrichment were ignored. In addition, the approach did not recognise the need for both structure and control of employee behaviour. The important issue of procedures, standards, and rules that guided employees towards the achievement of organisational goals were ignored.

These problems however notwithstanding, today, it is interesting to note that the focus of the human relations era is the backbone of more recent employee involvement programmes that have been found to increase the productivity of workers and increase the profits of organisations that adopt them.

1.1.4 Behavioural science

Expanding on the human relations school of thought of including academic findings from various other disciplines such as psychology, political science, sociology, and biology, the behavioural science era was born. Behavioural science focuses more on the total organisation and less on the individual. It examines how the workplace affects the individual worker and how the individual worker affects the workplace. Some feel that the modern-day fields of organisational behaviour (OB), the study of employee behaviour in an organisation; organisational development (OD), the process of changing employee and organisational attitudes and beliefs; and human resource management (HRM) grew out of the behavioural science era.

1.1.5 Personnel management

Personnel departments began to appear in organisations around the 1940s and were concerned with doing something about conflicts between employees and management. Early personnel administrators were called Welfare Secretaries.

Personnel management (PM) started around the 1950s. It was initially considered as a record-keeping unit, which also coordinated annual company picnics. Its functions are limited and have been described as a management role which deals with recruitment, training, handling the relationship between unions and management, safety, and departure of employees. By 1960–70s, however, it had reached a mature stage. Essentially, PM viewed people or employees as cost that must be reduced. Its role was narrowly viewed as record keeping and management of employee compensation.

During the 1980s, several external factors changed the face of how employees are managed. These factors created a strain on the relationship between employees and their employers and necessitated the need to bring in professional 'people persons' to the handle the work relation. These, among other things, led to the birth of HRM.

1.1.6 Human resource management

The full concept of HRM emerged in the 1980s. This was the time when issues like restructuring, downsizing, mergers, and acquisitions were becoming critical organisational issues. Its legal ramifications, policies, and procedures called for professionalism in the field of people management. By the 1990s, the face of HRM had changed completely; it had become recognised, empowered, and sophisticated to manage diverse employee needs.

Unlike PM, HRM's position is that employees are the most valuable asset in an organisation, and they must be developed and properly maintained to achieve overall organisational objectives and strategy.

According to some writers, there is no significant difference between PM and HRM. For them, it is just an old wine in a new bottle. This assertion is not true because the emphasis and approach of the two are different. With HRM, the emphasis is on treating people as a very important resource. Moreover, the two complementary goals sought in HRM are increased organisational effectiveness and the satisfaction of individual employee needs. Thus, the HRM approach does not see organisational goals and employee needs as exclusive but rather mutual and compatible.

There are some principles underlining the HRM approach which include the following:

- Employees are the key resources in every organisation, and therefore, if they are managed and developed effectively, they are likely to increase an organisation's productivity in the long term.

- A conducive work environment must be created so that employees are able to develop and utilise the skills, knowledge, and abilities they possess to its fullest and to the benefit of them and their organisation.

- Employers must follow legal policies and practises to satisfy the economic and emotional needs of the employees.

1.2 Defining Human Resource Management

HR practices play a key role in attracting, motivating, rewarding, and retaining employees. Like many other terms, various people have defined the subject in different ways including the following.

HRM is the function within an organisation that focuses on recruitment of, management of, and providing direction for the people who work in an organisation. HRM examines what can or should be done to make employees more productive and satisfied. It is the effective management of people at the workplace.

It can be said to be a broad range of specialised functions related to the individual in the workplace. These functions include but are not limited to recruitment and selection, performance appraisal, training, compensation, and many more. It also involves activities undertaken to attract, develop, and maintain an effective workforce within an organisation. Basically, HRM means managing the potentials and capacities in people in order to achieve both the individual and organisational objectives. The potentials and capabilities in peoples are often summarised as their knowledge, skills, abilities, and other characteristics such as their attitudes, discipline, health, and creativity.

Armstrong (2006) sees HRM as a strategic and coherent approach to the management of an organisation's most valued assets: the people working there who individually and collectively contribute to the achievement of its objectives. HRM has to do with policies, practices, and systems that influence employee behaviour, attitudes, and performances. Boone and Kurtz (1996) also define HRM as the process of acquiring, training, developing, motivating and appraising a sufficient quantity of qualified employees to perform the activities necessary to accomplish organisational objectives and developing specific activities and an overall organisational climate to generate maximum worker satisfaction and employee efficiency.

1.3 Why Study Human Resource Management?

Sometime when you come across a book and intend to read it is often normal to wonder how a particular subject relates to your interest or career aspirations. Whether you are a student or already working or you plan to be working in an HR department or not, the study of HRM is very relevant to you provided you intend to work with people or in an organisation. In fact, every aspect of the people who work in an organisation has to do with HRM. For instance, acquiring the requisite staff to work with, designing jobs, developing skilful employees, improving performance as well as compensating employees rightly all fall under HRM.

In addition, to be able to effectively work with other people, it is important to understand how they behave. It is also vital for every prospective employee to have a fair idea of how their recruitment and selection process are undertaken. Studying HRM will also enlighten individuals as to how some global, economic, technological, and legal issues are facilitated so that both employers and employees achieve their goals and interests.

1.4 Functions of Human Resource Management

HRM is a management activity which, among other things, serves the interest of employees, meets the needs of business and management, and harmonises HR strategies with organisational policies, goals, and objectives. It also adds value to businesses and helps employers to gain the commitment of their employees. Figure 1.1 gives a summary of the human resource processes.

There are several functions and activities that relate to HRM. It must, however, be noted that each organisation may perform unique functions since their business activities may vary from one another.

The functions of HRM include but is not limited to the following:

i. Complying with equal employment opportunities or equal opportunity and other employment legislations

ii. Determining knowledge, skills and abilities needed for a job through job analysis

iii. Designing the job description and specifications

iv. Undertaking human resource planning

v. Recruitment and selection of employees

vi. Organising interviews and seeing to the actual placement

vii. Induction and orientation

viii. Training and developing employees

ix. Providing employee compensation, benefit, and motivation

x. Managing the performance of employees including appraisals

xi. Providing coaching and mentoring opportunities for employees

xii. Promoting positive labour relations

xiii. Providing occupational health, safety, and well-being

xiv. Ensuring discipline and providing counselling

xv. Overseeing employee transfers, retirements, demotions, and dismissals

Figure 1.1: The Human Resource Processes

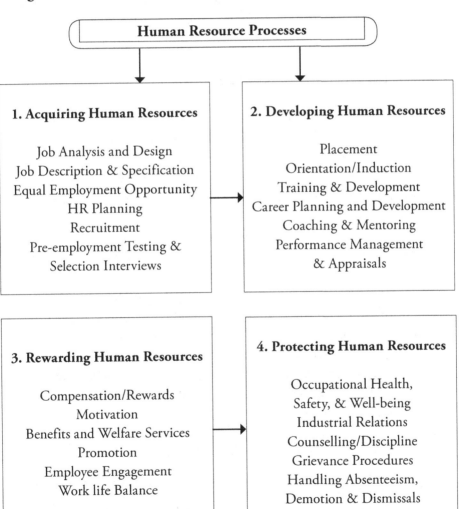

1.5 Importance of HRM in Achieving Organisational Effectiveness

For every organisation to achieve effectiveness, three important elements are needed. These include the organisation's mission, vision, and strategy; the organisational structure; and the management of human resource who will assist the organisation to achieve its objective.

The organisation's mission, vision, and strategy encompass the broad declaration of the organisation's purpose that identifies the organisation's products and customer and distinguishes it from its competitors. It includes the cluster of decisions about what goals to pursue, what actions to take, and how to use resources to achieve goals. These are important factors in any organisation since it defines where the organisation is going.

The organisational structure is also an important feature because it is the formal system of task and reporting relationships that coordinates and motivates organisational members so that they work together to achieve organisational goals. Without a proper structure, there will be chaos, and the smooth running of organisations will be impossible.

Among these three elements, however, it is people who do the work and create ideas that enable an organisation to survive; hence, they are considered the most important of the three. In fact, people are so powerful such that they can limit or enhance the strength and weaknesses of an institution. Human resources are central to building a competitive advantage in the organisation. There is no doubt that for the organisation to remain competitive in today's rapidly growing global market, they need to ensure that their human resources are managed effectively and efficiently. HRM contributes to organisational effectiveness in many ways including the following:

- Helping the organisation to reach its goals

- Employing the skill and abilities of the all employees efficiently

- Providing the organisation with well-trained and well-motivated workers

- Increasing to the fullest, employee's job satisfaction and self-actualisation

- Developing and maintaining a quality of work-life that makes employment in the organisation desirable

- Communicating HRM policies to employees

- Helping to maintain legal, ethical, and socially responsible policies and practices

- Systematically managing change to the mutual benefit of all employees.

1.6 Roles and Responsibilities of Human Resource Managers

Managers in organisations play various critical roles and are assigned specific responsibilities. HR managers usually work hand-in-hand with other line managers; however, their responsibilities are distinctive. Typically, HR managers are responsible for advising and counselling, providing varied services, formulation and implementation of policies as well as advocating for employees.

1.6.1 Advising and counselling employees

HR managers are expected to be knowledgeable about both internal and external issues relating to employment. They act as advisors and counsellors to supervisors, operation managers, as well as the chief executives on employment matters. Thus, they usually provide 'free consultancy' services to almost all categories of employees. HR managers are very helpful when it comes to needing vital information to make informed decision about employment issues.

1.6.2 Providing various human resource services

Moreover, HR managers provide a wide range of human resource services for their organisations. These include recruiting, selecting, orientation, training and development, appraisal, handling complaints, compensation and benefits management, motivation, and many more. Indeed, the various services represent most of the functions of HRM.

1.6.3 Formulation and implementation of policies

HR managers propose and draft human resource policies as well as review existing policies for their organisations. These policies, however, have to be approved by the board and CEO of the organisations concerned. The policies may include issues relating to compensation, discipline, demotion, dismissal, promotion, and the like. They are also responsible for ensuring that the policies they formulate are thoroughly implemented.

1.6.4 Advocating for employees

Another important role that HR managers play is serving as employee advocates. They serve as the voice of the employees by listening to any problems employees may have and present them to management. This has the tendency of creating a favourable working environment, and disputes and disruptions become minimal.

1.7 Skills and Competencies of Human Resource Managers

To be able to perform the HRM function effectively, HR Managers need to have some skills and competencies including the mastery of business, mastery of HRM, mastery of change, and personal credibility.

1.7.1 Mastery of business

HR managers are expected to have a good general knowledge and understanding of their business operations. They are usually expected to be aware of issues relating to their organisations both internally and externally. When customers, government agencies, or the general public need some basic information about the organisation, the HR person must be able to assist. This is to say they must not be familiar with only HRM issues.

1.7.2 Mastery of human resource management

The HR manager must be abreast with changes in their field of expertise. This may include training packages, labour laws, and compensation. This also means that in this era of globalisation, being abreast with only local HRM issues is not enough anymore. The mastery of HRM must include what has and is happening internationally with regards to HRM.

1.7.3 Mastery of change

Change is constant, and undoubtedly, there will be changes from time to time. HR managers must develop and have the ability to manage change. These abilities will include developing interpersonal and influence skills, problem-solving skills, as well as being innovative and creative in handling situations.

1.7.4 Personal credibility

Due to the advocacy role that HR managers play, they must have integrity in the eyes of the people they deal with. They must earn the trust of employees and customers alike. They must have good relationship with all the people they interact with. HR persons must be fair in dealing with people and must be guided by the values of their organisations and profession.

1.8 Consequences of Poor HRM in Organisations

Improper management of an organisation's human resource can lead to several consequences for the organisation. These can include the following:

1.8.1 Hiring the wrong person for a job

If recruitment and selection is not given the needed attention and time, organisations may end up hiring the wrong people into the organisation. This can create a lot of problems including poor or reduced productivity and profitability. When wrong people are put in positions that they do not fit in, it is the organisation that will suffer.

1.8.2 High employee turnover

Poor HRM can lead to people leaving the establishment frequently. Turnover is usually costly to the organisation because it means new employees have to be acquired. Besides, those who are already trained leave with every experience and development they have received. It is important to manage HRM properly because some employees are indeed valuable and their departure can affect the organisations.

1.8.3 Waste of time and money on interviews

Poor HRM can also lead to wasting of time and money on interviewing new applicants. Most organisations depend on interviews as a major aspect of the selection process, and excessive turnover can be both time-consuming and expensive.

1.8.4 Poor employee performance

When human resource is not well managed, issues such as performance appraisal may be ignored, and this will mean lack of measuring performance at specific intervals. Managing the performance of employees is critical to the development of an individual. Ignoring it can thus affect the performance of a whole team, department, or the organisation as a whole.

1.8.5 Court actions

Litigation may ensue due to poor management of human resource in an organisation. Wrongful policy interpretations that are followed and used to penalise employees can later create legal problems. Moreover, a possible hidden criminal record of an employee can set this off a court action. However, if employees are properly managed and the HRM activities are accurately undertaken, these problems can come to light in good time and suitably solved.

1.8.6 Close down

At worst, poor management of HRM can lead to the close down of an organisation. Several situations can contribute to such a problem. This could include a situation where there has been a problem of a possible wrongful treatment of human resource.

1.9 Contemporary Challenges of Human Resource Management

The competitive challenges that organisations and for that matter HRM face today are numerous, and they include intense competition, downsizing and delayering, quality improvement, managing employee work-life-balance, globalisation, endorsing technological developments, change management, developing human capital, containing costs, and retaining adept employees. Some of these challenges are further discussed below.

1.9.1 Globalisation

Globalisation is bringing about an increasing burden on HR managers as well as their employees. The term simply refers to the increasing removal of barriers to the movement of people, goods, services, information, and funds across geographical boundaries and barriers. The trend is towards offering customers 'anything, anytime, anywhere' around the world. Globalisation brings about new opportunities such as joint ventures, regional trade, and political alliance. However, globalisation has certain adverse effects on and implications for HRM, and these adverse effects are discussed below.

A growing number of organisations do not want to operate in just one country but rather develop more global operations. As companies go global, they have to deal with complicated issues related to different geographical areas, cultures, laws, and business practices. This implies that HR managers must train all their staff who work overseas to be able to comply with what pertains in their subsidiary countries. Issues like compensation packages, legal issues, understanding cultural diversities, and other requirements of their geographical location must be brought to bear. This is a serious challenge to HR managers.

In addition, globalisation brings on board the integration of various cultures. Culture includes the social factors affecting the values, beliefs, and actions of diverse group of people. For instance, American and European cultures are coming along with the goods and service imported into developing countries such as Ghana. Textbooks and other knowledge sources are also exposing people to and influencing cultures, some of which are beneficial and others are not. International companies carry some of their cultures to their new locations, and to keep your alliance with them, HR managers need to be abreast with them and also train their employee to do the same.

Another issue that organisations and employees need to deal with is their counterparts and customers from different countries, different legal, monetary, and economic environments. HRM is becoming complex, and being an expert in local HRM practice and laws alone is not enough. HR managers are therefore needed to be abreast with human resource issue the world over. Democracy and human rights is a concept that is now all over the world. Hence, issues such as equal employment opportunity or equal opportunity are no longer limited to the advanced countries. It is a challenge for HR persons to be well versed with these issues so that they do not flout the laws of other countries thereby putting the organisation in trouble.

1.9.2 Endorsing technological development

The technology that an organisation employs in their production and service delivery greatly affects the skills and abilities that the employees of the organisation must acquire. Technology can be described as the combination of skills and equipment that managers use in the design, production, and distribution of goods and services. Advancements in computer technology have dramatically changed the nature of work and the way employees interact at work with data and people. Companies are using technology to change the way they do business, and any organisation, which is not familiar with technology, cannot attain competitive advantage.

Technology is changing the face of HRM. Employers now need higher skill and knowledge for planning, decision-making, and problem-solving. Embracing new technological trends could pose a problem for some employees. Training becomes of great importance and a challenge. To convince employees to change from their old ways and to get them to train becomes a problem that HR managers have to shoulder.

One major change technology has brought about is the emergence of the use of software such as Human Resource Information System (HRIS). HRIS is an integrated system designed to provide information used in HR decision-making. It is designed to improve the efficiency with which HR data is compiled and to make human resource records a more useful source of information. This software has many uses, and some organisations use it to perform HR functions such as human resource planning, recruitment, training, payroll and benefits, planning of promotions, storing HR data, and health and safety activities.

The challenge is that HR managers themselves must first learn and be acquainted with the software and also train or ensure that their staffs are properly trained. Convincing a filing clerk of many years, for instance, to suddenly go and train to use a new technology for filing could be a challenge. However, the HR manager has the job of persuading staff to change from their old ways and use new technologies. Despite the many uses of HRIS, it poses security challenges since there are web-based HRIS option, and these need to be addressed.

1.9.3 Change management

Change is *a constant,* and it is regularly occurring in organisations. Hence, organisations are always under pressure to change so as to meet changing needs and situations or risk going out of business. Today, no organisation can maintain the status quo and survive for long. There are two types of change that organisations face. They are proactive and reactive change.

Proactive change is change initiated to take advantage of targeted opportunities, often before others see such opportunities. Reactive change, on the other hand, is the kind of change that occurs after external forces have already affected performance and compelled an organisation to react or face the consequences.

Change is a people's affair; it is people and their behaviour that must change or be changed. Consequently, change management is an HR responsibility. For organisations to change, people must change, and for managers to assist people to change, they need to understand people. Several issues can trigger change in organisation, and it is important that change is managed gradually to achieve results. Communicating change and successfully implementing it to the latter is a challenge that HR persons have to contend with.

According to Bohlander, Snell, and Sherman (2001), organisational change effort often fails for the following reasons.

- When organisations do not establish a sense of urgency for the change
- When there is no powerful coalition to guide the effort
- When organisation do not have leaders who are visionary
- When organisation lack leaders who communicate the vision
- When there are obstacles to the new vision and they are not removed
- When there is not systematic planning short-term 'wins' are created
- When victory is declared too soon
- When organisation do not anchor or secure changes in the corporate culture

1.9.4 Developing human or intellectual capital

Human capital can be described as the knowledge, skills, and other capabilities of individuals that have economic value and tremendous impact on an organisation. The fact that organisations compete through people emphasises the reality that success increasingly depends on an organisation's ability to effectively manage human capital. In developing human capital, organisations must do three important things which are retaining human capital, utilising human capital, and developing assignments for the human capital.

Retaining human capital simply implies that organisations must strive to hold on to their valued human capital. This is because among other things, when employees leave the organisation, they take with them any investment made in their development such as their training, development, and other experience. Sometimes some employees cannot be easily replaced; it is therefore important for HR persons to find ways of retaining their varied employees.

The value of knowledge management comes from application and not storage; hence, when human capital is retained, it must be utilised. *Utilising human capital* means that, apart from investing in employee training and development, organisations must find ways of utilising the knowledge and skills that their employees currently possess. Often employees have knowledge and skills that are hidden and not in use; therefore, HR people must find a way of unearthing these potentials and utilise them for the benefit of both the individual and organisation.

HR persons must also ensure that organisations engage their employees in activities and process that enhance knowledge exchange and mutual learning. *Developmental assignments* among other things involve finding ways of promoting teamwork and effective communication which are valuable in any organisation.

1.9.5 Containing costs

Due to the global changes and intense competition worldwide, organisations are forced to improve efficiency, lower costs, and increase productivity. In order to remain competitive, companies are employing several strategies to cut down cost. It is a known fact that labour cost is one of the huge expenses that organisation face that is estimated to about 50 percent of profit. Hence, measures such as downsizing, outsourcing, and productivity enhancement are employed by some organisations to contain or cut cost, and these methods come with their own challenges.

Downsizing can be explained as a planned elimination or cutting down of jobs. Other terms used are retrenchment, layoffs, and rationalization of the workforce. Generally, downsizing brings about increase in worker productivity and higher incomes for retained workers. However, the exercise demoralises some employees thereby affecting their performance, and HR persons must deal with these issues.

Employee outsourcing means hiring outsiders (individuals or companies) to perform jobs or tasks that could be done internally by the organisation. For instance, up until the 1980s, many large companies in Ghana had their own security departments, but most companies have currently outsourced these services to private secret companies.

To contain cost, productivity must also be enhanced. Productivity is defined in terms of the output per person within a given period. Organisations have the duty of increasing productivity by either reducing inputs or by increasing employee output. Worker productivity is the result of the combination of three factors which are employee abilities, motivation, and work environment. Productivity or work performance will suffer if there is any problem or weakness with any of the three factors that constitute productivity. It behoves HR managers to see to it that all the necessary factors for increased productivity is available.

With respect to *ability,* issues such as recruitment, selection, training, and development must be enhanced. For employees to be *motivated,* their job enrichment, promotions, coaching and mentoring, feedback, and rewards must be properly monitored. *Environment* encompasses empowerment, teamwork, leader support, conducive working condition, and organisational culture.

1.9.6 Retaining adept employees

Competent human resources can assist organisations to achieve the optimum use of other resources and consistently contribute to effectiveness and continuous improvement of the organisation. Competitive organisations worldwide rely on their employees to provide innovative solutions to the problems they might have. Indeed, in a world where competition is high and technologies, processes, and products can be easily duplicated by competitors, employees are the key and most reliable resource that can keep an organisation a step ahead of its competitors. The dynamic business environment has brought to bear a lot of organisational challenges, one of the prominent being retaining adept employees. Pfeffer (2005) affirm that acquisition, development, and retention of talent form the basis for developing competitive advantage in many industries and countries. Accordingly, for any organisation to thrive and remain competitive, it is important that it attracts and retains adroit human resources. This implies that employee retention plays a vital role in the growth of organisations and thus HR managers must do all in their power to retain their employees, and this is a real challenge.

Employee retention is an increasingly important challenge for organisations as the age of the knowledge worker unfolds (Lumley, Coetzee, Tladinyane, & Ferreira, 2011). Presently, the labour market belongs to employees, because talented candidates in the global job skills market have the luxury of choice (Harris, 2007). Employees, both new and experienced, are realising that they have more discretion in their choice of organisations to work with. Meanwhile, employee turnover is costly and can negatively affect organisational effectiveness and employee morale (Kacmar, Andrews, Van Rooy, Steilberg, & Cerrone, 2006).

The cost of replacing workers is high, finding skilled employees can be difficult, and investments in training are less secure (Lochhead & Stephens, 2004). Cascio (2006) affirms that the costs associated with recruiting, selecting, and training new employees often exceed 100 per cent of the annual salary for the position being filled. Thus, every turnover of skilful employees come at a cost and the combined direct and indirect costs associated with one employee leaving ranges from a minimum of one year's pay and benefits to something more substantial. Moreover, when knowledgeable employees leave an organisation, the consequences go far beyond the substantial costs of recruiting and integrating replacements. Consequently, most employers are seeking better ways to manage turnover in order to retain valued human resources and sustain competition and high performance.

The main purpose of employee retention is to prevent competent employees from leaving an organisation as this could have adverse effect on productivity and profitability (Samuel & Chipunza, 2009). Employee retention brings all kinds of benefits especially since globalisation, and the creation of regional economic blocs have increased labour mobility across nations. Also companies that keep their employee are likely to gain an advantage over their competitors by reducing overall labour costs and improving productivity. Meanwhile, retaining the workforce is one of the major contemporary challenges that HRM faces.

Several factors determine whether an employee stays or leaves an organisation. These factors include the compensation the organisation offers, training and career development opportunities, the culture of the organisation, employee relationships, job satisfaction, work-life balance, recognition, and empowerment. Although organisations may not be able to institute all the aforementioned practice, it is important that they find out which of them boost retention. This is because retaining talent with critical skill sets is acknowledged by organisations as vital to the achievement of business growth and the building of organisational competencies.

PART TWO

LEGAL ENVIRONMENT OF HUMAN RESOURCE MANAGEMENT

2 EQUAL EMPLOYMENT OPPORTUNITY AND HUMAN RESOURCE MANAGEMENT

Learning Objectives

After reading this chapter, you should be able to

- Understand the concept and development of equal employment opportunity

- Identify the major factors that have contributed to equal employment opportunity

- Recognise the laws that have implications for equal opportunity in the United States of America and Ghana

- Comprehend discrimination and the various categories of discrimination

- Evaluate how equal opportunity can be implemented in organisations

- Recognise the difference between reverse discrimination and affirmative action

Introduction

The legal aspect of managing human resources is very important, and organisations which decide to ignore it will risk incurring huge costs due to litigation, creating negative public image and having to endure other forms of damage to their organisations.

The laws and regulations of equal employment opportunity (EEO) which is also known as equal opportunity cuts across every aspect of HRM: recruitment, selection, promotion, compensation, discipline, and training. From the 1990s, most organisations across the world have been sued and have incurred huge losses because they violated the laws of EEO. Some organisations have had to pay millions of dollars to settle numerous sexual harassment (SH) claims, and they are now very determined to comply with the required laws.

Due to its importance, every HRM specialist or generalist must be aware of the EEO or equal opportunity laws in their country of operation and abide by it accordingly. In fact, all other managers must master it too.

2.1 Explaining Equal Employment Opportunity

Simply put, EEO is the treatment of individuals in all aspect of employment whether recruitment, training, promotion, and the like in a fair and non-biased way. Basically, EEO implies that individuals should be treated equally in all actions related to employment.

EEO is not just a legal issue but an emotional one too, and that is why organisations and managers for that matter must be cautious with the way they treat people irrespective of their colour, age, sex, physical condition, nationality, or ethnic backgrounds. It can be said to be an emotional issue because an individual does not decide which colour he or she wants to be or which nationality he or she wants to belong to. Hence, discriminating against people with respect to such issue is highly unfair. It should be stressed that blatant and intentional discrimination in employment is illegal and perpetrators could be dealt with.

2.2 Emergence of Equal Employment Opportunity

In December 1955, the civil rights movement was sparked off when Rosa Parks, an African-American Lady from Alabama, rebuffed to give up her seat in a bus to a white man and was arrested. The ramifications of this later led Congress to pass civil right laws. People like Dr Martin Luther King, Jr. were very influential during this era.

EEO emerged from the USA, and by mid-1950s and early 1960, a non-discriminatory employment had become a strong social concern. The influence of the USA in the world economy is so profound that what happens there quickly spreads to other continents and countries through various means including the media, textbooks, and educational system. It is therefore not surprising that equal opportunity is now a worldwide issue accepted and respected by most countries including Ghana.

2.3 Factors Contributing to Equal Employment Opportunity

Over the years, three main factors have contributed to the development of EEO. They are the changes in societal values, the economic status of vulnerable groups such as women, minorities, and people with disabilities, and the emerging roles of government laws and regulations.

2.3.1 Changes in societal values

The standard of compensating people according to their work and contribution rather than the colour of their skin, sex, ethnic, or any other criteria is gaining strong grounds in many, if not all, societies. Unlike previously, it is now acceptable in societies that people who work hard should be able to advance to the highest level and this is being practised by several countries.

Similarly, pressure is being mounted on the few countries that have not yet put these values into practice, to stop discriminating and allow people to reach their highest potential irrespective of who they are.

2.3.2 Economic status of vulnerable groups such as women, minorities, and people with disabilities

Today, the role of women have changed from the kitchen to the office, and from housekeeping to executive positions. Women can now be found in almost any job, and their economic status has been a major issue throughout the world.

Equally, the plight of disabled persons and their right is being echoed everywhere. They have formed associations to fight their social and economic rights. No more pity, but rather fair treatment and equality is what they demand. For example, in Ghana, the disability act has now been passed. The physically challenged association constantly request for walkways and easy access to places where they find it difficult to have access to.

In other parts of the world, it is now common to see minority as members of staff in a predominately white or black organisation. Establishments are striving to recruit minority so as to create a balance in their workforce and also cater for the economic imbalances that may exist.

2.3.3 Government laws and regulations

With the pressure from all around the world, most governments have passed laws and regulations to protect the right of individuals in social and economic life. Employers are now mandated to comply with the increasing number of laws to protect employees against unfair treatment and discrimination.

An example is the Equal Pay Acts of 1963 which enjoins organisation not to discriminate with pay, benefits, and pension schemes. This means that equal jobs and rewards for people with equal skill, effort, and responsibilities. All these factors have indeed contributed to the development and continuous growth of EEO.

If EEO cuts across all aspects of employment, then HR managers must consider some pertinent issues with respect to HRM issues such as recruitment, interviews, training, and promotion among others.

2.4 Equal Employment Opportunity and Employment Issues

If EEO indeed cuts across all aspects of employment issues, then it is imperative that HR experts consider what is right with regards to recruitment, interviews, training, and promotion.

2.4.1 With regards to recruitment processes, organisations must ensure the following:

- Accurate and up-to-date job descriptions which are not sex-biased are drawn

- They avoid exaggerated job criteria in person's specification

- They guard against sex/race stereotypes in advertising and recruitment

2.4.2 With reference to interview processes, organisations must ensure the following:

- They provide appropriate training for all interviewers

- Only trained people conduct interviews no matter their position

- Avoid asking applicants questions that are discriminatory

2.4.3 Persons who design training programmes in organisations must ensure the following:

- Women and men have equal opportunity to participate in training and development programmes

- The selection process does not discriminate against women and ethnic minority.

2.4.4 Promotions in organisation must be monitored so as to ensure the following:

- There is improved performance appraisals and review processes to minimise bias

- Past discrimination practices in selection for promotion are avoided

- Employers do not presume that women do not want promotion and thus higher responsibility.

2.5 Highlights of the Law that have Implications for Equal Opportunity in the United States of America and Ghana

Various countries have different laws that cover equal opportunity. Tables 2.1 and 2.2 illustrate the highlights of the laws that have implication for equal opportunity in the USA and Ghana.

Table 2.1: The Laws on EEO in the United States of America

The law	Summary of the provisions of the law
Equal Pay Act of 1963	This law require employers to provide equal pay for equal work done, irrespective of the individual's gender. It is· important to note that before this law, it was common for women to be paid less than men for the same type of work they did.
Title VII of Civil Rights Act of 1964 (amended in 1972, 1991, and 1994)	The Act prohibits discrimination in employment on the basis of race, colour, religion, or national origin. It also created the Equal Employment Opportunity Commission to enforce the provisions of the law.
Age Discrimination in Employment Act of 1967 (amended in 1986 and 1990)	With this law, discriminating against persons 40 years of age or older in any area of employment because of their age is prohibited in both private and public employment. However, there are exceptions to this rule where age is a bona fide occupational qualification.

Equal Employment Opportunity Act of 1972	This provision strengthens the Equal Employment Opportunity's enforcement and extends coverage of the law to government employees, employees in higher education, and other employers and employees.
Pregnancy Discrimination Act of 1978	Pregnant people are not supposed to be discriminated against. This Act broadens the definition of sex discrimination to include pregnancy, childbirth, or related medical conditions. It disallows employers from discriminating against pregnant women in employment benefits if they are strong and capable of performing their job duties.
Americans with Disabilities Act of 1990	It is prohibited to discriminate in employment against persons with physical or mental disabilities or the chronically ill. It directs employers to make reasonable accommodation to the employment needs of people with any form of disability. Employers with 15 or more employees must abide by this law.
Civil Rights Act of 1991	This Act provides for compensatory and punitive damages and jury trial cases involving deliberate discrimination. It requires employers to demonstrate that work practices are work-related and consistent with business necessity. This law covers the US citizens working for American companies abroad.

Table 2.2: The Law on Equal Opportunity in Ghana

The law	Summary of the provisions of the law
1992 Constitution	Article 17 (2) of the Constitution of the Republic of Ghana declares that all persons are equal before the law. 'A person shall not be discriminated against on grounds of gender, race, colour, ethnic origin, religion, creed or social or economic status'.
	Article 17 (3) For the purposes of this article, 'discriminate' means to give different treatment to different persons attributable only or mainly to their respective descriptions by race, place of origin, political opinions, colour, gender, occupation, religion or creed, whereby persons of one description are subjected to disabilities or restrictions to which persons of another description which are not granted of persons of another description are not made subject or are granted privileges or advantages which are not granted to persons of another description.
	Article 24 (1) Every person has the right to work under satisfactory, safe and healthy conditions, and shall receive equal pay for equal work without distinction of any kind.
	Article 24 (2) Every worker shall be assured of rest, leisure, and reasonable limitation of working hours and periods of holidays with pay, as well as remuneration for public holidays.

	Article 24 (3) Every worker has a right to form or join a trade union of his choice for the promotion and protection of his economic and social interests.
	Article 25 (1) All persons shall have the right to equal educational opportunities and facilities and with a view to achieving the full realization of that right – basic education shall be free, compulsory an available to all.
Human rights Act (Act 456)	The Commission on Human Rights and Administrative Justice (CHRAJ) enforces this Act based on complaints from employees and the general public. The act prohibits discrimination based on ethnicity, religion, sex, age, disability, or marital status. The Act, however, may allow discrimination based on Bona-Fide Occupational Qualification.
Part XVII – Unfair Labour Practices of the Labour Act, 2003 (Act 651)	Section 127 (1) prohibits discrimination against any person with respect to the employment or conditions of employment because that other person is a member or an officer of a trade union. A person who so discriminates against another person is guilty of unfair labour practice.
Employment of Persons with Disability, Part V of the Labour Act, 2003	Section 49 of the Act states that persons with disability who enter the public service shall be appointed on the same terms as persons without disability, irrespective of whether they are allowed to work few hours; and shall be classified in accordance with their previous period of qualifying service for the purposes of promotion and other public service awards.

Section 50 allows that the employment of a person who suffers disability after the employment, shall not cease if his or her residual capacity for work is such that he or she can be found employment in the same or some other corresponding job in the same undertaking, but if no such corresponding job can be found, the employment may be terminated by notice.

Unfair termination of employment, Labour Act, 2003

Section 63 (1) The employment of a worker shall not be unfairly terminated by the worker's employer.

(2) A worker's employment is terminated unfairly if the only reason for the termination is:

(a) that the worker has joined, intends to join or has ceased to be a member of a trade union or intends to take part in the activities of a trade union;

(b) that the worker seeks office as, or is acting or has acted in the capacity of, a workers' representative;

(c) that the worker has filed a complaint or participated in proceedings against the employer involving alleged violation of this Act or any other enactment;

(d) the worker's gender, race, colour, ethnicity, origin, religion, creed, social, political or economic status;

(e) in the case of a woman worker, due to the pregnancy of the worker or the absence of the worker from work during maternity leave;

(f) in the case of a worker with a disability, due to the worker's disability;

(g) that the worker is temporarily ill or injured and this is certified by a recognised medical practitioner;

(h) that the worker does not possess the current level of qualification required in relation to the work for which the worker was employed which is different from the level of qualification required at the commencement of his or her employment; or

(i) that the worker refused or indicated an intention to refuse to do any work normally done by a worker who at the time was taking part in lawful strike unless the work is necessary to prevent actual danger to life, personal safety or health or the maintenance of plant and equipment.

(3) Without limiting the provisions of subsection (2), a worker's employment is deemed to be unfairly terminated if with or without notice to the employer, the worker terminates the contract of employment

(a) because of ill-treatment of the worker by the employer, having regard to the circumstances of the case; or

(b) because the employer has failed to take action on repeated complaints of sexual harassment of the worker at the work place

(4) A termination may be unfair if the employer fails to prove that,

    (a) the reason for the termination is fair; or

    (b) the termination was made in accordance with a fair procedure or this Act.

2.6 Bona Fide Occupational Qualification

Although discrimination in any form is not permitted, there is a leeway for organisations in certain situations. A bona fide occupational qualification (BFOQ) is a permitted limited exemption for employers. BFOQ is a suitable defence against discrimination based on age, religion, sex, or national origin where it is an actual qualification for performance of the job.

For instance, under this provision, an older person could legitimately be exempted from working on designer clothes for teenagers. Moreover, a prospective employee who insists on wearing a headgear in a hairstylist's saloon because of his or her religious belief when he or she in fact needs to expose his or her hairstyle to attract customers can be refused the opportunity of getting the job. Issues regarding religious way of dressing, holidays, and the like can be addressed under this legal provision.

BFOQ is a justifiable reason for discrimination based on business necessity, health, and safety. Business necessity can be interpreted as business or work-related practice that is necessary for the safe and efficient operation of an organisation. It must, however, be emphasised that, in spite of these exemptions, reasonable accommodation is advised. Additionally, EEQ does not apply to discrimination based on race or colour.

2.7 Discrimination

How would one even know they have discriminated against someone or they are being discriminated against? Discrimination means to make a distinction, that is, to separate one person or group of persons from another based on some 'acceptable' criteria. It also means treating people differently or offering them differing treatment where the difference is based on their race, colour, religion, sex, (ethnicity) nationality, age, or disability status.

In some sense, discrimination is allowed in organisations. However, the basis for selecting one job candidate over the other must be clearly made known to all. Generally, EEO is designed to eliminate discrimination. Over the years, the definition of discrimination has changed; however, two criteria that are currently stressed are unequal treatment and unequal impact.

2.7.1 Unequal treatment

This refers to a situation where a particular practice is considered discriminatory if it applies different standards or treatments to different groups of employees or applicants for employment. For instance, if men and women are treated differently when they apply for the same job, it can be considered as unequal treatment.

2.7.2 Unequal impact

This refers to a situation where a practice is said to be discriminatory if it has the effect of negatively affecting certain groups of people disproportionately. Thus, if an employment or selection policy is designed to deliberately screen out certain group of people out of proportion, that policy or practice is considered discriminatory. For example, if the same selection test is used for degree holders and those who do not have any degree, the impact will be unequal since the graduates are likely to do better and thus stand the chance of being selected over those with lower qualifications.

2.8 Categories of Discrimination

Discrimination in employment can usually be categorised into one of the following three categories: disparate treatment, disparate impact or past discrimination.

2.8.1 Disparate treatment

Disparate treatment is sometimes known as direct discrimination. It refers to the intentional discrimination that involves treating one group of persons or employees differently from other employees.

2.8.2 Disparate impact

This is usually an indirect form of discrimination and refers to those seemingly neutral job qualifications, which are considered necessary for effective job performance but have adverse impact on members or a class of people. For example, if a job requires people of a particular height only to apply, persons who are not in that category are indirectly being discriminated against.

2.8.3 Past discrimination

Past discrimination is the situation where employment practices indirectly perpetuate or carry on the effects of past discrimination. For instance, if an employer insists on referrals from existing employees before offering employment to other prospective entrants, and if most current employees have systematically come from a particular group, they will consequently recommend people of their kind to the detriment of those who do not belong to this 'group'.

Another categorisation is that discrimination can also be either *objective or subjective.*

- In HRM, distinction must be based on clear job-related criteria to be regarded as objective or fair discrimination. For instance, if a university degree is accepted as a requirement for a job and it is made known to applicants and also used as a means of shortlisting and selection, it is an objective kind of discrimination because everyone is aware of the required qualification.

- Subjective discrimination, on the other hand, is termed unfair. It is usually a situation where different standards or criteria are used to, for instance, select prospective employees for the same job and where the selection criterion is only known by the employer. In this situation, the employee is usually in the dark as to the criteria the employer is using for the selection. For instance, if the employer prefers graduates from public universities to the government universities but does not give this information to the prospective applicants, then this kind of discrimination can be said to be subjective.

2.9 Different Types of Discrimination

Discrimination can take a lot of forms and is governed by various Acts. These forms include sex discrimination, age discrimination, place of origin discrimination, disability discrimination, and race discrimination.

2.9.1 Sex discrimination

Sex discrimination simply means discriminating against a person based on their sexual category or gender. Women are predominantly victims to this form of discrimination. In the United Kingdom, for instance, sex discrimination is regulated by the Act 1975 (c. 65) and sub-divided into direct discrimination, indirect discrimination, and victimisation.

- Direct discrimination refers to treating a person less favourably based on their sex. For example, refusing to employ women because you think they are weak for a job even though they have the required qualification.

- Indirect discrimination, on the other hand, refers to a situation where terms or conditions attached to a particular job make it indirectly discriminatory, and it cannot be said to be objective irrespective of one's sex. Sometimes employers turn not to realise its effect.

- Victimisation occurs when employees regardless of their sex are treated less favourably due to the fact that they have made some allegations of discrimination, given evidence or intending to do either of the two.

Equal Pay Act 1970 is an anti-sex discrimination legislation which ensures that both men and women are entitled to same terms and conditions including pay. Sex discrimination laws are sometimes extended to include pregnancy discrimination and SH.

- A number of employers are known to treat female employees or job applicants differently because of pregnancy or their capacity to become pregnant in the course of employment and this is known as the *pregnancy discrimination*. The Act that governs this kind of discrimination is the Pregnancy Discrimination Act 1978. In Ghana, the Labour Act, 2003 {Section 63 (2e)} prohibits an employer from terminating the appointment of a pregnant woman for reasons of her pregnancy or the absence of the worker from work during maternity leave.

- **Sexual harassment** is any form of unwelcome advances or conduct of a sexual nature that a reasonable person would find offensive, whether physical, verbal, or environmental. According to the Ghana Labour Act, 2003 (Act 651), SH means any unwelcome, offensive, or importunate sexual advances or request made by an employer or superior officer or a co-worker to a worker, whether the worker is a man or woman. SH will be discussed in more details later in this chapter.

2.9.2 Age discrimination

Age discrimination in employment occurs when an employer discriminates against a person in terms of recruitment, selection, compensation, promotion, or other conditions of employment due solely to that individual's age. In addition, employers have a duty to maintain a work environment that is free from age discrimination. Both recruitment and retiring ages are now legal issues being battled with in some European countries.

The Age Discrimination in Employment Act of 1967 makes it unlawful to discriminate especially against applicants between ages 40 and 65.

2.9.3 Place of origin discrimination

This is discrimination against a person on the basis of where the person comes from as may be inferred from the person's accent, facial marks, or other such indicators of origin. Like SH, creating a work environment that is hostile to an employee because of his or her place of origin also amounts to discrimination and is unacceptable.

2.9.4 Disability discrimination

Disability discrimination refers to discrimination against people due exclusively to the physical or mental impairment that limits them in one or more major life activity. Disability discrimination is common in all societies, and governments in most countries try to protect the disabled or physically challenged.

Some countries have laws governing disability discrimination such as the Disability Act of 1990 of the USA and the Disability Discrimination Act 1995 which came into force in the UK in December 1996. In Ghana, in addition to the provisions on disability in the Ghana Labour Act of 2003, a more comprehensive disability law was passed in 2006 by the government to deal with varied facets of disability.

2.9.5 Race discrimination

Race discrimination refers to making employment decisions regarding a person due solely to colour of their skin or race. Like SH, creating a hostile work environment for a person due solely to race, ethnic origin, or colour of skin amounts to discrimination.

2.10 Strategic Options Open to an Organisation in Complying with Equal Employment Opportunity

An organisation usually has several choices to make with regards to EEO, and they can decide to be proactive or reactive, on the breadth of its focus, on the depth of its EEO plan, on the 'degree of tie' between its EEO plan and its overall strategic plan, and on the degree of formality in its approach.

2.10.1 Proactive or reactive approach towards equal employment opportunity

The proactive approach involves the organisation anticipating and planning ahead in meeting EEO requirements. The organisation can take initiative to develop and implement EEO policies to avoid discriminatory policies and practices.

The reactive approach, however, means that the organisation does very little forward planning and is forced by circumstances such as threat of legal action or court orders to comply with EEO. Although being proactive about a situation is often better than waiting to just react, it is the duty of the organisation to decide on which approach they think is suitable for their circumstances.

2.10.2 Breadth of focus

An organisation may decide to focus narrowly on meeting some aspect of EEO in making employment decisions. For instance, they may decide to focus on disability discrimination and not worry so much about other aspects of EEO.

Another organisation may decide to cover a broader scope of EEO in performing its human resource functions. Again this is the choice and decision of the organisation in question.

2.10.3 Depth of equal employment opportunity plan

Deciding on depth of EEO plan means deciding whether the EEO plan should cover only a few employees such as the top and middle management alone or it should cover all employees throughout the whole organisation.

2.10.4 Choosing a degree of tie with strategy

An organisation's policies can be loosely tied to its overall strategic plan or firmly integrated with the strategic plan of the organisation through strategic human resource planning. Organisations have the choice to either tie EEO to their strategy or do otherwise.

2.10.5 Degree of formality

An organisation can choose to have an informal plan that depends on the knowledge of its managers or human resource staff. Alternatively, they can decide to have a formalised plan that clearly spells out in writing the organisation's EEO policies and practices. When it is formal, it is easier for every member of the organisation to be aware of it.

2.11 Implementation of Equal Employment Opportunity in Organisations

The implementation of EEO plan involves six major steps, and they are discussed below:

2.11.1. Commitment of senior management

For an organisation to implement EEO effectively, the first step is for senior management particularly, the CEO, to show commitment to employment equity and take initiative in that regard. When other employees see that those at the higher level are committed to a policy, it is sometimes easier for them to follow accordingly.

2.11.2 Data collection and analysis

The organisation must gather data on the profile of its labour force and analyse it to determine where it stands in relation to EEO. Some types of data that must be collected include salary distribution, sex, access to training, promotion, and the like. Statistics on gender equality, age, and other possible basis of discrimination must also be assessed and analysed.

2.11.3 Review of the employment system

After gathering information on its workforce, the organisation must then review its employment system, that is, its human resource activities and practices pertaining to recruitment, selection, training and development, promotion, compensation, discipline, and termination of appointment. This will assist them to know how well or otherwise they are doing with regards to EEO.

2.11.4 Establishment of work plan

After reviewing the employment system, the organisation must develop a work plan for the implementation of the actual EEO plan. The work plan should outline what EEO goals are to be achieved and the proposed actions that must be taken to achieve them.

2.11.5 Implementing the equal employment opportunity plan

Implementation means putting a plan into action. It is a very important stage in the whole process and must be handled critically. The implementation of an EEO plan requires commitment on the part of senior management. There must be clear definition of roles and responsibilities, provision of training, and the allocation of the necessary resources.

2.11.6 Monitoring, evaluation, and revision of the plan

Once a plan is implemented, it must be monitored and evaluated from time to time so as to ensure that the plan is being followed and that equity prevails in the performance of all HRM functions. With time, the plan could be revisited and revised if need be.

2.12 Other Issues Related to Equal Employment Opportunity

2.12.1 Reverse discrimination

In attempting to redress past discrimination, an organisation may give preference to the group that has been discriminated against to the extent that non-members of the designated group might complain that they are being discriminated against. The group could be those in the minority race, women, older persons, and those with disability.

For example, if an organisation feels that women have been discriminated against for a long time and the way to deal with the problem is to give preference to women even if they are not as qualified for employment, then reverse discrimination is being perpetuated. The male counterparts, on the other hand, may complain that they are being discriminated against if they feel that the attempt to correct past discrimination has gone too far.

In such cases, the organisation's management is usually caught between the correction of past discrimination and the complaints from the new complainants.

2.12.2 Affirmative action

Affirmative action is an attempt by employers to analyse their employment policies and develop an appropriate action to correct or redress discrimination in the past or even present. It is a process whereby employers identify problem areas, set goals, and take positive corrective steps to enhance opportunities for people who are or have been discriminated against in the past. For instance, if preferential treatment is given to designated groups in such matters as recruitment, promotion, and training, an organisation may decide to use affirmative action to right this wrong.

The action taken may involve allocating special quotas to members of the designated groups as they may not stand a chance if merit or performance is a given criterion used for selection purposes. Affirmation action has been used widely in an attempt to redress past discrimination against blacks and women in the USA. In a gist, it is about following specific guidelines to achieve balance and having representative workforce.

3 SEXUAL HARASSMENT IN THE WORK ENVIRONMENT

Learning Objectives

After reading this chapter, you should be able to

- Trace the historical background of sexual harassment

- Identify the main types of sexual harassment

- Recognise the perpetrators and conduct that constitute sexual harassment

- Describe the causes and consequences of sexual harassment

- Comprehend the roles and responsibilities of employers and employees in issues relating to sexual harassment

Introduction

Sexual Harassment (SH) is one of the most pressing problems in the work environment. The work environment here denotes anywhere someone is working to earn a living or anywhere one is practicing his or her profession. SH is a 'big issue' and a great challenge to a reasonable number of organisations the world over. Although SH is an aged dilemma, it is an emerging issue in HRM that presents a great challenge to a reasonable number of organisations worldwide. Apart from its devastating effect on the victim's emotional stability, it also impacts greatly on his or her ability to work effectively. It also affects an organisation's image and profitability.

Sexually harassing conduct causes devastating physical and psychological injuries to a large percentage of employees in workplaces all over the world. SH in the work environment is among the most offensive and demeaning torments an employee can undergo. It exacerbates the economic conditions of victims and damages their ability to achieve equality with their fellow employees. In the United States, survey research has reinforced the view that SH is a problem in the workplace and that it represents huge cost to businesses.

3.1 Historical Background of Sexual Harassment

While most histories of SH begun in 1964 when the United States Congress passed Title VII of the Civil Rights Act and created the Equal Employment Opportunity Commission (EEOC), Constance Jones in her book *Sexual Harassment* identified incidents of SH back to the 1830s when increased numbers of women began working in the textile mills in New England. She noted that printers in Boston conducted a campaign of intimidation to force women out of their jobs in that industry in 1835. Of course, there was no term to describe this course of action; the term 'sexual harassment' was coined by feminists in the 1960s.

SH is a violation of human rights and a prohibited form of violence against the dignity of humankind; it is endemic, often concealed but present in many organisations. Regrettably, most people are unaware of what constitute SH, for example, the abuse of familiarity such as addressing people by 'honey', 'baby', 'sweetie', 'darling', and 'dear' in the workplace. Again, some perpetrators do not know the consequences of their actions on their victims. Combating it is crucial, and both employers and employees must endeavour to discourage it.

It is interesting to note, however, that, today, SH is not about women alone because men are also sexually harassed in the workplace. According to the EEOC Fiscal Year Report 2007, the number of complaints filed by men is rapidly increasing.

The numerous consequences emphasise why SH is not only a serious problem but also a legal issue and a grave offence in almost every country. It is illegal; a violation of human rights and a prohibited form of violence against the dignity of humankind. In fact, SH in the workplace is a punishable offence under Title VII of the US Civil Rights Act of 1964. In Ghana, sexually harassing behaviour is equally unacceptable and is punishable by law.

3.2 Sexual Harassment Defined

The definition of SH differs from country to country and from one institution to another. Although the USA was the first country to enact laws concerning this issue, many jurisdictions outside the United States have adopted their own definitions intended to cover essentially the same forms of undesirable conduct. Some of the definitions for different countries are discussed below.

The EEOC in America, from whom most institutions and legislature draw their definition, defines SH as 'unwelcome sexual advances, requests for sexual favours, and other verbal or physical conduct of a sexual nature when:

- Submission to such conduct was made, either explicitly or implicitly, a term or condition of an individual's employment,

- Submission to or rejection of such conduct by an individual is used as the basis for employment decisions affecting such individual's employment, or

- Such conduct has the purpose or effect of unreasonably interfering with an individual's work performance or creating an intimidating, hostile, or offensive working environment'.

In the UK, the Discrimination Act of 1975 was modified to establish SH as a form of discrimination in 1986. It states that 'harassment occurs where there is unwanted conduct on the grounds of a person's sex or unwanted conduct of a sexual nature and that conduct has the purpose or effect of violating a person's dignity, or of creating an intimidating, hostile, degrading, humiliating or offensive environment for them. If an employer treats someone less favourably because they have rejected, or submitted to, either form of harassment described above, this is also harassment'.

In India and Pakistan SH is termed 'Eve teasing' and is described as unwelcome sexual gesture or behaviour whether directly or indirectly such as sexually coloured remarks; physical contact and advances; showing pornography; a demand or request for sexual favours; any other unwelcome physical, verbal/non-verbal conduct being sexual in nature. The critical factor is the unwelcomeness of the behaviour, thereby making an impact of such actions on the recipient more relevant rather than the intent of the perpetrator.

The Czech Republic explains SH as an undesirable behaviour of a sexual nature at the workplace if such conduct is unwelcome, unsuitable or insulting, or if it can be justifiably perceived by the party concerned as a condition for decisions affecting the exercise of rights and obligations ensuring from labour relations.

According to the Chartered Institute of Personnel and Development, UK, SH is 'any unwanted behaviour that violates dignity or creates an intimidating, humiliating or offensive environment'.

Section 175 of the Ghana Labour Act, 2003 (Act 651) defines SH as any 'unwelcome, offensive or importunate (persistent) sexual advances or request made by an employer or superior officer or a co-worker to a worker, whether the worker is a man or woman'.

3.3 Types of Sexual Harassment

There are two legally recognised types of SH as identified by the EEOC, and they are quid pro quo and hostile environment.

3.3.1 Quid pro quo sexual harassment

Quid pro quo (Latin word for 'this for that' or 'something for something') is where an individual's submission to or rejection of sexual advances or conduct is used as a foundation for employment decisions like recommendations, promotion, and other types of opportunities. It is basically 'sexual bribery'. An example is the exchanging of sexual favours for job benefits or the promise of salary increment after cooking for the managing director. Thus, quid pro quo harassment can take a form of threat ('have sex with me or I won't give you your promotion') or offers ('if you have sex with me, I can help your career').

3.3.2 Hostile environment sexual harassment

This occurs when an unwelcome sexual conduct has the purpose or effect of unreasonably interfering with job performance or creating an intimidating, hostile, or offensive working environment. To be precise, it involves creating an environment which makes the life of an employee uncomfortable, stressful, and unpleasant.

3.4 Perpetrators of Sexual Harassment

SH used to be perpetrated against women. Today, the issue has taken a different turn and men suffer it too and must therefore have the same rights as women to the protection of their dignity.

- The harasser may either be a man or woman; thus, both men and women sexually harass each other

- It is usually between a superior or supervisor and a subordinate

- A subordinate can equally harass a superior

- Colleagues also harass each other

- Customers/clients, visitors, contractors on site and other non-employees can also perpetrate SH

3.5 Conduct that Might Constitute Sexual Harassment

There are several conduct that might constitute sexual harassment. These conducts can be physical, verbal and visual. Unfortunately, some people do not even know that their behaviours are offensive to other people. Below are some of such sexually harassing conducts.

3.5.1 Physical conducts

Physical conducts that might constitute SH includes but not limited to

- Actual or attempted rape or sexual assault

- Touching or rubbing oneself sexually in front of another person

- Stalking; hanging around a person without legitimate reason

- Blocking, leaning over, intentionally brushing up against, or invading someone's personal space in a way that indicates a desire for sexual activity

- Giving personal gifts that are unsolicited

- Assault in retaliation of person refusing sexual advance

- Touching that is sexual in nature, such as massaging, touching a person's clothing, hair or body, hugging, kissing, patting, stroking, grabbing, and pinching.

- Actual or attempted rape or sexual assault

- Stalking; hanging around a person without legitimate reason

3.5.2 Verbal conducts

Verbal conducts that might constitute SH includes but not limited to

- Direct demand for sexual favours, or asking personal questions about one's sexual life

- Making kissing sounds, whistling, smacking, or other noises suggesting sex or catcalling

- Use of demeaning names such as 'Cutie', 'Sugar', 'Sweetie', 'Honey', 'Darling', 'Hey baby,' 'Doll,' 'Babe,' 'Hunk,' 'Girl,' or 'Boy' (when referring to an adult), 'Dear,' 'Pussycat,' or 'Broad'.

- Referring to men or women by their private body parts

- Telling sexually explicit jokes or stories, telling sexist jokes or stories, turning work discussions to sexual topics, or using sexual innuendoes during work discussions

- Telling lies or spreading rumours about a person's sex life, discussing sexual activities or sexual teasing

- Making lewd or suggestive comments regarding an employee's appearance (body, clothing, anatomy, or looks) or personal life
- Making sexual advances or repeated requests for dates even after recipient indicates that they are unwelcome and the like.

3.5.3 Visual conducts

Visual conducts that might constitute SH includes but not limited to

- Public displays of pornography
- Sexually suggestive graffiti or exploitive posters, pin-ups, calendars, cartoons or magazine clippings
- Sending sexually explicit email messages
- Viewing pornography via the internet in the work environment
- Leering, eyeballing, looking someone up and down, and staring at an individual or an individual's private body parts

3.6 Some Causes of Sexual Harassment

The causes of SH may be many, and they may also vary from person to person and from situation to situation. They however include the following:

i. Lack of organisational policy on SH

ii. Ignorance and lack of knowledge on some specific on-the-job behaviours that constitute SH under the law

iii. Sometimes teamwork transcending professionalism

iv. Sheer lustfulness and macho beliefs like 'real men pinch bottoms'

v. Some women believe their highest calling is to be popular with men or that 'real women look sexy' so they dress anyhow forgetting they may be perceived 'anyhow'. This behaviour can invite sexual advances at work.

vi. Some women who see sexuality as their only power base, play along.

vii. Poor moral values, marital problem, separation, divorce, and the like

viii. It could also be a power game where some men feel threatened by the career advancement of women and therefore tend to harass them.

ix. Again, some people use SH attempts as humour or enjoy in demeaning other people

3.7 Consequences of Sexual Harassment

With respect to *employees or victims*, the emotional consequences are several. Some face low self-esteem, panic, stress, anxiety, humiliation, frustration, and high blood pressure among other things. Depending on the extent of the harassment, that is, if assault or rape ensues, the HIV virus could be contracted leading to AIDS and sometimes death of the victim. This suggests that SH cannot be regarded as something trivial.

The harasser who is either a superior or another employee also faces their own challenges. When found out, they are likely to lose self-respect, integrity, and any influence they may have at the workplace. Depending on the magnitude of the offense, their appointment may be terminated, their career jeopardised, and they can even be sued and jailed.

The impact of SH on an *organisation* is equally expensive. The positive image of the organisation can be tarnished when embarrassing headlines and lawsuits from victims is made public. Of course, no one will want to work at a place where they could be sexually harassed. It will therefore be difficult to attract potential applicants to such organisations. It can even lead to loss of key and competent employees, and the organisation's customer base can also be affected.

SH can destroy positive working relationships between employees, lead to absenteeism due to sickness, and increase employee turnover since most people cannot be coerced to work in a climate where integrity and decorum is not upheld. Once performance is lowered, there is likely to be decrease in productivity and eventually profitability will suffer. SH can increase the financial burden of an organisation with respect to recruitment, compensation for victims, and adopting measures to regain lost corporate image.

Employers have the obligation to take action when they become aware that SH has occurred. New rulings of the US Supreme Court make it possible for employers to be liable for up to $50,000 SH damages even if they are totally unaware of the behaviour. In this vein, a 1999 survey by the Society for Human Resource Management reports that 62 per cent of companies offer SH prevention training programs and 97 per cent have written SH policies.

3.8 Responsibility of Employers

Employers have a big role to play to curb SH at the workplace. Indeed, the EEOC requires all organisations with more than fifteen employees to have policies and procedures to deal with SH. Among other things, organisations have to do the following:

i.   Develop a policy against SH and make every employee aware of the policy. The policy must clearly define what constitute SH and the information must be brought to the notice of all employees.

ii. Investigate complaints and allegations of SH that is brought to their notice promptly and thoroughly. In performing this duty, they must first encourage people to come forward with complaints about SH and also assure them of confidentiality when complaints are made.

iii. Appropriate disciplinary measures must be taken against offenders. This can help to deter others from following the same conduct. Employers have the obligation to take action when they are aware that SH is occurring or has occurred.

3.9 Role of Employees or Victims

i. Employee must understand their rights. They have a right to a work environment free from intimidation, hostility, or harassment. Violation of this right is an offence.

ii. Victims must object at the time of harassment. They must be able to tell the harasser that the behaviour is unwelcome. They must be sure to say 'NO' clearly, firmly, and mean NO. The response can prevent future harassment from the person, especially if the harasser does not realise the behaviour as offensive.

iii. The victim must tell someone about the incident. They can talk to a trusted friend, colleague, or counsellor. It is important to ask for both formal and informal advice and support to help stop the harassment.

iv. It is necessary to document what happened. Victims must keep a record of what happened or is happening. Make note of dates, places, times, witnesses, and the nature of the harassment. The information will become very vital if the victim decides to make a formal charge.

v. The victims must write a letter or send an email. Sometimes an email or letter to the harasser can be an effective way to communicate objections to certain behaviours. It should state (a) the facts of the situation, (b) the effects the behaviour has had on the individual, and (c) the caution that the victim wants the behaviour to stop.

vi. The employee or victim must report the problem to the appropriate personnel. This could be the HR manager or the appropriate authorities responsible for handling such situations in the organisation.

It is important to emphasise that SH laws and policies adopted at the international, national, and organisational levels are not meant to inhibit normal socialisation at work or relationships based on mutual consent. Rather, these laws are aimed at distasteful conducts which serve as obstacles to the freedom and equal progression of employees in the work environment.

PART THREE

WORK ANALYSIS AND JOB DESIGN

4 ANALYSING JOB REQUIREMENTS

Learning Objectives

After reading this chapter, you should be able to

- Explain the term job analysis and its importance

- Understand the meaning of some important HR terms related to jobs

- Know the reasons for recruiting employee

- Identify the methods of recruiting from within and outside the organisation

- Comprehend the advantages and disadvantages of recruiting from within and outside the organisation

- Identify ways of improving the effectiveness of external recruitment

Introduction

An organisation is a collection of people who work together and coordinate their action to achieve goals. It can also be seen as an entity that takes input from the surrounding environment and transforms those inputs into goods or services. Employees play a very crucial role because they do all the work in the organisation sometimes with the help of machines. When an organisation intends to build a high performing hiring process, they need to follow some logical sequence to achieve that objective. One of such processes is known as job analysis. This chapter explains job analysis its importance as well as some key terms used in relation to jobs.

4.1 Job Analysis Defined

Job analysis is basically the process of studying jobs in an organisation it defines the structure of a specific job. It is a fundamental course of the pre-employment process because it involves the studying and collecting information relating to the operations and responsibilities of a particular job. Analysing a job leads to a wealth of information about a definite job. Job analysis can be explained as a systematic analysis of each job for the purpose of collecting information as to what the job holder does, under what circumstances the job is performed and what qualifications are required for doing the job. Put differently, job analysis is a systematic procedure followed to identify the tasks, duties, responsibilities and working conditions associated with a specific job as well as the skills, knowledge, abilities, and other necessary characteristics required to perform that job. Job analysis can also be defined as a process of examining jobs by collecting data in order to identify their main features and determine in detail the particular duties and requirements and the relative importance of these duties for a given job.

Job analysis is central to all human resource activities and decisions because it is necessary for the performance of all the various human resource management functions such as job design, job evaluation, recruitment, selection, training and development, performance appraisal, compensation and career development. The ultimate purpose of job analysis is to improve organisational performance and productivity. When a professional job analyst properly undertakes, a job analysis it produces two important sets of information or documents namely; the job description and job specification which are the task to be performed and the attributes needed to perform the job well.

4.2 Job Description

Job description is one of the main product of a job analysis. It is a written description or statement of the tasks, duties, and responsibilities of a job to be performed. It represents a written summary of the job as an identifiable unit in the organisation. It can also be explained as factual statement or written document which narrates the job contents in an organized and systematic way by describing, what tasks to be performed by a worker and how they are to be performed.

It usually consists of the following:

- The job title, for example, human resource officer, accounts officer, marketing manager, and so on.

- The job identification section indicates, for example, the location of the job and the person to whom the jobholder will report to.

- The job summary or overview of the job describes the purpose of the job and the main outputs expected from the jobholder.

- The job duties or functions indicate responsibilities, social interactions, equipment and tools used on the job, working conditions of the job, and other relevant characteristics of the work environment.

4.3 Job Specification

The second product of job analysis is job specification and it evolves from the job description. It outlines the personal qualifications and skills a person must have in order to perform the duties outlined in the job description. It is the statement of the needed knowledge, skills, and abilities of the person who is to perform the job. Job specification covers factors such as knowledge and skills required, training undertaken, professional qualification, key responsibilities and characteristics required to complete the given job. Skills relevant to the job may include the following:

- The qualifications of the prospective job holder

- Previous work experience they may have

- Education and specialised training the individual must possess
- Knowledge, skills and other special abilities
- Responsibilities they may have to assume
- Personal and emotional characteristics
- Mental alertness/abilities
- Sensory demands such as sight, smell, and hearing
- Communication skills needed

Figure 4.1: A Diagram Explaining the Products of Job Analysis

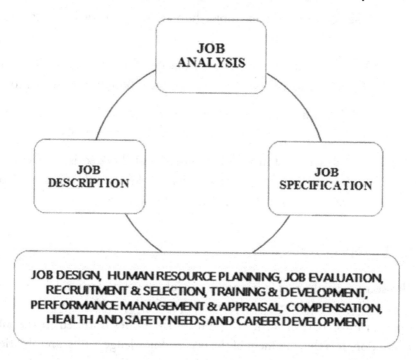

4.4 Methods of Collecting Job Related Information for Analysis

Several methods may be used individually to collect job analysis data. It must be noted that, a combination of these approaches may be employed depending upon the need of a particular organisation. The following are some of these methods:

- Interviewing people currently working on the job or their supervisors
- Interviewing supervisors
- The use of expert panels
- Sending out structured or open-ended questionnaires
- Direct observation of people at work
- Diary method

4.5 Some Benefits of Job Analysis

Apart from being a pre-employment process, job analysis undoubtedly provides a number of benefits to organisations. Some of these importance are discussed below.

i. It helps to measure as many job-relevant characteristics as are feasible, so that important characteristics needed are not overlooked

ii. It establishes similarities and differences in jobs thereby assessing the relative importance of one job to other jobs

iii. It helps establish an internally fair and consistent job structure

iv. It helps to identify job candidates with the highest potential to become top performers thereby minimizing pre-hire error

v. It is a means of obtaining concrete and direct first-hand job-related data on the duties associated with a particular job

vi. It helps to identify the possible risks associated with the job responsibilities

vii. It helps to obtain a more specific and accurate job descriptions and job specification

viii. It provides the basis for selecting employees thus it helps HR people to make improved decision during the hiring process

ix. It helps to Identify critical competencies required for success on the job

x. It helps to get the best possible output for job design and re-design

xi. It provides a critical basis for developing a more equitable compensation management plan

xii. It helps in the identification of the skills and abilities required for an employee to perform well on the job and it can be a legal defense for hiring an individual

xiii. It is also needed to improve issues such as training and development, performance appraisal, health and safety, and some legal consideration

xiv. It makes it easier when there is a need to make replacement decisions when an employee exit the organisation

4.6 Limitations of Job Analysis

i. Preparing a very useful job analysis can be time and labour intensive and costly

ii. There are usually inherent personal biases in the entire nature and process of job analyst

iii. Sometimes the sources of data are limited for the process

iv. Job analysis cannot forecast or predict the future requirements of a job in situations where there is a major change in industry norms.

v. Although it helps to predict what is to be expected on the job, the actual experience, difficulties, job related queries cannot be fully covered by job analysis

vi. In respect to the methods of collection data on job analysis there is sometimes lack of co-operation from employees

vii. Sometimes using a single data source renders the analysis ineffective

viii. Intangible qualities such as mental abilities cannot be directly observed

ix. Analyzing jobs requirements involves a lot of human effort

x. In some cases, the job analyst may not possess the appropriate skills

4.7 Terms Related to Job

There are some important terminologies that relates to jobs and they are discussed below.

4.7.1 Task

A task is a logically related set of actions required for the completion of a well-defined unit of a job. For example, 'change a tyre' is a task for the job of a mechanic. Changing a tyre consists of a set of actions.

4.7.2 Duty

A 'duty' is a set of tasks that are logically related. For example, for a nurse, one major duty area is 'to administer prescribed medication to patients.' The administration of medication can take different forms, each form constituting a task in itself. For instance, administering intravenous injection is a task in the broad duty field of administering medication.

4.7.3 Job

A job is a group of related activities and duties. It can also be defined as a unit of work consisting of activities that have been formally grouped so that they may be assigned to one person or a group.

4.7.4 Position

A position is the different duties and responsibilities performed by only one employee. There are as many positions in an organisation as there are employees.

4.7.5 Job family

A job family is a group of two or more individual jobs with similar characteristics.

4.7.6 Job analysis

Job analysis is the process of collecting data to identify and determine in detail the particular duties and requirements and the relative importance of these duties for a given job. It usually produces job description and job specification,

4.7.7 Job description

Job description is a written statement of the tasks, duties, and responsibilities of a job to be performed. It represents a written summary of the job as an identifiable unit in the organisation.

4.7.8 Job specification

Job specification outlines the personal qualifications and skills a person must have in order to perform the duties outlined in the job description. It states the relevant and needed knowledge, skills, and abilities required of the person who is to perform the job.

4.7.9 Job evaluation

This is a systematic determination of the relative worth of a job within an organisation that results in an organisation's pay system. The outcome of job evaluation is the development of an internal structure or hierarchical ranking of jobs.

4.7.10 Person specification

This tells you not only about the job but also provides a blueprint of the ideal person to do that job and details the personal attributes and qualities associated with successful performance.

4.7.11 Job rotation

This is the moving of a person from one job or task to another in an attempt to add variety and help remove boredom. It may also give the individual a holistic view of the organisation's activities and be used as a form of training.

4.7.12 Job enlargement

This is a method of designing jobs that increases the number of tasks performed by a job incumbent without increasing the level of responsibility. It is sometimes called horizontal job design and makes a job structurally bigger. It can also be explained as increasing the scope of the job and the range of tasks that the person carries out.

4.7.13 Job enrichment

Job enrichment has to do with enhancing a job by adding more meaningful tasks and duties to make the work more rewarding or satisfying. This method designs a job such that employees can satisfy needs for growth, recognition, and responsibility while performing the job. Job enrichment involves vertical job enlargement and aims to give an individual a more meaningful and challenging job. It incorporates motivating or growth factors such as increased responsibility or autonomy.

4.7.14 Job design

Job Design can be explained as the process of defining how work will be performed and the tasks that will be required in a given job. It involves the conscious efforts to organize tasks, duties and responsibilities into a unit of work to accomplish positive objectives.

5 JOB DESIGN AND THE CHANGING NATURE OF WORK

Learning Objectives

After reading this chapter, you should be able to:

- Understand the concept of job design

- Comprehend the changing nature of work and the need for job design or redesign

- Define job design and know the elements and process of job design

- Recognise the roles of employers and employees in the job design process

- Appreciate some peculiar issues or problems of job design

- Learn how the dimensions/principles of job design can be influenced

- Know the advantages and disadvantages of job design

Understand the various techniques and of job design

Introduction

There are swift changes in today's organistions. Firms are growing rapidly due to technology and digital transformation and this is challenging the traditional work patterns. Technology is changing the skills that employers seek and how people work and achieve results. Thus employees today need to be good at complex problem-solving, teamwork and flexibility. It is therefore important that jobs are designed or re-designed properly so that when competent employees join an organisation they will be motivated to improve the productivity and profitability of the organisation. Alternatively, if the jobs are designed poorly it will result in absenteeism, high labour turnover, conflicts, grievances and other employee/employer challenges. Job design integrates work content, method, rewards and the qualifications required for each job in a way that meets the needs of workers and the organisation at large.

5.1 The Concept of Job Design

Although not usually considered as an incentive, job design can have a significant impact on employee motivation as well as retention. A study by Harvard Business School researchers also concluded that job design is a primary driver of employee engagement. Job design also known as work design or task design is a very important function of human resource management specifically, staffing. It is related to the specification of contents and relationship of jobs in order to satisfy technological, organisational, as well as the personal requirements of the employee. Generally, job design involves the systematic attempt to organise tasks, duties and responsibilities into a unit of work to achieve certain objectives with the managers deciding the individual job tasks and authority. It can also be explained as the process of defining how work will be performed and the tasks that will be required in a given job. Put differently, job design is the process of work arrangement or re-arrangement aimed at reducing or overcoming job and employee dissatisfaction arising from repetitive and mechanistic tasks or duties.

According to Michael Armstrong, "Job design is the process of deciding on the contents of a job in terms of its duties and responsibilities, on the methods to be used in carrying out the job, in terms of techniques, systems and procedures, and on the relationships that should exist between the job holder and his superior, subordinates and colleagues." Davis (1966) defined job design as "The specification of the contents, methods, and relationships of jobs in order to satisfy technological and organisational requirements as well as the social and personal requirements of the job holder." It is a very important concept because its principles are geared towards how the nature of a person's job affects their attitude and behaviour at work, and aims at improving job satisfaction, quality of work and reducing employee problems. It must be noted that, to achieve employee satisfaction and maximum performance results, existing jobs can also be re-designed which is basically changing the tasks or the way work is performed in an existing job.

Job design aims at satisfying specific objectives for both the organisation and employee. It helps the organisation to achieve it requirements in terms of operational efficacy, quality of products and/or services and increases productivity. For the employee, job design also aims at satisfying the needs of the individual with respect to their interest, challenge and accomplishment thereby providing for job engagement and commitment to carrying out their jobs well. Thus job design aims at improving job satisfaction, in order to improve quality and to reduce employee grievances and it associated problems.

5.2 Designing Efficient Jobs

Whenever employees execute tasks efficiently, not only does the organisation benefit from lower costs and greater outputs, but the employees also turn out to be satisfied and less fatigued. Research show that, the above point of view has for years formed the foundation of classical industrial engineering, which looks for the simplest way to structure work in order to optimise efficiency. Usually, applying industrial engineering to a job reduces the difficulty of the work and makes it simple for anyone to be trained quickly and easily to be able perform the job. It must however be noted that, such category of jobs however, tend to be highly specialised and repetitive. In spite of the genuine benefits of industrial engineering, an emphasis on efficiency alone can create jobs that are so simple and repetitive and this can lead to boredom. Sometimes, workers performing such jobs may feel their work is insignificant, worthless or of little importance to the organisation which in actual fact may not be the case. Hence, organisations must endeavour to combine varied approaches in designing efficient jobs.

Other issues worth noting in designing efficient jobs is the variety of tasks in the job to be performed as well as the autonomy the job holder may possess. An effective design clearly defines the means through which and the extent to which tasks are executed by an employee. A workers favourable reaction to the design can lead to greater achievement, higher performance levels, greater job satisfaction, less absenteeism, and lower turnover. To the organisation, this can be translated into higher productivity, lower costs and higher profitability. Thus an efficient design is beneficial to both the employer and employee who are and must always be partners in the job design and re-design process.

To have an efficient design both the employer or human resource person and the employee must play critical roles as depicted in the table below.

Table 5.1 Roles of the Employer and Employee in the Job Design Process

Employer/Human Resource Person	Employee
Ascertain job design needs.	Assist in how to efficiently design the job.
Assist in job design and re-design.	Give feedback about reaction to the job designed.
Support line managers and employees to adjust to empowerment and teamwork issues.	Espouse a positive attitude and always be willing to change.
Monitor and evaluate job designed and consider alternatives if need be.	Be responsible for continually learning new ways of doing your work.
Develop workplace accommodation to cater for the change.	Suggest and request for job accommodation whenever needed.
Accommodate employees, empower them and facilitate teamwork.	Assist each other throughout the process and learn to work in teams.

5.3 The Four Elements of Job Design

In determining how well to design jobs to achieve optimum result some vital elements need to be considered so as to satisfy both the employer and employee needs. The engage for success white paper series No. 2014-01, identified four element or basic principles of job design. These elements in are job content, job context, work relationships and line manager.

5.3.1 Job content

The actual content of the job should be designed to assist the employee to find his or her work meaningful and a very significant part of the whole. In addition, people need to have a sense of responsibility, and be able to see the link between the work they undertake and the end results of their work. Where possible, job content must permit employees to use their current skills and develop new ones that will contributes to a 'whole piece' of work in the organisation. Employees must feel that the work they do matters and makes a difference. They must have a sense of autonomy and they should receive consistent and constructive feedback from their line managers.

5.3.2 Job context

The context of the job has to do with factors such as ergonomic job design, work setting, technology, and flexible working options such as flextime, telecommuting and job sharing. When designing jobs, these contextual features need to be considered because it is common knowledge that a sense of autonomy arises in part when employees feel they have some choice and control over the context within which they work. Similarly, in order to experience the safety which according to Kahn (1990) is very crucial for engagement, employees need to feel their job is environmentally and ergonomically healthy and secure.

5.3.3 Work relationships

Studies have shown, and it is also common knowledge that employees are more likely to be engaged and feel belonged in an organisation when they find themselves in an open, trusting and harmonious work settings. Jobs in the modern economy are more likely to be interdependent, hence job design needs must consider not just the job itself, but also the way the job holder is anticipated to interact with those around them.

5.3.4 Line manager

The line manager has a very important role to play in bringing the individual's job design to life. Simply having a job that is well-designed will not count much without a knowledgeable and supportive line manager. The line manager needs to be available and part of the process and work procedure in order to be able to provide useful and timely feedback for the job holder. The constructive feedback will then aim at improving the work performance and overall productivity of the organisation.

5.4 The Process of Job Design

The job design process involves structuring work and designating specific activities at individual or group levels. It also determines, the responsibility of an employee, the authority he or she enjoys over the work, scope of decision-making, level of satisfaction and productivity. Hence it is important to consider certain factors so that the reason for the design is achieved. The human resource professional, line manager as well as the job holder play critical roles in this process. The process of job design must include the following:

5.4.1 Define the task to be performed

The key requirement for the job design process is for the stakeholders to clearly define the task an individual employee is supposed or expected to perform. The task is the piece of work assigned to an individual and he or she is required to perform it within the given time frame. It is a logically related set of actions needed to be undertaken in order to complete a well-defined unit of a job.

5.4.2 Methods and procedures

The methods and procedures that will be used to carry out the job must also be determined from the commencement of the design. The method that will ensure that time is used judiciously must obviously be the considered choice since optimum use of time is critical for the organisation.

5.4.3 Harmonisation of work

It is crucial that the line manager and HR professional ensures that there is harmonisation of work. Put differently, as much as possible, there should be no conflict between jobs. Each job must be clearly designed and defined and there must be no overlaps whatsoever.

5.4.4 Motivate the employee

The employer must decide on how to design jobs that will motivate the employee. Thus the level of motivation that is required to be prescribed for an individual to get his or her work completed accurately and successfully must be considered.

5.4.5 Resources allocation

The employers must also determine the amount of resources that is needed to be allocated to the execution of a particular job. Judicious use of resources is encouraged and every effort should be made to use the organisation's resources prudently while designing the job.

5.4.6 Monetary rewards

It is imperative that the monetary rewards attached to the job is considered at the job design stage. This is because sometimes employees agree to perform assigned duties based on the compensation they are likely to receive. A fit between the job and its performer usually increases efficiency, satisfaction and timely execution.

5.4.7 Scope and reporting authority

The scope and reporting authority must be clearly stated. Clear lines of authority prevent confusion as to which supervisor an employee should obey in cases where contradictory directions are given to the job holder. Clear chain of command must definitely be part of the process.

5.5 Dimensions or Principles of Job Design

Some key principles or dimensions must be taken into consideration when roles are being designed and they include Skill variety, Responsibility,

Autonomy, Task Identity, Task Significance, Feedback, Participation in decision making, Recognition and support, and Working environment.

5.5.1 Skill variety

To develop and increase the interest of employees, the skill variety dimension of their job must always be considered. Skill variety is the degree to which a job requires various activities, necessitating the worker to develop a variation of skills, abilities and talents. Greater variety in a job can improve the significance, challenge and commitment of the employee in the role or task they are expected to perform. Employees must be able to utilize their skills and develop or acquire new ones while dealing with a particular job. Repetitive tasks on the other hand may offer little challenge and can lead to lose of interest and dissatisfaction by the role holder.

Diversity of variety means more than merely adding an extra but similar duty. For example, photocopying different documents from different departments cannot be explained as variety. Instead some other significant and different task can be incorporated to make the job more meaningful and challenging. Alternatively, it must be noted that too much variety can also be a source of conflict and frustration. Thus the optimal aggregate of variety will differ based on the individual, the position they occupy, and the needs of the job.

5.5.2 Responsibility

Individual employees ought to feel responsible for the work they are doing, either as individuals or as members of a team. Their work or roles must be clearly defined so that they can know that they are personally responsible for the positive outcomes or negative consequences that may occur as a result of their actions. If the responsibilities are clearly stated, then the job holder and their supervisor will be better able to discern if the obligations of the position are being delivered or not. It is very crucial that the employee is able to appreciate the significance of the work they carry out and where it fits in the overall purpose of the organisation they work with.

5.5.3 Autonomy

Usually autonomy goes hand in hand with responsibility. It is the degree to which the job provides the employee with significant freedom and discretion to plan out their work and determine or regulate the procedures in the job. Autonomy means giving more independence or scope to and individual to regulate and control their own work within the agreed structures or parameters set for the job. Thus the employee will need to possess some rights or exhibit some discretion in some areas of decision making within the overall framework of their job. This is usually motivating and to some extent helps the employee to innovate and employ methods of working that will bring positive results. Autonomy in most situations, helps the jobholder experience greater personal responsibility leading to success his or her work performance.

5.5.4 Task identity

Task identity is the degree to which the job requires employees or jobholders to identify and complete a workpiece with a visible outcome or result. Employees often receive more satisfaction from doing a 'whole' piece of work; that is, performing a task from beginning to the end. This is more likely to occur when a task or job has a distinct beginning and end which is clearly evident or apparent to the job holder and possibly others who work with or around him or her. It is greatly desirable that employees see the end results of the work they have produced, either on their own or as a part of a team. Thus employees attach more value and experience satisfaction in a job when they are involved in the entire process rather than being responsible for just a part of the entire work.

5.5.5 Task significance

Task significance questions how important a job is to other people and what impact it creates on their lives and that of others. Thus the degree to which one's job affects other people's lives and the effect can be either in the immediate organisation or the external environment. Put differently, it is the extent to which an identifiable piece of work affects, or is important to others within or outside one's organisation. When an employee is aware of other people's reliance or dependence on the work he or she is doing it can contribute to his or her job satisfaction. Employees feel more important in a job that extensively improves the physical or psychological well-being of others than a job that has limited effect on other people.

5.5.6 Feedback

Feedback is usually necessary for improving performance hence organisation must endeavour to establish good relationships and open feedback channels. Generally, employees benefit from information on how they are doing on the job and this helps them feel motivated and contribute to their development in the roles they play in an organisation. Providing genuine feedback is principally the responsibility of one's line manager and this can be done through regular one-to-one meetings to discuss work objectives. However, team members can also provide useful feedback. Supervisors must be able to communicate to their staff on frequent basis. Constructive feedback should not be given once a year or only during the time of appraisals,

Feedback should include the standard of the employee's performance, the target they had to meet, and possibly how they relate to the overall operation of their session, department or organisation as whole. It is important that in some cases a role provides the holder with an opportunity for interaction with other employees, who in turn will be important sources of feedback at many levels. In some instances, colleagues and customers are also encouraged to give appropriate feedback, recognition and support to members of staff and this is known as the 360-degree feedback.

5.5.7 Participation in decision making

Most employees want to be part of decision making processes especially when the matters directly affect their work. This is because most of the time as a result of their work experiences they may have considerable potential to contribute. Also, generally, employees are far more likely to act upon and own decisions that they have been part of. When job holders are merely informed about matters affecting them and the work they undertake, it can be considered as communication; however, it is more rewarding and motivational if they are actively involved in the decision making process.

It is worth noting that, sometimes it is better for employers and employees to exchange ideas. This is because unless people can partake in the discussion of matters that affect their work, they may not be fully satisfied or contribute their full potential in their job. Participation and contribution of ideas can be encouraged through team, sectional, departmental or institutional meetings.

5.5.8 Recognition, support and safe working environment

Generally, most people aspire to have jobs that contribute to their self-worth, especially through acceptance and recognition by their supervisors and fellow employees. If this does not occur sometimes some employees may feel isolated and have negative feeling about their work due to its nature and this can greatly affect performance. It is therefore very important that employees are recognized and supported throughout their career. Employers need to encourage sound working relationships between individual employees, provide clearly defined areas of responsibility and also provide support and boost team work.

Another important principle of job design is that jobs must be designed to support a safe and healthy work environment. The work environment must be free from all forms of harassment, it must be non-discriminatory and issues of occupational health, safety and hazard prevention must be accorded utmost importance

5.6 How to Shape or Influence the Dimensions/ Principles of Job Design

For organisations to achieve their aims and objectives, it is important that employers and employees influence or shape the dimensions or principles of job design. It must however be noted that the actions to be taken which will yield positive impact hugely depends on the employer. Some of the actions that can be taken to positively shape the dimensions of job design already discussed above are thoroughly discussed in the table below.

Table 5.2 How to Influence the Dimensions/Principles of Job Design

No.	Dimension/Principle	Action to be taken to impact positively
1.	To improve *skill variety*	Employers must provide ample opportunities for employees to undertake several activities or tasks and sometimes allow them to combine jobs, necessitating the worker to develop a variation of skills, abilities, talents and commitment.
2.	To influence *responsibility*	The roles of the employee must be clearly defined and they must be personally held accountable for the positive outcomes or negative consequences that may occur as a result of their actions or inactions.
3.	To inspire *autonomy*	Provide the employee with significant independence and discretion to plan their own work systems, make decisions and regulate procedures within the agreed structures or parameters set for the job.
4.	To influence *Task identity*	Employers must structure jobs such that the jobholders can identify and complete a workpiece with a visible outcome/result because employees are often more satisfied from doing a 'whole' piece of work; that is, performing a task from beginning to end.

5.	To affect *task significance*	Individual jobs designed must be important and structured to affect other people's lives either in the immediate organisation or the external environment; because employees feel more relevant if their job extensively improves the well-being of others.
6.	To obtain *feedback*	Supervisors must establish open, frequent and constructive feedback channels since it is necessary for improving performance. Employees usually benefit from information on how they are doing on the job and this helps them feel motivated and it contributes to their output and development.
7.	To encourage *participation in decision making*	Employers must create situations where they can exchange ideas with their employees because generally, job holders are more likely to act upon and own decisions that they have been part of. Participation in idea generation and decision making can also be attained through regular institutional meetings.
8.	To promote *recognition, support and safe working environment*	Employers must encourage sound working relationships between individual employees, provide clearly defined areas of responsibility, provide support and recognize and reward hard work. Also jobs must be designed to promote safe, healthy and non- discriminatory work environment.

5.7 Advantages and Disadvantages of Job Design

Like most concepts, job design which essentially assist the employee to eventually grow at both personal and professional levels has other great advantages. Similarly, there are some drawbacks of job designs based on the technique adopted. This session discusses such dichotomy.

5.7.1 Advantages of effective job design

i.   Job design can help create a job profile which will motivate employees at the work place.

ii. When jobs are well designed it can reduce the level of dissatisfaction employees experience on the job and improve work relationships.

iii. Job design also guarantees that the job is simplified or broken down to employees and this is helpful particularly for those who have limited skills.

iv. When jobs are designed effectively, it can assist employees to appreciate a wider set of roles and eventually settle in on the most suitable role for them.

v.   Jobs appropriately designed exposes the training and development needs of employees and when this is positively considered it can increase employee productivity.

vi. Job design help employers to understand the employee output, work load, efficiency, and the number of hours required for a particular kind of schedule or work as well as the needed rest.

vii. Job design is a continuous and ever changing process and it helps employees make adjustments to workplace changes thereby promoting their personal and professional growth.

5.7.2 Disadvantages of job design

Although job design is aimed at reducing dissatisfaction, enhancing motivation and engaging employees at the workplace this is not always the case. There are some setbacks that plague job design and some are discussed below.

i.   The job simplification method of job design can lead to monotony and its associated boredom.

ii.   Job design can be costly and time consuming to the organisation.

iii. The ever changing nature of job design can be a source of worry and discomfort to employees who are change averse.

iv.   Job design does not necessary fix all the problems employees may have with their job and it can even end up with more disgruntled employees.

v.   Job design might not be feasible or applicable to all organisations.

vi.   Rotating employees as a method of job design can affect the flow of work and sometimes impede the quality of output.

vii. Job dissatisfaction after a supposedly effective job design can lead to frustration and frequent absenteeism.

5.8 Issues or Problems of Job Design

When jobs are well-designed it will make the work of the employee interesting and satisfying; for the employer the outcome will be increased performance and productivity. However, several issues affect or plight job design and these problems can be broadly categorized under there major headings namely; organisational factors, environmental factors, and behavioural factors.

5.8.1 Organisational factors

Job design can be influenced by organisational factors such as the nature and characteristics of work, work flow, organisational practices and ergonomics. Due to the various elements of job, the design is expected to classify various tasks into logical sets of jobs. Under the nature of work, the various tasks can be categorized as planning, performing, monitoring, controlling and evaluating. Jobs must also be designed to improve physical abilities of employee, that is, satisfy issues of ergonomics so as to ensure effectiveness and productivity.

Every organisation has its own culture and it determines ways that tasks are carried out. The culture also affects the way jobs are designed at the workplace and it is important that they are aligned to the interest of employees and unions as a whole so as to reduce conflict.

5.8.2 Environmental factors

Environmental factors are worth considering since it affects job design extensively. These issues embody both the internal and external factors such as the employee's availability, knowledge, skills, and capabilities as well as socio economic and cultural scopes. When the job designed is overly challenging and beyond the skills and abilities of the employee it can lead to job dissatisfaction and decreased productivity. Today, jobs are becoming more employee than process centered. Hence the design should focus on the employee and their competency to perform at their optimum.

5.8.3 Behavioural or human factors

Behavioural or human factors relate to the human need that must be satisfied to ensure or promote productivity at workplace. These factors include issues such as autonomy, feedback and diversity. Autonomy must be encouraged since it promotes an environment which is free from fear. It also indorses or encourages, employee creativity and can lead to improved efficiency and effectiveness.

It is also vital for employees to receive constructive feedback about their performance since feedback is an essential ingredient for work performance. Another behavioural factor is the level of diversity. A job should usually be sufficiently diverse or varied and interesting. This is because repetitive jobs often lead to monotony and boredom hence diversity must be considered when a job is being designed.

5.9 Techniques of Job Design

When jobs are well designed, it can proffer non-monetary motivation and provide greater level of satisfaction to employees especially when they are able to fulfil their assignments and increased work responsibilities. To the employer adopting the right techniques in job design can translate into higher levels of productivity and profitability. There are a number of important techniques that organisations can adopt when designing jobs. These include job simplification, job rotation, job enlargement and job enrichment and these are discussed below.

5.9.1 Job simplification

This technique of job design assumes that complex work can be broken down into simple, repetitive tasks to maximize efficiency and its associated profitability. Thus a challenging job can be broken down into smaller parts then each task is assigned to a particular worker who will perform that task over a long period of time. The employee thereby gains proficiency and flexibility in performing that task having done it repeatedly. Put differently, the technique is used to breakdown complex jobs into relatively simpler or easier sub-parts with the intention of reducing the physical and mental efforts or strain required to perform the job and also enhance the performance and productivity of the employee.

5.9.2 Advantages of job simplification

Some advantages of job simplification technique include the following:

i.   The training costs of simplified jobs are minimal or practically nonexistent because usually lower level of skill is needed to perform simplified jobs; the organisation thus saves training cost.

ii.   Each parts of a job or task are assigned to different employees to perform overtime so they end up gaining speed, mastery and become very efficient at what they do.

iii. The Physical and mental efforts that an employee requires to perform a complex task is minimized since different employees are expected to perform a small portion of the previously larger and complex job.

iv. The proficiencies that the employees gain in the jobs assigned to them overtime translates into increased productivity on the part of the employee and its resultant profitability to the organisation.

5.9.3 Disadvantages job simplification

Some setbacks of job simplification technique include the following:

i. When employees perform the same task over and again, it may lead to boredom and monotony.

ii. Tedium situations can lead to increase in the mistakes employees make, absenteeism, and sometimes workplace accidents.

iii. On the whole, the quality and quantity of output can be adversely affected due to simplification.

iv. Sometimes job simplification can have negative consequences, the overall productivity of the organisation can be adversely affected, and the organisation may end up experiencing losses.

5.10 Job Rotation

In order to promote flexibility and in the work environment, jobs are designed such that employee roles will be rotational. Job rotation allows employees to horizontally serve their tasks in different organisational levels. Thus it is a systematic movement of workers from one job to another after a specified period of time without changing the actual job content. When the roles of workers are rotated, they experience different positions and responsibilities at various levels and become multi-skilled employees with enhanced abilities or capabilities in the organisation. Job rotation also reduce monotony of work and help an employee to acquire varied skills required for performing different tasks in the organisation. It is also intended to enhance motivation, develop employee outlook, increase productivity, and improve an organisation's performance.

5.10.1 Advantages of job rotation

Some advantages of job rotation include the following:

i.   It assists management of organisations to explore and discover the hidden talent of individual employees.

ii.   The experience of rotation enables employees to realise or ascertain their own interest and this help in creating the right employee job fit.

iii.   Job rotation reduces the monotony of work and makes the work more interesting

iv.   It helps the employee to develop a wider range of experiences thereby broadening their skills and knowledge.

5.10.2 Disadvantages of job rotation

Some disadvantages of job rotation include the following:

i.   Job rotation can lead to frequent interruptions in the work since employees can be moved around at any time and this can interrupt the work routine.

ii.   The employees who looking for a more challenging assignments may still feel frustrated if tasks he is asked to perform is too simple.

iii.   Sometimes it is difficult for some employees to cope with other team members in their newly assigned stations.

iv.   With some employees there is always the fear of getting a more hectic or tedious work when they are rotated from one place to another.

5.11 Job Enlargement

According to Hulin and Blood (1968) job enlargement is the process of allowing individual workers to determine their own pace (within limits), to serve as their own inspectors by giving them responsibility for quality control, to repair their own mistakes, to be responsible for their own machine set-up and repair, and to attain choice of method. Simply put, job enlargement denotes an increase in the number of tasks an employee performs thereby increasing the diversity of their job but at the same level. The employees are pushed to adapt new tactics and procedures on their own. Job enlargement sometimes known as horizontal job loading or expansion refers to increasing the number of tasks an individual performs in an existing job and widening the breadth of their responsibilities at the same level in the organisation.

In other words, job enlargement means increasing the scope of duties and responsibilities of an individual by adding the related activities to his or her existing job profile and usually without any modification in his or her authority and level in the hierarchy within the organisation. Thus, job enrichment is a job design technique which is used to broaden or increase the scope of an employee's same-level activities they perform with the intent to increase his or her responsibility and duties and minimise the boredom that he or she may be facing with an existing job duties.

5.11.1 Advantages of job enlargement

The following are some advantages of job enlargement:

i. Job enlargement aims at increasing employee flexibility and reducing monotony by providing the employee more variety of tasks.

ii. It helps increase an employee's interest, satisfaction and efficiency in work they perform.

iii. Usually there is no training cost associated with job enlargement since employees are not required to get additional training for the task-related activities they are assigned to perform.

iv. Through trying new things, employees can eventually learn to develop new skills without being taken too far out of their comfort zone and this is motivational.

5.11.2 Disadvantages of job enlargement

Some disadvantages of job enlargement are as follows:

i.   Monotony and boredom do occur gradually over a period of time

ii.   Employee can consider this approach as a negative step taken by the management since they are required to do more task or activities for the same amount of remuneration

iii.   Sometimes worker unions may push or argue for increased pay because of the increased workload

iv.   The technique sometimes tends to be costly in the long run since some employees may require additional training to acquaint themselves with their enlarged jobs.

5.12 Job Enrichment

Job enrichment has to do with increasing the depth of a job by expanding it vertically. It increases the employees' autonomy over the planning and implementation or execution of their own work, leading to self-assigned responsibilities. Thus job enrichment is an increase in the meaningfulness of the work and the responsibilities of an employee since it is designed to allow workers more control over their work. Job enrichment can therefore be explained as a technique used to increase the satisfaction among the employees by delegating higher authority and responsibility to them and thereby enabling them to explore and fully utilize their skills, knowledge and abilities.

Unlike job enlargement which increases, the employees' tasks horizontally with the same level of challenge, job enrichment is represented or characterised by the varied range of tasks and challenges with different levels of difficulties. This technique redesigns the job and offers the job holder the autonomy to plan, organise and control his or her job – thereby providing increase both the depth and scope of their work. Thus job enrichment adds a few more motivators to a job to make it more rewarding and satisfying. It may improve the work by giving employees more challenge, more responsibility, more complete task, more opportunity for growth and more chance to be innovative and contribute their ideas to the organisation.

5.12.1 Advantages of job enrichment

Some advantages of job enrichment are as follows:

i.   When the employees bear more responsibility for their work it can provide them with new learning skills, overall job satisfaction, and growth in the field of work.

ii. Enrichment can lead to increase in the employee morale due to recognition, provide a sense of accomplishment and get them to produce top results leading to increase of profitability of the organisation.

iii. By giving authority to the employees to perform higher level jobs, organisations prepare its employees to occupy high-level positions in the near future which is also known as succession planning.

iv. Job enrichment also creates a positive and better working environment, reduces boredom and absenteeism in the workplace and this can eventually change the outlook of the organisation.

5.12.2 Disadvantages of job enrichment

Some disadvantages of job enrichment are as follows:

i.   One of the limitations of job enrichment is that it eventually changes as well as increases the work load of employees with usually no additional remuneration and this does not please employees.

ii. Sometimes, employees may prefer to have their jobs enriched but they may not possess the necessary knowledge, competences and qualifications to meet the new challenges and this becomes stressful.

iii. There is, generally, a tendency on the part of the management to impose job enrichment on workers rather than applying it with their consent and this can have a negative impact on employees.

iv. Although job enrichment remains an effective technique for motivation since it provides recognition, sometimes employees need to learn additional skills and this is usually tough them and can also affect the standard of work.

Figure 5.1: A Diagram Depicting the Various Techniques of Job Design

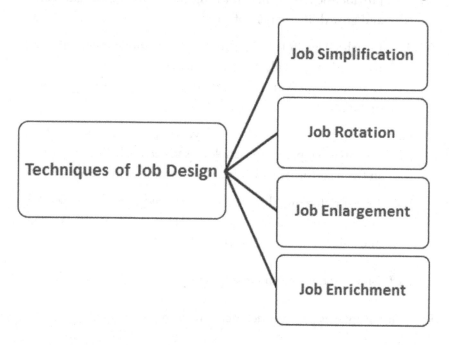

It is vital to note that, there are contemporary trends in job design. Today, jobs are not designed based on only the traditional techniques discussed. The exigencies of the times have led to the introduction and usage of modern job design leanings which provides flexibility in the working life of the employee. Such techniques include flextime, compressed work week, job sharing and telecommuting. These modern-day trends will be thoroughly discussed in chapter seventeen, which focuses on work-life balance.

PART FOUR

METHODS OF ATTRACTING HUMAN RESOURCES

6 HUMAN RESOURCE PLANNING

Learning Objectives

After reading this chapter, you should be able to

- Understand human resource planning

- Identify some important reasons why organisations plan for human resource

- Recognise the major stages of the human resource planning process

- Evaluate the techniques in forecasting demand for human resources

- Appreciate how to overcome the challenges in human resource planning

Introduction

Before organisations decide to employ new people, it is crucial that they first think and plan carefully towards it. Human Resource Planning (HRP) is a very important HR function. From time to time, organisations engage in activities that will help them to forecast their current and future needs for human resources. HRP is simply a process of determining or projecting the future employee needs of an organisation in both quantitative and qualitative terms and planning towards it. It can also be explained as the process of anticipating and making provision for the movement of people into, within, and out of an organisation.

6.1 Human Resource Planning Defined

HRP is the process of analysing and identifying the need for and availability of human resources so that the organisation can meet its objectives. It is all about getting the right people at the right time doing the right things for the benefit of their organisations and themselves. The purpose of HRP is to deploy human resources as effectively as possible, where and when they are needed in order to achieve organisational goals. Organisations that wish to remain competitive in today's challenging business world must undertake this exercise. HR experts must and are usually involved in this procedure.

When done well, HRP makes more effective and efficient use of people at work; there are more satisfied and better developed employees, and there is ample time for more effective EEO planning.

6.2 Some Important Reasons for Human Resource Planning

The following cover some reasons why it is important to undertake HRP:

i.   Without HRP, an organisation is not likely to use the human resources it has efficiently; thus, there could be more employees than needed in a particular department and a fewer number in another department within the same organisation.

ii. HRP gives a better chance to employees to participate in planning their own careers and their training and development. Advance planning also gives employees a better chance to utilise their talents. Employees are more likely to have greater satisfaction with their jobs, and this could lead to lower absenteeism and turnover, fewer work-related accidents, and higher quality of work.

iii. Advance planning enables an organisation to take EEO requirements into account while making recruitments, selection, training, and development decisions. Without advance planning, an organisation can be violating EEO requirements without knowing. Of course, flawing the laws can have legal implications and can lead to litigation.

iv. Without advance planning, an organisation is not likely to do recruitment, selection, and training of employees effectively. HRP helps organisation to determine recruitment levels and thus avoid expensive and unsatisfactory panic measures adopted to meet production targets.

v. HRP also helps to settle on the right proportion of qualifications and training levels workers should possess. It also assists an organisation to anticipate possible redundancies and prevent such situations.

vi. HRP helps organisations to monitor the ratio of human resource cost to other cost of production. This will promote the judicious use of the already scarce organisational resource. HRP will prevent situations where there is adequate HR but insufficient materials and machines.

vii. It helps to plan towards future workspace requirements like offices, proper ventilation, staff canteens, equipment and machines, residential facilities, and other employee health and safety measures.

6.3 Stages of the Human Resource Planning Process

The HRP process consists of five essentials stages. They include the following:

i. Environmental scanning or situation analysis

ii. Forecasting demand for employees

iii. Forecasting or analysing supply of employees

iv. Balancing supply and demand considerations

v. Development of plans for action

6.3.1 Environmental scanning or situation analysis

Environmental scanning is the systematic monitoring of the major external forces influencing an organisation. Here also lies the interaction between strategic planning and HRP; both start with environmental scanning.

The forces which an organisation must monitor in environmental scanning include the following:

- Economic factors – generally or regionally

- Competitive trends – such as the use of new processes and introduction of innovations

- Technological changes – such as office automation and computerisation.

- Political and legislative issues, including laws and administrative rulings

- Social and cultural concerns – such as child care and educational priorities

- Demographic trends – age, literacy, increased or decreased life expectancy

In addition to these factors, organisations may conduct cultural audits to learn about the attitudes and activities of the workforce. Cultural audits involve getting information about how an organisation's culture reveals itself to employees and how it can be influenced or improved.

6.3.2 Forecasting demand for employees

Forecasting the demand for employees is determining the number and types of workers needed to meet the future objectives of the organisation.

In forecasting the demand for employees, the following factors are taken into account:

- Demand for the company's products and services and market fluctuations

- General economic climate and trends

- Availability of raw materials – this can affect production and hence HR

- Technological trends in the industry

- The company's competitive strategy such as mergers and acquisitions

- Absenteeism and staff turnover

- Financial resources and organisational growth

- Government policies such as age limitation or retention, health, and safety

- Internal problems such as unexpected labour unrest

6.3.2.1 Techniques in forecasting demand for human resources

Organisations may use quantitative and/or qualitative techniques in forecasting demand for employees.

6.3.2.2 Quantitative forecasting techniques

Quantitative forecasting could include trend analysis, regression analysis, time series, and many others. These are all mathematical tools used to project the demand for human resources.

- Trend analysis can be used as a quantitative forecasting technique. This technique involves the use of quantitative methods or statistical methods, such as regression analysis, to forecast employment requirements. Often the first approach is to identify a key indicator or business factor such as sales and plot a historical trend of the factor in relation to the number of employees. The ratio of employees to the indicator or business factor (e.g. sales) will give the productivity ratio. The demand for human resource is calculated by multiplying the business by the productivity ratio.

6.3.2.3 Qualitative forecasting techniques

With regards to qualitative forecasting techniques, management forecasts and Delphi technique can be employed.

- Management forecasts are the opinions and judgments of supervisors and departmental heads who from experience are knowledgeable about the organisation's future employment needs. They send their forecasts to the HR department for compilation and comparison to previous year's forecast. The people who undertake this process use their experience and intuition in the process. With these opinions, the HRP experts are able to come up with projections for the coming year.

- Delphi technique also known as expert estimate is a technique developed by the Rand Corporation in the 1940s, and its purpose is to get the most reliable consensus of opinion of a group of experts. Someone who serves as an intermediary sends a series of questionnaires to the experts, asking them to give their best estimates of employment trends in the coming year. The Delphi technique attempts to reduce the element of subjectivity from forecasts by using experts whose forecasts are obtained independently. In addition, because the forecasts are often obtained more than once and averaged out, the averages are expected to be more reliable.

6.3.3 Forecasting supply of employees

Forecasting the supply of employees has to do with determining if there will be sufficient number and types of employees to fill available anticipated vacancies in the organisation. The process of forecasting supply of employees involves tracking current employment levels in the organisation and making future projections. In forecasting the supply for future employees, an organisation must analyse the internal labour supply and external labour supply situations.

With the internal labour supply, the following tools can be used:

- Staffing tables may be prepared and used to summarise existing jobs in the organisation, the number of employees occupying those jobs, and vacancies that exist.

- Skill inventories involve taking stock of the skills, knowledge, and abilities that employees currently have and what they will need in the future. A skill inventory lists all employees and indicates each employee's education level, past work experience, career goals, special skills and abilities, and training and development aspirations of the employee.

- Markov analysis is a technique that may be used to show the percentage and actual number of employees who remain on each job from year to year, and the proportions of those who are promoted, demoted, and transferred or those who leave the organisation.

- Replacement charts is a useful tool in HR planning. It provides the list of all the current jobholders and also identifies persons who are available for possible replacements should any opening occur.

HR managers must consider external supply of labour when there is inadequate internal supply of employees for promotions or when the organisation is filling entry-level vacancies. Factors which influence external labour supply include the following:

- Population density and profile or educational level of the people you are considering

- Mobility of labour or pattern of immigration

- The unemployment rate

- Government policies regarding employment

- Competition for human resources since this affects attracting and retaining employees
- Local transport facilities proximity to work and city centre

6.3.4 Balancing supply and demand considerations

After analysing the supply of and the demand for future workers, the two forecasts are compared to determine what action to take. The staffing possibilities will depend on whether there are shortages or surpluses of employees.

In situations of labour shortages, the organisation has the following options:

- Hiring full-time staff
- Hiring part-time staff
- Asking employees to work overtime
- Recalling laid-off workers

In a situation where there is labour surplus, the organisation can follow any of the options below:

- Staff layoffs
- Terminations
- Demotions
- Retirement

It must be noted that all these options come with their own consequences.

6.3.5 Development of plans for action

After the first four stages have been exhausted, there is a need for an action plan to be drawn. The action plan will enable the organisation to achieve the goals set in some proper sequence. The action plan will usually be based on the information gathered through the various stages, any analysis undertaken, and the available alternatives that may exist. The final plan that will be followed must be sanctioned by the management of the organisation.

6.4 Overcoming Challenges in Human Resource Planning

As with every organisational process, performing the HRP function could also come with some challenges. The following are some ways that problems with HRP can be curbed.

i.   Information is critical in any planning process. Having the right information at the right time for good planning is crucial. Information about the internal and external environments must be collected and analysed. It is important that the experts undertaking the process spend time to get the right information and thoroughly evaluate it.

ii. Some aspect of HRP could be technical. To get it right, it is important that organisations engage the service of people with the right expertise to undertake the process.

iii. Time is very vital in undertaking HRP. It is therefore important that organisations set aside ample time for the exercise. This is necessary because generally, it takes a considerable amount of time to get the right information and also interpret data correctly.

iv. Another way to overcome the problems of HRP is to identify current trends and come up with predictions, which are accurate given the said situation. Monitor circumstances as they unfold and see how they compare with actual plan and perform the necessary updates so that future uncertainties can be dealt with.

v.   The use of software could also be an important factor in undertaking HRP. A human resource information system which is an integrated approach to the gathering, storing, analysing, and controlling the flow of information throughout an organisation on its human resources could be a useful tool.

7 RECRUITMENT OF EMPLOYEES

Learning Objectives

After reading this chapter, you should be able to

- Understand the reasons for employee recruitment

- Know the reasons why employers undertake recruitment activities

- Identify the methods of recruiting from within an organisation

- Comprehend the advantages and disadvantages of recruiting from within the organisation

- Understand the methods of recruiting from outside the organisation

- Appreciate how to improve the effectiveness of external employee recruitment

Introduction

Before an organisation can fill a job vacancy, it must find people who are not only qualified for the position, but are also willing to do the job. Hence, recruitment can be explained as a set of activities an organisation undertakes to attract job candidates who have the abilities and attitudes needed to help the organisation achieve its objectives. Put differently, recruitment is the process of locating and encouraging potential applicants to apply for existing or anticipated job openings. It is all about influencing the right people with the right skills willing to do the job to apply for a particular job opening at the right time.

7.1 Reasons for Employee Recruitment

There are several reasons why employers undertake recruitment activities. They are as follows:

- To fill in vacancies or positions. These vacancies may have been created either through retirement, resignations, expansions, or turnover.

- For succession planning purposes. Succession planning is the process of identifying, developing, and tracking key individuals who will be groomed to succeed top-level personnel who leave the organisation. In some cases, organisations may decide to be proactive and recruit solely for the purposes of future succession.

- Due to unforeseen happenings, sometimes organisation can undertake recruitment activities so that they may have a ready pool for quick selection when need be.

Recruitment can be done from within organisation or outside the organisation. Whether or not a particular job will be filled from within the organisation or from outside will depend on the availability of personnel for the pending position, the organisation's HR policies and the requirements of the job to be staffed. Some organisations may decide to fill entry-level positions through promotions and transfers and use this as a source of motivating or rewarding hard-working employees.

7.2 Methods of Recruiting from Within the Organisation

Some of the methods that can be used for recruitment from within the organisation include utilising technology, job posting, organisation's publications, personal approach, and when necessary, recall of laid-off employees.

i. Organisations can use technology to create a database that contains the complete records and qualifications of each employee within the organisation. If the database is efficient and updated regularly, it helps employers to easily locate qualified employees. It also becomes easier to locate qualified employees when it comes to identifying people to recruit from within the organisation

ii.   Job posting is another method that can be used for recruitment from within. It consists largely of posting or displaying vacancies on bulletin or notice boards. In addition, it may also include the use of designated posting centres so that employees will be aware of available vacancies from time to time.

iii. Sometimes organisation's publications can also be used as a means of recruitment from within. Newsletters, bulletins, direct mail through the intranet or internet, and special handouts contain the information regarding the available vacancies.

iv.   Personal approach is a situation where supervisors or heads of department can also approach individual employers they think are suitable about a pending position and encourage them to apply. If they apply for the job, this also becomes a form of recruitment from within.

v.   When it becomes necessary, an organisation can use laid-off workers to fill vacancies. Laid-off workers can represent investments made by the organisation and re-calling them can serve as motivation for future better performance. However, this will largely depend on the organisation's policies and the rationale for laying-off the employees concerned.

7.2.1 Advantages of recruiting from within the organisation

The advantages of internal recruitment are numerous and include the fact that

i.   Organisations can capitalise on the investments made in recruiting, selecting, training, and developing its current employees.

ii.   It serves as a reward for employees for their past performance and is intended to encourage them to continue their efforts.

iii. It improves morale and motivation in the organisation. It gives other employees a reason to anticipate that similar efforts by them will lead to recognition and promotions.

iv. Vacancies filled through transfers broaden the job experiences of employees and make them more acquainted to the organisation's climate.

v. It is less expensive with respect to both time and money spent on the employees

vi. Productivity results come quickly because of familiarity of employees at the workplace

7.2.2 Disadvantages of recruiting from within the organisation

Recruitment from within the organisation has some limitations including the following:

i. It may narrow the scope of expertise and people available to be interviewed for the position.

ii. Internal recruitment can result in infighting and ultimately lower morale

iii. If it is not done well, it can create complacency since some employees will think no matter what they do, they will be promoted if they serve some number of years.

iv. Some positions require specialised training and expertise which may not be available in the organisation.

v. Also the money that may have to be spent on some employees before they fit in their new positions and perform well may be too costly.

vi. It may bring about inbreeding because new ideas and approaches from the wider and competitive market do not readily get to the organisation.

7.3 Methods of Recruiting from Outside the Organisation

In several instances, organisations will have to do some recruitment from outside the organisation. Even in cases when vacancy at the top has been filled internally, some lower-level position becomes vacant and needs to be filled from outside. The external recruitment sources that organisations use include advertisements, unsolicited applications and resumes, the use of the internet, employee referrals, employee referrals and recommendations, educational institutions, employment agencies, and executive search firms.

- Advertisements are the most common method of attracting applicants from outside the organisation. Radio, television, billboards, posters, electronic mails, and other media may be employed in advertising. These forms of media have the advantage of reaching a large audience of possible applicants. It may however be burdensome because many people without the requisite qualifications may apply hoping that the employer will not find the specifications they require and so invite them.

- Unsolicited applications and resumes are another source of external recruitment. Most employers will receive unsolicited applications and curricula vitae (CVs) from individuals who may or may not be good prospects for employment. This source cannot be ignored even though many applicants may not be qualified. Such applications must be dealt with tactfully. Good public relations dictate that any person contacting an organisation for a job should be treated courteously and respectfully. If there is no hope for employment, the applicants concerned must be dealt with tactfully and frankly.

- Some organisations also use the internet as a means of recruiting externally. These organisations create a space for the uploading of resumes and the filling of application forms online. This helps build up a strong database of potential employees. However, this will be burdensome to scan through all applications since some may not qualify for any position.

- Employee referrals and recommendations on who to hire to fill a particular position have in some cases been one of the good sources of external recruitment. Sometime, through this means, the right people are brought into an organisation. This is largely because employees are hesitant to recommend somebody who will not perform satisfactorily. However, if not handled properly or when used too often, employee referrals may encourage nepotism and equal opportunity issues.

- When looking for young applicants with formal training in specialised areas or for retraining to staff positions in the organisation, educational institutions are perhaps the first place to look. The organisation should, however, be willing and ready to offer further training to these applicants so that they are able to fit well into their custom needs. This is because most of these applicants would have had little or no work experience. In Ghana, some organisations go to universities to look for possible trainee applicants.

- Employment agencies or centres and executive search firms are other useful sources for external recruitment. Sometimes organisations use these agencies to fill their vacancies. These agencies tailor their services to the specific needs of their clients. Whiles the private employee agencies help the unemployed find jobs and charge fees for their services, the public agencies are government or state agencies responsible for gathering unemployment data and assisting the unemployed to fill those vacancies. The public agencies among other things perform their services by advertising the qualifications of the unemployed to potential employers. The executive search firms, on the other hand, help organisations search for the right calibre of staff to fill key positions. They are often called 'headhunters' and do not advertise positions but seek out relevant candidates with requisite qualification. When they get the required person to fill the position, the search companies are paid by the clients and not the job candidates.

Others sources of external recruitment may include religious bodies, social groups, professional organisations, and labour unions. It must be noted that the competence of the employees needed at a particular time will dictate what source of external recruitment the organisations may adopt. Moreover, each method that will be adopted has its own advantage and disadvantage.

7.3.1 Advantages of recruiting from outside the organisation

There are many advantages associated with recruitment from outside the organisation, and they include the following:

i.   There is usually a new breath of ideas and attitude brought to the organisation by externally recruited staff.

ii. Externally recruited employees usually come with a lot of morale dictated by their need to prove themselves worthy of the investment and confidence shown in them.

iii. There is a larger pool to select potential employees, and this enhances the organisation's chance of getting good material.

iv. Sometimes external recruitment makes it easier and cheaper for employers to get high calibre of people than to train or retain internal employees.

v.   In situations where the organisation needs to fill in specialised positions, it becomes easier because there are wide range of options to select from. External recruitment makes it relatively easier to get the choice of candidate without having to train and retrain an internal employee to fill the vacancy.

7.3.2 Disadvantages of recruiting from outside the organisation

The disadvantages of recruiting externally are various and include the following:

i.   Usually the investment that organisations have to make is higher because there is the need to retrain and accustom external applicants to several organisational policies they may not be familiar with.

ii.   In situations where several internal staffs are by-passed to pick an 'outsider', there may be a lot of confrontation. Sometimes negative competitive spirits may roar its head right from the initial stages.

iii.   It may take a longer time for employees recruited from outside to adjust before actual productivity begins.

iv.   In certain situations, the people recruited from outside the organisation may unknowingly be spies and can create problems for the organisation.

v.   External recruitment could be costly and time-consuming as compared to internal recruitment.

7.4 Improving the Effectiveness of External Employee Recruitment

Although organisations spend a lot of time and money in their external recruitment processes, sometimes the desired result is not obtained. Usually, the potential employees or candidates may either not have the required educational background or qualification. This situation sometimes prolongs the whole process unduly, and with regards to external recruitment, sometimes the advert or method used may have to be done all over again. This situation can, however, be enhanced if organisations employ the right and qualified people to undertake the process and also provide candidates with realistic job preview.

The size of an organisation usually determines who undertake the recruitment function. Large organisation may hire professional HR recruiters to undertake the function for them. Smaller organisations, however, may decide to do it on their own. Regardless of who carry out the recruitment, it is very important that they have a good understanding, knowledge, skills, and expertise required to perform the recruitment function.

Instead of providing the applicant with just a job preview, which often only highlights the positive working conditions of the particular job and the organisation, HR professionals have argued the need for a realistic job preview. A realistic job preview includes a tour of the candidate's potential working area, together with a discussion of the negative health or safety considerations. This system produces enhanced communication, honesty, and openness as well as realistic job expectations, and this helps the applicant to make an informed choice. With this, recruitment is likely to be successful.

PART FIVE

EMPLOYEE SELECTION AND INTERVIEWS

8 SELECTION OF EMPLOYEES

Learning Objectives

After reading this chapter, you should be able to

- Understand some of the reasons for selecting an employee
- Identify the different categories of the selection criteria
- Know the techniques for gathering information about potential employees
- Analyse issues on reliability and validity in the selection process
- Recognise the various categorisation of employment tests that organisations undertake

Introduction

Although recruitment and selection is often heard being mentioned together, they are two distinctive human resource functions. While recruitment has to do with inviting prospective applicants to apply for the job, selection involves the process of choosing individuals who have relevant qualifications to fill existing or projected position. According to Ivancevich (1998), employee selection is the process by which an organisation chooses from a list of applicants, the person who best meets selection criteria for the available position. Thus, selection can be explained as the methods that managers use to determine the relative qualifications of job applicants and their potential for performing well in a particular job.

8.1 Reasons for Employee Selection

There are various reasons why employers carry out the selection function. Some of these reasons are explained below.

i.   Careful selection is important because of the legal implications for an organisation due to unfair discrimination and incompetent hiring.

ii. When applications received are too many which is often the case, the selection process is the right way to identify and select the desirable ones. This process of sieving so as to get the right candidates out of the lot is also known as shortlisting.

iii. Selection also enables employers to set aside the unqualified applicants before they get into the organisation and become costs.

iv. HR people and others responsible for employment do not want to be held liable for negligent hiring, for instance where the records and background of the applicant are not thoroughly checked. To achieve this effective selection must be done.

v.   Another important reason for the selection exercise is to correctly predict the performance of the persons to be selected.

The overall goal of employee selection is to maximise 'hits' and avoid 'misses'. Hits are accurate predictions of the performance of the person selected, while misses are situations where the applicant selected does not perform satisfactorily and hence the prediction is wrong.

8.2 Categories of Selection Criteria

A good job analysis makes selection quite easy because it makes what is needed obvious. Job analysis is critical to the determination of selection criteria. In addition, a selection system must distinguish between the following:

- characteristics that are needed at the time of hiring

- those that are systematically acquired during training

- those that are routinely developed after a person has been put on the job

The process starts with the application letter. The applicant's CV then expatiate on the following:

- Educational background is the abilities and characteristic needed for success on some jobs. The requirement may range from a degree in any field or in a specialised area or certain grade point average.

- Work experience gives the indication of the past performance on a similar job or any other job and sometimes gives an indication of the future.

- Physical characteristics will usually denote the height, weight or structure, and appearance of the prospective applicant.

- Other personal characteristics may include, for example, attitude, interest, hobby, age, and marital status where necessary.

8.3 Techniques for Gathering Information about Potential Employees

Many people applying for a job may not be qualified or be the right type of persons. It is important that the HR persons or managers undertaking the selection process finds out all they can about the applicant, including what they can or cannot do. Generally, what a person has done in the past best indicates future performance. The HRM person must therefore use appropriate techniques to discover a person's past performance and future possibilities. The techniques for gathering information about potential employees and the qualities or characteristics to look out for are summarised in Table 8.1.

Table 8.1: Methods to Gather Information about Potential Employees

Techniques	Qualities to look for
1 Preliminary screening or interview	Obvious misfit from outward appearance and conduct of applicant or interviewee
2 Biographical inventory from application or resume blanks	Whether the applicant has adequate educational and performance record
3 Various types of tests	
Intelligence test	Whether the applicant meets the minimum standards of mental alertness and ability.
Aptitude test	Whether the applicant has specific capacities for acquiring particular knowledge or skills
Proficiency or achievement test	Whether the applicant can demonstrate the ability to do a job
Interest or inventory test	Whether the applicant has professional interest in the job
Personality test	Whether the applicant has the personal characteristics required for the job
Polygraph or the lie detector test	Assess applicant's tendency to tell lies using a mechanical device
Honesty and integrity test	Pencil and paper test to assess applicant's tendency to be honest and dependable.

4	In-depth interview	Whether applicant lacks necessary innate ability, ambition, or other qualities
5	Verifying biographical data from references	Check for unfavourable or negative reports on past performance
6	Physical or medical examination	Check to ensure that the health of an applicant can meet the requirements of the job. The law states that medical examinations must be directly related to the requirements of a job. Normally, an applicant will not be asked to do a medical examination until an offer of employment has been made.
7	Personal judgment	Look out for the overall competence and ability to fit into the organisation
8	Work samples	Where necessary, examine samples of work produced by the applicant

8.4 Reliability and Validity of Selection Processes and Decisions

Selection processes and decisions always raise questions of reliability and validity.

8.4.1 Reliability

Reliability refers to the expectation that a test or selection procedure will yield the same result over time. In other words, reliability is about the consistency with which a selection procedure or test produces the same results for a given person or group of persons. Thus, a test is reliable when it measures the same thing consistently. For example, if a tape is used to measure the sides of a desk and the same result is obtained each time the measurement is taken, then the measure is reliable. With regards to a selection process, reliability can be explained as the extent to which two or more methods, for instance, an interview and a test yield similar results or are consistent.

Illustration:

(a) Assume that a group of interviewers judge the performance of a number of applicants twice – two days apart. If the marks they award individually vary for the same interviewee on both occasions, then their tests are not reliable.

(b) Assume you interview a person and also give the person a test; if the person passes the test but fail the interview, then the two results are not consistent.

(c) Assume two raters rate an individual; one person rates the individual high whilst the other gives a low rating to the same individual, then the inconsistent results indicate unreliable measurement. Decisions based on such results will not be a good predictor.

8.4.2 Validity

Validity is the degree to which a test or selection procedure measures attributes that are of interest. Validity raises the question as to whether a test measures what it is claiming to measure. Whenever one gives a test or asks questions to make a selection decision, it is assumed that the test is measuring certain attributes that predict job performance. It is vital that the test does not measure something that is not related to job performance. In a more technical sense, validity refers to inferences made from the use of a procedure, and not the procedure itself. Table 8.2 illustrates the various approaches to validity and their meaning.

A test must be validated before it is used for selection purposes. There are two reasons for validating tests before using them. First, validity is related to employee performance or productivity and hence accurate prediction that the person selected will actually perform. Second, EEO regulations stress the importance of validity in selection procedures. This is to ensure that irrelevant criteria are not used in making selection decisions that in effect treat some people unfairly.

Table 8.2: Types of Validity and Their Meaning

Approaches to validation	Meaning of the approach
Criterion-related validity	This refers to the extent to which a selection tool predicts, or significantly correlates with important elements of work behaviour.
Concurrent validity	Refers to the extent to which test scores (or other predictor information) match criterion data obtained at about the same time from current employees.
Predictive validity	This is the extent to which applicants' test scores match criterion data obtained from those applicants or employees after they have been on the job for some period of time.
Cross-validation	This verifies the results obtained from a validation study by administering a test or series of test to a different sample possibly drawn from the same population.
Content validity	This can be explained as the extent to which a selection instrument such as a test adequately samples the knowledge and skills needed to perform a particular job.
Construct validity	This means the extent to which a selection tool measures a theoretical construct or trait such as emotional competence, intelligence, taking risk, and creativity. It usually measures those traits that cannot be observed directly but are assumed to exist.

8.5 Employment Tests

An employment test is an objective and standardised measure of a sample of behaviour that is used to gauge a person's knowledge, skills, abilities, and other characteristics in relation to other individuals (Bohlander et al., 2001). The various types of employment tests are summarised in Table 8.3.

Table 8.3: Categorisation of Employment Tests

Type of employment test	What it measures
Aptitude test	This measures a person's capacity to learn or acquire skills
Achievement test	Measures what a person knows or can do right now
Cognitive ability test	Measure mental capabilities such as general intelligence, verbal fluency, numerical ability, and reasoning ability.
Personality and interest inventories	Measure disposition and temperament. The five dimensions of personality are as follows: (a) Extroversion – degree to which someone is talkative, sociable, active, aggressive, and excitable or emotional. (b) Agreeableness – degree to which someone is trusting, amiable, generous, tolerant, honest, cooperative, and flexible. (c) Conscientiousness – degree to which someone is dependable and organised and perseveres on tasks. (d) Emotional stability – degree to which someone is secure, calm, independent, and autonomous.

	(e) Openness to experience – the degree to which someone is intellectual, philosophical, insightful, creative, artistic and curious.
Physical ability test	These are tests used to assess a person's physical abilities especially for potentially dangerous jobs such as those that involve endurance, strength, height, working with smoke, etc.
Job knowledge test	This is a type of achievement test designed to measure a person's level of understanding about a particular job.
Work sample test	This test requires applicants to perform tasks that are actually part of the work required on the job.

8.6 Assessment Center

Assessment center is a very useful tool for employee selection. Although it is called a center, it is actually not a place, but a process in which candidates are evaluated as they participate in a series of exercises. The situations presented to the candidates usually resemble what they might be called upon to handle on the job. These exercises at the assessment center focuses on the kind of skills and abilities required to effectively perform the higher level jobs. Most often it is used in identifying employees who have managerial potentials or for filling first-level managerial openings. It increases an organisation's ability to select employees who will perform successfully in management positions. Evaluation is based on a collection of instruments and exercises designed to diagnose an individual's development needs based on initiative, leadership skills, and ability to work effectively in a group setting. The exercise usually takes two to three days, and multiple raters are involved.

The assessment center selection process employs multiple methods to assess candidate's competencies to take higher responsibilities in the future. The exercises include formal meetings, tests, exercises, events, group discussion, and the like. Sometimes candidates are put in a conference setting to discuss various topics with or without designated group roles. The participants are given very little instruction on how to approach the subject matter. Each participant must, however, make some contribution in the group, and their performance is evaluated by an assessor.

8.7 Summary of the Steps in the Selection Process

The steps used in selecting applicants may vary depending on the size of the organisation concerned, the position to be filled, and other circumstances of the employment. The following are some general steps most organisations use in selecting employees.

i.   Completion of application form

ii.   Shortlisting or initial screening

iii.   Initial interview or interaction with employees or immediate supervisor either face-to-face or on phone

iv.   Employment testing (e.g. aptitude and skill tests, presentation, group exercise, assessment centres)

v.   Background investigation or pre-interview checks (e.g. ID and sickness checks, right to work checks, work permits, and criminal records)

vi.   Formal Interview

vii.   Reference check to ensure that family members are not serving as referees and other documents

viii.   Medical examination

ix.   Final selection decision and offer of contract

9 JOB SEARCH, CURRICULUM VITAE AND COVER LETTERS

Learning Objectives

After reading this chapter, you should be able to

- Understand what one needs to do in searching for a job

- Know some tips for writing *curriculum vitae* and cover letters

- Explain job interviews and how it is conducted

- Identify the various types of interviews and the people involved in the interview process

- Learn how to be successful in an interview

Introduction

A successful job search process involves matching the needs and principles of an individual with those of an organisation. Indeed, getting a dream job is one of the desires of any job applicant. Though the process may be competitive, prospective candidates must also be proactive and endeavour to put in the needed effort to secure the right career. It is worth mentioning that the job you do will eventually have considerable impact on your life. It will Influence your

- Standard of living

- Status in society

- Feeling of satisfaction and happiness

- Sometimes friends you make

117

To find the right job, there are some analyses that one has to make. Once you settle on these issues, it will help you to prepare a good CV which may help you in your actual job hunt. They include the following:

- Do an intrapersonal analysis of yourself – this will help you to know what you actually want in terms of work. Know your values, skills, expertise, and qualification

- Determine your professional aspiration – in the next few years, where do you intend to be?

- Know your needs and interests – is it money, prestige, time with family, or a secured job that interest you?

- Know the type of people you will want to associate with – note that you will be spending a minimum of seven hours at the workplace five times in a week

- Research about the organisation you want to work with – it is important to decide whether you prefer to work in a small or big organisation

9.1 Tips for Writing Curriculum Vitae

What is a curriculum vitae?

In the search for job, a Curriculum Vitae (CV) is very vital. It is the first document a prospective employer sees about you. It is important that the CV is written so well that it leaves a strong impression on the employer such that they will not be able to turn you down from an interview. The CV is a marketing brochure through which a prospective employee sells him or herself to a potential employer. It is a summary of one's educational background, research, work experience, and other professional experiences. Usually, the basic objective of the CV is to secure the prospective applicant an opportunity to be invited for an interview.

It is vital to emphasis the right things in the CV, especially if you think, any of your achievements gives you a cutting edge over others for a particular opening, for instance, if you are a fresh graduate but a first-class student, it is necessary to stress that. You may not be able to write a perfect CV at the first trial; hence, you need the patience to draft and redraft it depending on the job you need.

9.2 Some Dos and Don'ts of Curriculum Vitae Writing

9.2.1 DOs

i.   Draft and redraft your CV until you are satisfied with it. Do make your CV visually appealing. Look at how others have done theirs and ask for help if you need it.

ii.   Do start your CV with general contact information which includes your name, address, telephone number, email address, and fax number, if necessary.

iii. Write a brief but attractive or appealing career summary at the beginning of the CV.

iv.   Include a section on your contact information, education, and experience.

v.   Include these sections on honours and awards received depending on your strengths and interests.

vi.   There could be a section on professional activities, for example, committee memberships, intern experiences, relevant volunteer work among others.

vii. Skills could include the knowledge of a second language and/or computer proficiencies.

viii. References (you may include this and rather not indicate they are available on request).

ix.   If you are an experienced candidate, then rather keep the focus of your CV on your work experience, responsibilities, and achievements. Rank your achievements in order of priority.

x.   Use words with more impact to reveal your influence over situations, for example, words like managed, achieved, coordinated, responsible for, and so on could be used.

xi. Put less important things on the second or back page or ignore them if they do not add anything to improve the document

xii. Use formal and not flashy font faces, for example, Times New Roman and Arial and possibly font size 12. Do justify your margins to keep your CV neat.

xiii. Write short sentences and keep the same tense throughout the document.

xiv. Do check your CV carefully for spelling, grammatical, and typographical errors.

xv. Do use formatting such as bullets, italics, or bold font sparingly, and use paper that is white or neutral not a colourful or glossy paper.

9.2.2 DON'Ts

i.   Do not try and do it all by yourself the first time. Do a draft and seek help from others, colleagues, friends, career specialists, members of faculty, etc.

ii. Do not lie about your candidature; it is possible that you will eventually be found out.

iii. It is not necessary to write the word résumé or CV on top of the document.

iv. Do not attach any photograph until you are asked to do so, unless it is a compulsorily requirement for the position.

v.   Avoid the usage of 'I', 'my' too often since it depicts self-centredness. Where possible, avoid a section on weaknesses. However, a weakness can be written in a positive way, for example, I find it difficult to tolerate lazy people.

vi. Do not state that references are available on request because if there are many applicants, it is likely that those who have their referees' contacts readily available will be contacted.

vii. Do not mention health problems in the CV. If you have some obvious health problem, inform the interviewer at the next stage in the selection process.

viii. It is not necessary to state current or expected salary on the CV.

ix. Do not write CVs that are too lengthy. Although there are no strict rules on the length, your CV should be professional and should include important data only. A minimum of two pages is usually ideal.

x. Avoid the use of abbreviations or jargons because the selection team may not know exactly what you mean.

xi. Do not include the following information which are not necessary: age, ethnic identity, political affiliation, religious preference, hobbies, number of kids, number of family members, sexual orientation, place of birth, height, and weight.

xii. Do not include information that is humorous because the CV is a serious document.

9.3 Cover Letters

Generally, it is important to attach a brief letter usually known as a cover letter to the CV. A cover letter can be a helpful tool to highlight your skills. It can be used to show how one's skills are appropriate for a particular job. A cover letter can also be used as a marketing tool; think of it as your personal sales brochure. You should use a cover letter anytime you use a CV. It can be used for email applications too. It should contain the following information:

Your cover letter should be in a standard business letter format.

- State where you can be reached by phone or email.

- Identify the job for which you are applying.

- Include the title and vacancy number, if any.

- Put down where you found out about the job, for example, newspaper advertisement or web page.

- If you were referred by someone, mention that person.

- Briefly highlight your skills and experience. Don't include all of the information found on your CV.

- Convince the employer of what he or she will gain by hiring you.

- Close the letter by stating what you would like to happen next, for instance, hope to hear from them or ready for an interview.

9.4 Tips for Job Hunt

Once the CV is done, you can start the proper job hunt. However, there are certain things which you must keep in mind as a job seeker and hunt for them accordingly.

9.4.1 Set a goal for your job hunt

Rather than applying for every job published in the newspaper or on the internet, it is better that job seekers try to analyse their application and skills and understand the type of profile they can fit into. Only apply to opening that are relevant to your interest so as to increase your chances of success. A lot of time is spent at the workplace, and one must therefore look for jobs that he or she will enjoy doing.

9.4.2 Search for jobs at all relevant places

The corporate world today has changed considerably. Job openings are not published just in the newspapers. The internet or websites has become a very strong medium for interaction between organisations and applicants. Similarly, placement consultants and agencies also play a vital role; hence, it is important to apply for relevant jobs through all these avenues. Send out your CV for organisations and consultants to consider it for their requirements. It is also important to attend job fares too; some banks and big companies organise it regularly.

9.4.3 Get in touch with decision makers

Where possible, try to get in touch with the decision-makers. Look out for the decision-maker in the organisations you intend to apply to and send your application directly to them. This could be the HR manager or whoever is directly in charge for the selection process. This will, however, not be possible if the advertisement states a particular place or address the application should go to.

9.4.4 Stay prepared

An opportunity does not seek time to knock at your door. Therefore, always keep yourself prepared to answer an interview call at any time. Be ready to attend an interview within the shortest possible notice.

9.4.5 Follow-up your job application

If you have applied to an organisation for a job and have not heard from them after a month or two, it is prudent to follow-up on your application with the appropriate contact person or the HR department. The follow-up will give you an idea about the status of your application and also help you in proving your seriousness for the particular job.

9.4.6 Do not overly stress with your job hunt

Do not let job hunt overpower yourself. The truth is that it is not easy to get a job these days. Also good things take time to come. Keep trying and be patient with your search.

9.4.7 Avoid negative thinkers

Keep yourself away from negative thinkers. Being surrounded by negative thinkers reduces your level of confidence and chances to perform properly in the interview. Do not give up. With time, you will surely get your dream job.

9.5 Types of interviews

Only few interviews in your life will be as important as an employment interview, so it is natural that you may feel nervous, anxious, or intimidated. The ways to handle these feeling is to research about the organisation, practice, and prepare for the interview.

Employment interview involves the interpersonal communication or exchange between a potential employer and a job applicant. Every organisation approaches the interviewing process differently. Indeed, there are different types of employment or selection interviews. They include non-directive interviews, structured interviews, situational interviews, behavioural interviews, and stress interviews.

9.5.1 Non-directive interviews

With this kind of interview, the applicant is allowed maximum amount of freedom in determining the course of the discussion. The interviewers ask general, broad, or open-ended questions. The kind of follow-up questions asked will depend on the direction in which the applicant takes the discussion.

9.5.2 Structured interviews

Structured interviews are a standardised set of questions asked, and all interviewees are rated against those questions. The questions may be situational questions, job knowledge questions, job sample or job simulation questions, and worker requirement questions. Standardised and structured interviews may reduce the possibility of charges of unfair discrimination because every applicant is asked the same question.

9.5.3 Situational interviews

With this kind of interview, an applicant is given a hypothetical situation or incident and asked how he or she would respond or react to it. The applicant's response is then evaluated against some pre-established standards.

9.5.4 Behavioural interviews

This type of interview focuses on actual performance or situation-based questioning and requires specific examples of past performance of the applicant. The applicant is asked to describe what he or she actually did in a given situation, for example, how did you deal with an angry customer in your former employment? The interviewers look out for things like any mistake you made and how you rectified it.

9.5.5 Stress interviews

This kind of interview is designed to create anxiety and put pressure on an applicant to see how the person responds. Stress interview aims at accessing how well interviewees can cope with pressure because the position may be stressful. The questions are usually aggressive and annoying. The best way for interviewees to handle this situation is to keep their cool.

9.6 People Involved in the Interview Process

Employment or selection interview can be carried out either by one person, two or more people or panel members.

9.6.1 One-on-one interviews

This takes place between the HR manager or their representative or the applicant's immediate supervisor and applicant only.

9.6.2 Two-or-three-member interviews

This is slightly different from the one-on-one because apart from the applicant, there are usually two or three other people present and involved in the process.

9.6.3 Panel interviews

With this process, various people including managers, supervisors, and colleagues form the interview panel. Usually five or more people are involved.

The panel members take turns asking questions, and after the interview, pool their observations to reach agreement on the status of the candidate.

9.7 How to be Successful in an Interview

9.7.1 Before the interview

- Do your homework or research about the company. Thus find out everything you can about the company, for instance, their salary range, their mission and vision, products and services, and some important policies. In your research, read the annual report, company brochure, information on the internet, and if possible, talk to people who work there and be well-informed.

- Anticipate, prepare, and practice likely questions and answers. Identify what you have to offer by way of your education, training, and experience. You must know what you have done and can do. In thinking of why you qualify for the job, there is no need for exaggeration; however, you must know all the skills, abilities, and talents you possess that will make you an excellent employee.

- In addition, prepare some questions you can ask the interviewers. Note and put together things and documents to take with you and make photocopies of certificates where necessary. It is important to know the exact directions to the venue of the interview.

- On the day of the interview, be mindful of your appearance. It is necessary to dress professionally and wear shoes that are comfortable. Excessive make-up and heavy perfume or fragrance are not necessary. Be sure to arrive on time at least thirty minutes early. Whatever happens, try to be yourself and relax.

9.7.2 During the interview

The following are some critical things to note during the interview:

- The interview starts immediately you are ushered in the interview room. From that time onwards every second count.

- Walk in confidently, and make sure you greet and sit when you are asked to.

- Introduce yourself with a smile and firm handshake. Maintain good eye contact throughout the conversation.

- Use formal language and be honest with your answers since it does not pay to tell lies.

- Listen and think carefully before you answer any questions asked. You can ask for clarifications if you needed it.

- Sit upright, maintain eye contact, watch your mannerism, try not to fidget, and beware of your non-verbal signals.

- It is important to show interest and enthusiasm in the whole process, rather than being passive and indifferent.

The following are some likely questions that may come up:

- Tell us about yourself – this is where you focus on your educational background and relevant training and experience.

- Tell us about us – this is where the research you have done about the company comes in handy. Mention some of the positive things you know about them, and clearly state why you are interested in this position.

- Why do you think you are the suitable candidate for this position? It is important to focus on your professional experience.

- How well do you work with others? This is where you focus on your teamwork, interpersonal and communication skill.

9.7.3 After the interview

In cases where interviewees want to make follow-up phone calls or write letters, it is acceptable. Interviewees use these options to ask if any additional material or information is needed; dispel any misconceptions that may have arose during the interview and express enthusiasm for the job. Sometimes people send thank you letters to appreciate the interviewers for their opportunity, time, and hospitality. Others will also ask for the status of their application. It is, however, very necessary to contact employers if you do not hear from them after a reasonable period of time.

9.8 Guidelines for Conducting Interviews for Applicants

- The venue for the interview must be ready before the commencement of the actual interview. Delays usually send wrong signals to prospective employees.

- The interviewers must definitely be trained in conducting interviews, and they must also be conversant with EEO issues

- The panel members must appoint and agree upon chairperson before the commencement of the interview.

- As much as possible, they do not have to 'scare' their candidates.

- Questions to be asked and marks to be awarded must be prepared before the interview.

- They must read through the applicant's cover letter, CV, and any other relevant document in advance.

- The interviewers need to check the identity of the applicant and cross-check original certificates.

- Interviewers must avoid any biases and stereotypes.

- They must also be in the position to answer questions from the candidates.

- They must also communicate the decision reached in a shortest possible time.

PART SIX

REWARDING AND RETAINING HUMAN RESOURCES

10 COMPENSATION AND REWARD SYSTEMS

Learning Objectives

After reading this chapter, you should be able to

- Know the meaning and basis for compensation

- Understand the components of total compensation

- Identify the importance of managing compensation

- Comprehend the different views that employers and employees hold about compensation

- Appreciate the factors that affect the wage mix

- Evaluate the uses of pay surveys and job evaluation as instrument used in pay systems

Introduction

Compensation is one of the oldest and established functions of organisations. To get people to work for you and to be able to sustain and retain them, you need to reward them for the effort they have expended. Indeed, without compensation, most people will not work for organisations. Employee compensation plays a very significant role in every organisation. It determines the kind of employees who are attracted into the organisation, those who are retained and how they perform in the organisation.

There is a fundamental assumption that money can influence behaviour; hence, a fair remuneration is understood to be the cornerstone of the contractual and implied agreement between employees and employers. The absence of adequate benefits can be one of the main factors contributing to employee intention to leave an organisation. Employees expect their employers to reward them fairly and equitably; hence, developing an appropriate programme is a very critical duty for HR departments. Today, due to the immense competition between organisations, compensation has become even more costly and challenging for HR persons and the organisation as a whole.

Most managers believe that money is the prime retention factor, and many employees cite better pay or higher compensation as the reason for leaving one employer for another (Mathis & Jackson, 2004). A number of studies have also established that highly competitive wage systems promote employee commitment and thus results in the attraction and retention of a superior workforce. As a result, some organisations may even provide compensation packages which are well above the market rate to attract and retain critical talents. This makes compensation and reward planning a vital dimension of effective HRM policies.

10.1 Compensation Explained

Compensation is an integral part of HRM which helps in motivating the employees and improving organisational effectiveness. Literally, compensation means to counterbalance, offset, and make up for or an exchange. Compensation is the total reward received by an employee in exchange for services performed for an organisation. Employee compensation includes all forms of pay and rewards received by employees for the performance of their jobs (Snell & Bohlander, 2007). According to Milkovich and Newman (1999), compensation refers to all forms of financial returns and tangible services and benefits employees receive as part of an employment relationship.

Compensation can be direct and indirect. Direct compensation includes employee wages and salaries, incentive payments, bonuses, and commissions. Whiles indirect compensation comprises the many fringe benefits provided by employers and non-financial compensation including health care, life insurance, subsidised lunch, leave policy, overtime, pension plan, and transportation policies. Both direct and indirect compensation can also be termed as extrinsic rewards. Another form of reward that employee can receive is the intrinsic such as recognition, promotion, positive working conditions, and interesting work

Compensation is the remuneration received by employees in return for their contribution to an organisation. It can also be described as the direct and indirect monetary and non-monetary rewards given to employees on the basis of the value of the job, their personal contributions, and their performance. These rewards must meet both the organisation's ability to pay and any governing legal regulations.

Compensation offers employees some level of security, autonomy, recognition, and improved self-worth, which consequently increases their sense of self-worth, leading to affective commitment (Döckel, Basson, & Coetzee, 2006). In addition, competitive pay and rewards motivate employees and reinforce positive behaviour. Employee benefit and rewards increase worker commitment to the organisation and reduce the tendency to think about other job opportunities. Organisations which provide adequate remuneration to their employees are persuading them to continue with their good work and remain with them for a long period of time. Table 10.1 summarises the employee total compensation.

Table 10.1 Employee Total Compensation

Compensation of employees	Extrinsic rewards	Monetary rewards	Hourly wage
			Salary
			Bonuses
			Commissions
		Benefits	Insurance
			Transport facilities
			Retirement/pension plan
			Paid holidays
			Paid public holidays
			Canteen services
			Medical services
			Recreation facilities
	Intrinsic rewards		Recognition
			Promotion opportunities
			Goof working condition
			Safe work environment

10.2 Basis for Compensation

Developing pay plan is very important to both small firms and bigger ones. Whereas paying too high will be expensive for the company, lower rates will guarantee poor quality of performance and frequent turnover. Equity and discretion are needed in this exercise.

Pay systems are designed and managed to achieve some specific objectives including efficiency, equity, and compliance with rules and regulations. Efficiency has to do with improving performance, quality, satisfying customers, and controlling labour cost. Equity deals with fair treatment for all employees, a 'fair day's pay for a fair day's work'.

Thus, equity focuses on designing pay systems that recognise both employee contributions and needs. As a pay objective compliance refers to conforming to the various government regulations and compensation laws in the country, changes in laws and regulations may necessitate adjustments to ensure compliance.

To get the right form of compensation, it is important that an organisation undertakes pay survey and job evaluation. Pay survey is the process of analysing compensation data gathered from other employers in a survey of the relevant labour market. Gathering external pay data is essential to keep the organisation's compensation externally competitive within its industry.

Job evaluation, on the other hand, is a systematic determination of the relative worth of a job within an organisation that results in an organisation's pay system. The outcome of job evaluation is the development of an internal structure or hierarchical ranking of jobs. Thus, it establishes internal relativities and provides the basis for designing an equitable grade and pay structure, grading jobs in the structure, and managing job and pay relativities. Evaluating jobs produce the information required to design and maintain equitable and defensible grade and pay structures. It also assesses the intended against the actual performance and the information is used for future adjustments.

Job evaluation can be analytical or non-analytical. Analytical job evaluation involves making decisions about the value or size of jobs, which are based on an analysis of the extent to which various defined factors are present in a job. These elements should be present in all the jobs to be evaluated, and the different levels at which they are present indicate relative job value. Examples of analytical job evaluation are point-factor rating and factor comparison.

Non-analytical job evaluation, on the other hand, compares whole jobs to place them in a grade or a rank order. The commonest non-analytical approach is to match roles as defined in role profiles either to standardised definitions of grades, bands, or levels or the role profiles of jobs that have already been graded. Another approach is to rank whole jobs in order of perceived value. Examples of this kind of evaluation include job classification, job ranking, and paired and comparison ranking.

10.3 Different Views of Compensation

Employees and managers have different view on compensation, and they are discussed below.

10.3.1 Employees' view of compensation

- Employees may see compensation as an exchange for services rendered or as a reward for a job well done.

- To some, it reflects the value of their personal skills and abilities, or the return for the education and training they have acquired.

- To others, it is the major source of personal income and financial security and thus a vital determinant of their economic and social well-being.

10.3.2 Managers' view of compensation

- For managers, compensation is a major expense to the organisation. Studies show that in many organisations, labour costs account for more than 50 per cent of total costs.

- Competitive pressure, both internationally and domestically, push managers to consider the affordability of their compensation decisions.

- Managers also treat compensation as a possible influence on employee work attitudes and behaviours and their organisation performance.

10.4 Factors Affecting the Wage Mix

The wage mix is usually affected by both internal and external factors and these are discussed below.

10.4.1 Internal factors

The component of internal factors include

    i.   Organisation's compensation policy

    ii.   Worth of a job which is obtained throough job evaluation

    iii.   Employee's relative worth in meeting job requirements

    iv.   Organisaion's ability to pay

10.4.2 External factors

The external factors that make up the wage mix are as follows;

    i.   Labor market condition

    ii.   Area wage rates

    iii.   Collective bargaining

    iv.   Cost of living

    v.   Legal requirements

10.5 Objectives of Compensation

Some of the objective of compensation are as follows;

    i.   To help organisations to pay market-competitive compensation

    ii.   To asist organisations to achieve both internal and external pay equity

iii. To ensure that all emloyess are fairly treated

iv. To promote open and understandable pay practices

v. To enable organsations to comply with all governmental compensation regulations

vi. To promote pay-for performance standards at the workplace

vii. To mesh employees' future performance with organisational goals

viii. To be able to control the compensation budget of organisations

ix. To attract new employees and talented employees into the organisations

x. To reduce unnecessary turnover and increase employee retention

10.6 Importance of Managing Compensation

There are numerous importance to managing compensation effectively in organisations. Some of these significance are discussed below.

i. Unless compensation is provided, no one will come and work for the organisation. Thus, compensation helps in running an organisation effectively and accomplishing its goals.

ii. An ideal compensation management structure motivates employees to work hard and improve their productivity as well as increase the organisation's productivity.

iii. Effective compensation management sees to it that all government and labour laws and legal regulations prevalent in the country are adhered to so that there are no disputes between the management and the employee unions.

iv. Good compensation management reduces employee turnover and helps in creating a great atmosphere to work in the organisation.

v. Salary is just a part of the compensation system; the employees have other psychological and self-actualisation needs to fulfil and compensation serves the purpose.

vi. The most competitive compensation will help the organisation to attract and sustain the best talent. The compensation package should, however, be as per industry standards.

vii. Employees may quit when compensation levels are not competitive, resulting in high turnover. To retain current employees, their compensation must be managed well.

viii. Compensation should reinforce desired behaviours and act as an incentive for such behaviour to occur in the future. Effective compensation plans reward performance, loyalty, experience, responsibility, and other positive behaviours.

ix. When compensation is high enough, it can attract qualified applicants. Pay levels must respond to the supply and demand of workers in the labour market since employers compete for workers. Premium wages are sometimes needed to attract applicants already working for others.

10.7 Challenges of Managing Compensation Effectively

There are several challenges of effectively managing compensation and five of the major ones are discussed below.

i. One of the major challenges of the managing compensation is the controlling of the huge labour cost associated with paying employee compensation. This is because employee costs constitute in some cases over 50% of an organisation's budget.

ii. Another challenge is how organisations can offer competitive pay in order to compete for and attract and retain the best available talent in the world market.

iii. Problems with internal equity is also a major challenge. When the value of an employee's work does not match his or her pay, or when employees consider themselves valuable and expects to be paid more than they receive, it can affect the existing pay systems and create problems for the organisation.

iv.   Another key problem of managing compensation is how the organisations can effectively manage executive compensation. This is a critical issue for both public and private organisations. Some organisations have been heavily criticized by their employees, shareholders and other stakeholders for creating compensation plans with large rewards exclusively for executives.

v.   Attempting and succeeding at design compensation packages that will successfully motivate employees to perform at their best tends to be a major challenge to organisations. Indeed the package which must recognize and reward employees for their contributions in a way that's affordable to the organisation is not easily achievable.

PART SEVEN

ASSESSING AND DEVELOPING ADROIT HUMAN RESOURCES

11 PERFORMANCE MANAGEMENT AND APPRAISALS

Learning Objectives

After reading this chapter, you should be able to

- Understand performance management and why it is necessary to manage employee performance

- Evaluate the elements in the performance management system

- Comprehend the importance of performance appraisal and the steps for developing performance appraisal systems

- Recognise the various people who should appraise performance

- Evaluate the methods and instrument of performance appraisal and some errors that can occur in rating employee performance

- Identify guidelines for effective performance appraisal interviews

Introduction

Performance Management (PM) became popular about two decades ago. PM is a very significant aspect of organisational success because it is the key process through which work is accomplished. However, less than a third of employees believe that their company's PM process assists them in improving their performance. Research also shows that PM is regularly ranked among the lowest topics in employee satisfaction surveys. Sometimes the employee annual review known as appraisals are often confused with PM. It must be stressed that the employee appraisals are just an aspect of the entire concept of PM. Indeed, PM uses various tools including performance appraisals to ensure that performance goals are achieved.

PM has a variety of meanings and has been used to describe various HR initiatives. It incorporates issues that are central to many other elements of HRM, such as appraisal and employee development, performance-related pay, reward management, and employee relations. However, the concept of PM adopts a future-oriented strategic focus and is applied to all employees in an organisation so as to maximise their present as well as future performances. PM is the totality of the day-to-day management activity and is concerned with how work can be organised in order to achieve the best possible result. For PM to be effective, it requires the effort of both employers and employees. Basically, effective PM can strengthen and augment the relationship between individual expectations, and departmental and organisational goals and objectives.

11.1 Defining Performance Management

By way of definition, PM has been explained differently by various writers. PM is a planned or strategic and integrated process which incorporates goal-setting, performance appraisal, and development into a unified and logical framework with the aim of aligning individual performance goals with the organisation's wider objectives (Dessler, 2003). Armstrong and Baron (2004) explain PM as a process of aligning or integrating organisational and individual objectives to achieve organisational effectiveness, with development as the prime purpose. According to the Society for Human Resource Management, PM is the organised method of monitoring results of work activities, collecting and evaluating performance to determine achievement of goals, and using performance information to make decisions, allocate resources, and communicate whether objectives are met.

Performance management is also seen as the policies, procedures, and practices that focus on employee performance as a means of fulfilling organisational goals and objectives (Lowry, 2002), Thus, PM establishes a framework through which performance of individuals can be directed and monitored, so as to identify their training needs and promote motivation and advancement through feedback.

11.2 Why Manage Performance?

It is important for HR managers to direct the performance of their employees for various reasons including the following.

i.   Managing performance will facilitate continuous review and ongoing development of individuals, teams, and department in the organisation

ii. The underlying assumption is that by managing the performance of the individual or team effectively, departmental and organisational performance are likely to automatically improve

iii. Equally when performance of individuals is managed, it can diminish frustration and discontent amongst team members and sometime poor performance of the organisation.

iv. PM has a significant role to play in enhancing organisational performance, by ensuring that all individuals understand their expected contribution to business objectives and are equipped with the skills and support to achieve this.

v.   It is important to manage performance because it promotes sharing of expectations between employers and employees.

vi. PM gives managers the opportunity to clarify what they expect individual and teams to do on a periodical basis. Likewise, individuals and teams can communicate their expectations of how they should be managed and how they need to do their jobs.

11.3 Performance Management System

It must be noted that PM is a process and not an event. It operates as a continuous cycle. Even though there is no universal model for PM, available literature suggests some important elements that must be present. Performance management is a system and starts when immediately employees are recruited and selected for the job.

The four elements in the cycle are as follows:

- Setting objectives during employee orientation/induction
- Reviewing and appraising employee performance annually
- Strengthening and developing new performance standards
- Providing support through employee counselling/therapy

11.3.1 Setting objectives during employee orientation/induction

It is important that as soon as the employees are selected to be part of an organisation, they must be informed about what is expected of them by way of performance standards. During the orientation and induction processes, employees must be made aware of what they need to do. This can be termed as the planning or goal-setting phase of the cycle. Their roles and responsibilities must be made very clear, and they must be told when they will be assessed, either after six months or annually depending on the policies of the organisation. Objectives set and results expected must be practical; also, any support by way of equipment and personnel must be made available to enhance performance.

11.3.2 Reviewing and appraising employee performance annually

Once the standard has been set, the next stage is appraising the employee's performance on the agreed period. Usually, performance appraisals are held annually. There are several ways that the performance of an employee can be reviewed. Basically, an appraisal is an open discussion about the employee's work done over a period of time and the criteria set. Appraisals will be further discussed on a later page.

11.3.3 Strengthening and developing new performance standards

Sometimes after the review, it will be evident that the standards have not been met, and this is where the third stage is initiated. Often employees will achieve almost all the target set. However, there are situations where they fail to achieve the standards due to issues like absenteeism, poor performance, deficient job description, work overload, lack of supervision and support, lack of ability to cope with the work, stress, and family and domestic problems. Depending on the cause of the failure to achieve the expected performance, the organisation can decide to strengthen the performance standards or even develop new standards. This is aimed at managing the failure to achieve the required standards subsequently.

11.3.4 Providing support through employee counselling or therapy

Depending on the issues that come out during the appraisal discussions, the employer may decide to either counsel the employee or suggest alternative remedies such as therapy. If the problem is family-related, such as abuse, difficult child, emotional or addiction, then counselling the employee is better than just developing new performance standards. In cases where the issues are ill-health or stress-related, then therapy could be the imminent suggestion. By providing this kind of support, you may be helping the individual to meet the expected performance standard. The performance management process is depicted in Figure 11.1.

Figure 11.1: The Performance Management Process

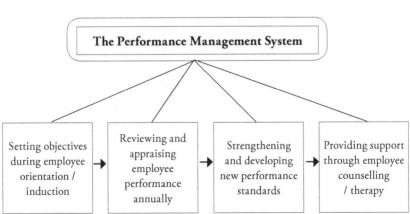

11.4 Performance Appraisal

Performance appraisal, review, or evaluation is the HRM activity that is used to determine the extent to which an employee is performing his or her job effectively. It is the name given to the regular, formalised, and recorded review of the way an employee is performing in his or her job. Put differently, appraisal interviews are performance review sessions that give employees feedback on their past performance and/or future potential.

Usually, the jobholder's immediate manager or supervisor carries out this exercise. It gives managers the opportunity to discuss a subordinate's performance record and explore areas of possible improvement and growth. It also provides an opportunity to identify the employee's attitude and feelings more thoroughly and thus improve communication. Many organisations operate performance appraisals regularly, usually annually, during which an individual's manager assesses performance, potential, and development. Thus an appraisal is a tool used for both evaluation and development of the employee. In evaluating, an individual's performance is thoroughly assessed and decisions are taken based on that. In developing, feedback relating to their performance, directions for future performance and training needs are discussed.

11.5 Importance of Performance Appraisal

Some importance of performance appraisals includes the following:

i.   Appraisals are useful for the development of the employee. It can help to evaluate previous training had and which employee needs more training, counselling, and mentoring.

ii.   It helps supervisors to make salary recommendations and the organisation to decide who should receive a pay rise and promotions and who should be laid-off. Hence, it is useful for rewards and compensation purposes.

iii. Appraisals also have a motivation effect which is to say, it encourages initiative, develops a sense of responsibility, and stimulates effort for improved performance.

iv. It serves as a legal defence for promotions, transfers, rewards, and discharges; thus, it serves as a tool for legal compliance.

v. With regards to HRP, appraisals serve as a valuable input for planning human resource need for the organisation.

vi. It is a communication too. It gives employees the opportunity to discuss job-related matters and performance standards regularly with their supervisors.

vii. It gives employees the opportunity to discuss any existing problems with other colleagues, domestic issues, and other barrier to effective performance. This when addressed will lead to the improvement of current performance.

11.6 Steps for Developing Performance Appraisal Systems

To achieve the needed results, organisations must develop some steps for the employee performance appraisal system. Some of the steps are discussed below.

11.6.1. Establish performance requirement

The organisation must determine the skills and outputs that will be evaluated during the process. This will not be different from the requirement in the job description as well as performance standards already agreed upon.

11.6.2 Select an appropriate appraisal method

There are several methods of appraisal. It is important that organisations select the appropriate method for the various types of employees to be appraised. Sometimes employees from different department may also require different methods of appraisal. No one method will be best suited for all situations.

11.6.3 Train supervisors and other appraisers

It is very crucial that the supervisors or persons responsible for appraisals are well trained to handle it. If they are well trained, it will enable them to prepare well and be fair and accurate in rating the employee performance. Inaccurate appraisal has diverse negative effect on the employee, and decisions may be taken based on a wrong fact; hence, training the appraisers is very important.

11.6.4 Discuss the method with employees

Before the day of the appraisal interview, the supervisor or the appraiser must discuss the methods that may be used with the appraisee. The discussion should focus on the areas of performance that will be evaluated and what the employee is expected to do by way of preparation before the day of the appraisal.

11.6.5 Give employees time to prepare for the interview

The person to be appraised should be given ample notice before the due date. It is an interview that has effect on decisions that will be taken on the employees' employment; hence, it is necessary that they prepare adequately. Appraisals should not be a surprise event but a well-planned and thought-out procedure.

11.6.6 Appraise according to work standards and not personal opinion

It is important that employees are appraised based on agreed and predetermined job requirement. Sometimes supervisors may have some reservations about the employees being appraised; however, it is necessary that this does not affect the appraisal procedure. The supervisor must focus on the work-related standards that have been set and not emotions.

11.6.7 Discuss appraisals with employees

The appraisal forms once agreed on and signed by both the appraiser and appraisee can be admissible in the law court. It is therefore important that the supervisor discusses the appraisal with the employee and allow them to make any input they may have. Areas of agreement or disagreement must be thoroughly discussed. Where expectations have been met, it must be made known to the employees, and any improvement must be discussed before signatures are appended.

11.6.8 Determine and agree on future plan

Feedback is another very important aspect of the whole process. It is therefore important that the supervisor and employee being appraised both agree on the future plan and way forward. This aspect also gives the employee the direction to follow to achieve continuous improvement and to meet future expectations.

11.7 Reasons Why Appraisals Fail

Appraisals fail due to many reasons, and they include the following:

i.   Some managers feel that the exercise is time-consuming and little or no benefit will be derived from the time and energy spent in the process.

ii.   Most managers/supervisors dislike the face-to-face confrontation of appraisal interviews because it is a platform for subordinates to speak their minds.

iii. Some managers are not sufficiently proficient or ready to provide appraisal feedback which is one of the important things in the whole process.

iv.   Most superiors turn to be bias even in well-organised systems, and the judgemental role of appraisal conflicts with the helping role of developing employees.

v.   Some appraisal systems or forms are archaic and do not ask the right questions, thereby lacking the needed answers, and this forfeits the main aim of the exercise.

11.8 Who Should Appraise Performance?

Apart from supervisors, different people such as the subordinate, peers, team members, and even customers can also appraise employees.

11.8.1 Manager/supervisor appraisal

This is performance appraisal done by an employee's manager and often reviewed by a manager one level higher.

11.8.2 Self-appraisal

This is done by the employee being evaluated, generally on an appraisal form compiled by the employee prior to the performance interview proper.

11.8.3 Subordinate appraisal

This is performance appraisal of a superior by a subordinate. This is more appropriate for developmental needs than for administrative purposes.

11.8.4 Peer appraisal

This is an appraisal conducted by one's fellow employees, generally on forms that are compiled into a single profile for use in the performance interview to be conducted by the employee's manager.

11.8.5 Team appraisal

An extension of the peer appraisal is the team appraisal. While the peer is on equal standing basis, the team appraisal will look at the overall contribution to the work team.

11.8.6 360 Degrees appraisal

This refers to the kind of appraisal that involves everybody the employee in question has some working relationship with including peers, superiors, subordinates, as well as internal and external customers.

11.9 Methods and Instrument of Performance Appraisal

There are several methods of appraising employee performance. They include the graphic rating scales, behavioural anchored rating scales, ranking, forced distribution, and 360-degrees appraisal.

11.9.1 Graphic rating scales

The graphic rating scale method of assessing employee performance is one of the oldest and most common methods. It is also a popular method with managers because among other things, it can be filled out quickly, and appraisers need little training to handle it. With this method, the managers do checks on the performance levels of their staff. It is a trait approach to performance appraisal whereby each employee is rated according to a scale of characteristic. Employers rate employees on some standard or attribute of work, for instance, behaviour and outcomes. Graphic rating scale allows the rater to mark an employee's performance on a continuum. The rating is usually done in a 1–5 likert scale with 1 representing 'satisfactory' and 5 'excellent'.

11.9.2 Behavioural anchored rating scales

The Behavioural Anchored Rating Scales (BARS) is a combination of rating scales. Instead of using broad employee attributes, the points on rating scale are critical incidents. BARS is a formatted performance appraisal based on making rates on behaviours or sets of indicators to determine the effectiveness or ineffectiveness of working performance. The form is a mix of the rating scale and critical incident techniques to assess performance of the staff. BARS is a numerical scale that is anchored by specific narrative examples of behaviours that range from very negative to very positive descript of performance. It is a complicated method of evaluating employee performance based on employee behaviour rather than attitude or assumptions about motivation or potential. BARS is a difficult and time-consuming scale to develop. Each job must be analysed and a list of critical incidents developed by experts in the job. Once the critical incidents are developed, they are matched to a set of performance scope that are then scaled from effective to ineffective performance.

11.9.3 Ranking method

As the name suggests, the ranking method lists all employees in a certain order – from the highest to the lowest or from effective to least effective or best to worst. This method is comparative and raters judge employees' performance in relation to each other instead of against an absolute standard. The advantage of ranking is that it is fast and easy to complete. Also this method does not allow the evaluator to rate everyone as high. A numerical evaluation given to the employee can be directly related to compensation changes and other employee considerations. Although some major errors are avoided with this method, it, however, fails to provide detailed feedback for employees since their strength and weaknesses are not obvious and future direction is unclear.

11.9.4 Forced distribution

The forced distribution method is similar to the ranking method. It is a comparative method of appraisal that requires raters to place a certain percentage of employees into each of several categories based on their overall performance. Thus, forced distribution requires that supervisors spread their employee evaluations in a pre-described distribution. For example, 10 per cent of the employees must be placed under 'unsatisfactory', whiles 30 per cent are placed under 'very good.' This method forces employers or raters to discriminate between employees; however, their absolute differences remain unknown and that is a shortcoming. Another problem with this method is that supervisors may not want or oppose the idea of placing some employees in the lowest or highest category.

11.9.5 360 Degrees appraisal

360 Degrees appraisal method is a multisource rating which is presently gaining popularity. This refers to the kind of appraisal that involves everybody the employee in question has some working relationship with. This is an appraisal based on the collection of performance data from a number of sources, including peers, superiors, subordinates, as well as internal and external customers. It is an alternative approach to traditional

form of appraisal. Although it may be time-consuming, usually, the problem of bias is limited with this kind of appraisal.

11.10 Approaches to Appraisals

There are several approaches to performance appraisal and some are discussed below:

11.10.1 Tell and sell approach

This kind of appraisal is best suited for new employees. The approach reviews the employee's performance, and then the reviewer tries to convince the employee to perform better. The information given to the appraisee is not a suggestion but rather a requirement.

11.10.2 Tell and listen approach

This method allows the employee to explain the reasons, excuses, and defensive feeling about performance. The supervisor then attempts to counsel or suggest the employee on how to perform better to overcome these reactions.

11.10.3 The problem-solving approach

This approach identifies problems that are interfering with employee performance. Both the appraiser and appraise discus the problems and try to find a solution together. Sometimes coaching, mentoring, or counselling efforts are suggested and discussed as measures that can help the employee to remove any barriers and set goals for better future performance.

11.11 Errors in Rating Performance Appraisal

Apart from errors such as personal preferences, prejudices, and biases, other possible ones such as leniency or strictness, central tendency, recency of event, and halo effect errors can obstruct an employee's appraisal process.

11.11.1 Leniency or strictness error

This is a performance rating error in which the appraiser tends to give employees either unusually high or low marks. With this, error ratings are grouped at the positive or negative end of the performance scale instead of spreading them throughout the scale. This could signify biases on the part of certain supervisors by consistently assigning high or low values to subordinates.

11.11.2 Central tendency or clustering in the middle error

This occurs when a rater avoids using high or low ratings and assigns average ratings to appraisees. Central tendency makes it difficult for making HRM decisions regarding compensation, promotion, and training needs because it fails to discriminate between subordinates.

11.11.3 Recency of events error

Recency error occurs when supervisors evaluate subordinates' performance based on work performed most recently. In this case, raters forget about past behaviour and focus on current behaviour. Generally, the above errors make it difficult to separate good performance from poor performance.

11.11.4 Halo effect error

Halo effect error occurs when a rater allows one particular aspect or behaviour of an employee's performance influence the evaluation of other dimension of performance. For instance, if a rater allows the fact that an employee is always punctual to cover up for her being very slow at work, a halo effect error has occurred. Halo error can be either a positive or a negative error, that is, the initial impression can cause the ratings to be either too low or too high. Furthermore, this occurs when managers allow high prominent characteristics of an employee to influence their judgment on each item in the performance appraisal.

11.12 Guidelines for Effective Performance Appraisal Interviews

i.   Schedule the appraisal date and inform the employee ahead of time, usually ten to fourteen days.

ii. Select a location that is comfortable and free of distractions. Your location should be a relaxed atmosphere, which will encourage a frank conversation.

iii. Assure the employee that the appraisal session is to improve performance and not to discipline them.

iv. Be specific and descriptive, not general and judgmental, discuss your differences and resolve them.

v.   Stress more on the positive aspect of employee's performance and focus criticism on performance and not personality characteristics.

vi. Maintain a professional and supportive approach during appraisal discussion, and do not argue with the person you are evaluating.

vii. Jointly discuss and design plans for taking corrective action for growth and development.

viii. Provide performance feedback, identify training and development needs, and give direction for future performance.

ix. Performance must be reviewed formally at least once a year but more frequently for new employees or those who are performing below standard.

12 EMPLOYEE TRAINING AND DEVELOPMENT

Learning Objectives

After reading this chapter, you should be able to

- Understand the difference between employee training and development

- Identify some factors that create the need for training and development

- Explain the systematic approach to training and development

- Assess the different training methods for non-managerial employees as well as managerial development

- Evaluate some factors that hinder learning and how to obtain and hold learners' attention

Introduction

Training plays a very important role in any organisation, and it is said to be the backbone of strategy implementation. In addition, organisations often compete on competencies which mean that it is the knowledge and expertise of their employees that give them an edge over their competitors. Thus, training plays a central role in nurturing and strengthening employee competencies. Most new employees join organisations with most of the qualification, knowledge, skills, and abilities needed to start working. Others may require extensive training before they are ready to make much of a contribution to their organisations. However, almost every employee needs some type of training on an ongoing basis to maintain effective performance or to adjust to new ways of work. Training and development programmes are usually designed to help improve procedures and performances of both employees and the entire organisation. Although they are often used together, they are different in concept and approach. Training programmes have definite goals and specific audience and are a vital part of the overall growth strategy of the employee and the organisation as well. Development programmes on the other hand, concentrate on the broader skills that can be applied in decision making and enhanced leadership skills.

12.1 Training Explained

Training is an effort initiated by an organisation to foster learning among its members. Due to changing trends in technology, organisational changes, and changes in tasks and the nature of jobs, it has become imperative for organisations to train their members. Training serves as a vehicle through which organisations increase the knowledge and skills of their members up to a level required for satisfactory performance. Thus, training is a way of teaching organisational members the method to perform their current jobs and helping them acquire the knowledge and skills they need to be effective performers. Put differently, training refers to a planned effort by an organisation to facilitate employees' learning of job-related competences. These competences include knowledge and skills that are essentially needed for the successful performance of their jobs.

12.2 Development Explained

Unlike training, development, on the other hand, is aimed towards broadening an individual's skills for future responsibilities. Development can be explained as any process aimed at preparing staff for future challenges and a variety of tasks that they may perform in future towards the achievement of organisational strategic goals. Development does not lead to any immediate and tangible benefits to the organisation, but rather future benefits. It makes the employee efficient enough to handle critical situations in the future, that is, how well the employee can equip himself for the future demands.

12.3 The Thin Line between Training and Development

From the discussions so far, it is noticeable that although the term training and development are often used together, there is a slight difference between the two terms. Many experts make a distinction between training and development. The former focuses on short-term performance concerns, whiles the latter is more towards broadening an individual's skills for future tasks. Thus, training usually is aimed for the short run, and development concentrates on the long run objectives. Also training programmes centres on a smaller number of technical skills such as upgrading of an employee's skills, whereas development tend to focus on a broad range of skills such as decision-making, planning, and motivation.

It must however be emphasised that the common practise in recent times, however, is to fuse the two terms into one single phrase – training and development. Training and development mean the combination of efforts or activities used by an organisation to increase the skill base of their employees.

12.4 Some Factors that Create the Need for Training and Development

There are several issues that make it necessary for organisations to train and develop their employees. Some of these issues include the following:

i. Globalisation

ii. Customer sophistication

iii. Social and legal changes

iv. Technological advancement

v. Organisational changes such as mergers, acquisitions, and downsizing

vi. For improvement of employee skills and performance

vii. To prevent managerial obsolescence

viii. For promotion and succession planning

ix. To satisfy employee growth needs

x. To solve organisational problems

xi. To prepare employees for promotion and managerial succession

12.5 Some Benefits of Training and Development

The importance of training for both new and experienced employees cannot be overemphasized. Below are some benefits of training and development in organisations.

i. Improves employee performance

ii. Increases employee satisfaction, value and morale

iii. Addresses weaknesses in skills of employees

iv. Creates an overall knowledgeable staff

v. Reduces persistent consultation and supervision

vi. Advances the adherence to quality standards and overall productivity

vii. Increases independence and innovation in new strategies and products

viii. Reduces employee turnover

ix. Improves employee retention

x. Boosts organisational profile and reputation

12.6 The Four-Phase Systematic Approach to Training and Development

The ultimate goal of training, is to contribute to the organisation's overall goals. Training programmes should therefore always be developed with this in mind. The agenda of training should show a connection between the strategic objectives of the organisation. Training programmes are designed and undertaken in a systematic way.

The systematic approach to training and development highlights the employment of a four-phase model: the needs assessment, programmes design, implementation, and evaluation.

12.6.1 Training needs assessment

The first phase in the systematic training approach is to assess the training needs. The main objective of training is to enable an organisation achieve certain objectives; therefore, assessing the need for training employees is a very important process. At this stage, some questions that may arise are as follows: what kinds of training are needed? Which department or section needs the training? Which persons in the designated department need them? As well as which methods will best be used to deliver the needed knowledge and skills to employees? These analyses are systematically utilised to ensure that the training is timely and focused on priority issues.

Training needs assessment is done in three different stages: the organisational analysis, task analysis, and person analysis.

i.   Organisational analysis

This is the first step in the needs assessment process. It involves identifying the broad forces that can influence training needs. Organisational analysis is an examination of the environment, strategies, and resources of the organisation to determine where training emphasis should be placed.

ii.   Task analysis

This involves reviewing the job description and specification to identify the activities performed in a particular job and the knowledge, skills, and abilities needed to perform them. The first step in task analysis is to list all the tasks or duties included in the job. The second step is to list the steps performed by the employee to complete each task. Once the job is understood thoroughly, the type of performance required, along with the skills and knowledge necessary for performance, can be readily identified.

iii. Person analysis

Person analysis involves determining which employees require training and which employees do not. This helps managers to determine what prospective trainees are able to do when they enter training so that the programmes can be designed to emphasise the areas in which they have deficiencies.

12.6.2 Training programme design

After the training objectives have been identified, the organisation must come up with an appropriate programme design. The second phase which is designing the training programme is also very crucial. It must be noted that the success of this stage depends largely on the organisation's ability to properly identify training needs. A well-designed programme will focus on issues such as instructional objectives, trainee readiness and motivation, principles of learning, and characteristics of instructors.

i.   Instructional objectives

These describe the skills or knowledge to be acquired and/or the attitudes to be changed. A clear statement of instructional objectives will provide a sound basis for choosing methods and materials and for selecting the means for assessing whether the instruction will be successful or otherwise.

ii.   Trainee readiness and motivation

Trainee readiness refers to both maturity and experience factors in the trainee's background. Prospective trainees should be screened to determine that they have the background knowledge necessary to absorb what will be presented to them. Trainee motivation is another precondition for learning. Individuals who are goal-oriented, self-disciplined, and persevering are more likely to perceive a link between effort they put into training and higher performance on the job. By focusing on the trainees themselves rather than on the training topic, managers can create a training environment that is conducive to learning. Six strategies can be used to motivate them:

- Use positive reinforcement

- Eliminate threats and punishment and be flexible
- Have participants set personal goals
- Design interesting instruction
- Break down physical and psychological obstacles to learning

iii. Principles of learning

Training is aimed at bridging a gap between the needs of employees and the organisation. One important step in this transition is giving full consideration to the psychological principles of learning. These are the characteristics of training programmes that help employees to grasp new materials, make sense of it in their own lives, and transfer it back to the job. Some of the principles of learning are listed below:

- Properly set goals and objectives of the training process
- The presentation of the training must make meaning in the lives and work of trainees
- Properly used models, illustrations, and audio visuals that enhance the mental capture of information
- Take into consideration the individual differences of trainees and adapt training to fit them
- Use a practical approach in training and allow trainees to put what they have learnt in theory into practice, both at the training centre and back to their workplaces
- Know whether to lump the training together with a short break or separate them over several hours with several breaks
- Ensure that there is feedback and reinforcement. This will give you some knowledge of the results achieved and serve as motivation to the trainees to further practice what they have learnt on their jobs.

iv.   Characteristics of the instructors

The success of any training effort will depend to a large extent on the teaching skills and personal characteristics of the people responsible for conducting the training. A good trainer is one who puts in an extra effort or demonstrates more instructional preparation. Some traits that can be seen in a good trainer include the following:

- Knowledge of the subject
- Interest in the subject
- Adaptability and flexibility
- Genuineness or sincerity
- Sense of humour
- Individual Assistance
- Enthusiasm

12.6.3 Training delivery or implementation

The whole concept behind training may be lost if it is implemented poorly. Thus, the heart of training may perhaps lie in the implementation phase. What will make the implementation successful is the making of the right choice as to which training method or combination of methods to use. Usually, it is suggested that training should be pilot-tested in order to ensure that it is appropriate and meets the need identified.

The delivery methods are several but not all are good for all occasions or calibre of trainees. Some methods are more suitable for training non-managerial employees, whiles others will be best suited for managerial employees.

12.6.3.1 Training methods for non-managerial employees

There are several methods which are deemed to be suitable for the training of non-managerial employees, and each of the methods has its own advantages and disadvantages. Some of the methods are discussed below.

i. On-the-job training

This is by far the most common method used to train non-managerial staff. With its ability to provide direct learning experience to trainees, it has been viewed by many to be potentially the most effective means of facilitating learning in the workplace. With this method, trainees are assigned to work on tasks with experienced employees. The trainee picks up knowledge directly from participating in the training activity and from observing how the experienced person works. It is necessary that the trainee follows the basic instructions given at intervals, before or after the work session.

ii. Apprenticeship training

With this method, individuals entering the industry are given thorough instruction and experience, both on and off the job, in the practical and theoretical aspects of the work. Though employee wages are usually less while they are in the apprenticeship programme, it still provides compensation while individuals still learn their trade.

iii. Cooperative training

This method combines practical on-the-job experience with formal classes. The term is typically used in connection with university programmes that incorporate part or full-time experiences with their normal course work. Expanded versions of this method allow employees to work by day and learn at night courses relevant to their careers. Some employers normally support this method because of its numerous benefits.

iv. Internships

Internship offers students the chance to get real-work experience while finding out how they will perform in work organisations. While organisations benefit by getting student-employees with new ideas, energy, and eagerness to accomplish their assignments, the students acquire a lot of experience during the process. Generally, universities award credits to their students after appraising their performance on internship programmes.

v. Classroom instruction

When thinking about training, the first thing most people think about is a classroom. The reason is that beyond its popularity in education, classroom training allows the maximum number of trainees to be handled by the minimum number of instructors. This method becomes useful particularly when information can be presented in lectures, demonstrations, films, and videotapes or through computer instruction.

vi. Programmed instruction

This is usually referred to as self-directed learning. It involves the use of books, manuals, or computers to break down the content of the subject matter into highly organised, logical sequences. This programme demands continuous response on the part of the trainee. After being presented with a small segment of information, the trainee is required to answer a question, either by writing it in a response frame or by pushing a button. The trainee is often told when they are right or wrong in their response. The major advantage of this is that training is individualised and at the own pace of the trainee. While it cannot guarantee that a lot more is learnt by trainees using this method, it typically increases the speed at which they learn.

vii. Computer-based training

Computer-based training, such as the computer-assisted instruction system, delivers training materials through a computer terminal in an interactive format. Computers make it possible to provide drill and practice, problem-solving instruction, and other sophisticated forms of individualised tutorial instruction.

viii. Audio–visual methods

This refers to using equipment and facilities that provide information in audio and visual formats for the appreciation and comprehension of trainees.

Video tapes and audio tapes, CDs, DVDs, and the use of equipment such as camcorders and projectors help to convey the information needed to be transmitted more efficiently. Teleconferencing or videoconferencing allows instructional programmes to be transmitted to many locations at the same time and permits immediate interaction among trainees.

ix. Simulation method

Sometimes it is impractical or unwise to train employees on the actual equipment used on the job. This is more so when the equipment involved is very expensive, highly technical, or fragile. This method emphasises realism in equipment use and its operation at minimum cost and maximum safety. The airline industry and the military are perhaps the pioneers in this method of training.

12.6.3.2 Training for managerial development

Various methods can be used in the training of managerial employees. Each of the methods has some advantages as well as shortcomings. Organisations must therefore explore the methods they deemed suitable for their managerial development.

i. On-the-job experiences

Some skills and knowledge can be acquired just by listening and observing or by reading. Others must however be acquired through actual practice and experience. By presenting managers with the opportunities to perform under pressure and to learn from their mistakes, on-the-job development experiences are some of the most powerful and commonly used techniques. However, just as on-the-job training for the first-level employees can be challenging, if not well planned, on-the-job management development can face similar problems. It should be well planned, organised, supervised, and challenging to the participants.

Not all on-the-job experiences are equal in their potential effectiveness for management development. Effective experiences and development usually occur when individuals are placed in a variety of challenging situations with problems to solve and choices to make under conditions of risk. These situations have the effect of motivating individuals to learn, provide opportunities, gain new ideas and knowledge, and practice their skills. It also enables the people being developed to apply knowledge and encourage new insights through reflection on previous actions.

Individuals can also gain experiences in a supportive environment with supervisors who act as positive role models and mentors, are supportive, and also provide counsel. The various on-the-job experiences are available for use by trainers. These include mentoring, staff meetings, coaching, job rotation, understudy assignments, action learning, and special projects. Some examples of challenging situations include the provision of new or increased responsibilities, special start-up assignments such as initiating a new programme or project, and handling human resource problems such as hiring and firing.

ii.   Seminars and conferences

These, like classroom instruction, are good for bringing groups of people together for training. Seminars and conference are used to communicate ideas, policies, or procedures. They are also good for raising points of debate or discussing issues usually with the help of a qualified leader who have no already made answers or resolutions. In this regard, they are used when attitude change is a goal.

iii.   Case studies

This method is particularly useful in a classroom situation. It can act as a good compliment to the classroom instructional method of training. By using documented examples, participants learn how to analyse and synthesise or put together facts, to become conscious of the many variables on which management decisions are based. This is generally used to improve upon the decision-making skills of trainees.

The case method forces trainees to grapple with exactly the kinds of decisions and dilemmas managers confront every day. In doing so, it redefines the traditional training dynamic in which the trainer dispenses knowledge and trainees passively receive it. The case method creates a classroom in which participants succeed not only by simply absorbing facts and theories, but also by exercising the skills of leadership and teamwork in the face of real problems.

Case studies are particularly important and useful where active participation is desired, team problem-solving and integration are possible, and analytic, problem-solving, and critical thinking skills are most important,

iv. Management games

With management games, players are faced with the task of making a series of decisions affecting a hypothetical organisation. The effects that every decision has on each area within the organisation can be simulated with a computer programme for the game. A major advantage with this technique is the high degree of participation it requires. It does not always need a computer because ordinary card slides may be used and played by several players depending on the objectives and intended learning.

v. Role play

Role play consists of assuming the attitudes, roles, and behaviour of others. The roles assumed are usually that of a supervisor or a subordinate who are involved in a particular problem. By acting out another's position, participants in the role playing can improve their ability to understand and cope with others. Role playing should also help trainees to learn how to counsel others by helping them to see situations from different perspectives. It is often used in training managers to handle employee issues relating to absenteeism, performance appraisal, and conflict situations.

At times, participants may be hesitant to try role playing. Successful role playing takes planning. Instructors should do the following:

- Ensure that members of the group are comfortable with each other
- Select and prepare the role players by introducing a specific situation

- Help participants prepare and ask them to describe potential characters

- Realise that volunteers make better role players

- Prepare the observers by giving them specific tasks

- Guide the role play enactment through the stages since it is not scripted

- Keep the role play as short as possible

- Discuss the enactment and prepare bulleted points of what was learnt

12.6.3.3 Obtaining and holding the learners' attention

Before people can learn any material, they must focus their voluntary attention on it. The desire to learn comes from within and it is spontaneous. To obtain and hold the learner's attention, the trainer must do the following.

- A good trainer must try to gain and maintain voluntary attention in every session he or she presents.

- Relate what you aim to teach to those subjects in which you know the trainees are interested.

- Introduce the session in such a way that the trainees will not only see and become interested in this relationship, but will want to learn more about it.

- Begin with a good story to which the trainees can relate. An effective trainer makes it his or her business to know the background of the trainees.

- Maintain the trainees' attention by doing all that is possible to facilitate their understanding and absorption of the material.

- Ensure that the trainee's learning is an active process in which the trainer and trainees are equal partners in terms of participation.

Some factors that hinder learning include the learning plateau, fatigue, and failure to concentrate.

- The learning plateau – at intervals, the rate of learning flattens out as the brain rests saturation: if the message is overloaded, the receiver rejects the excess and learning stops
- Fatigue – a tired receiver is not as receptive as an alert one
- Inability to concentrate – the longer the message, the more concentration decreases from beginning to end

12.6.4 Evaluation of training

After first three phases have been undertaken, the whole training and development programme must be evaluated so that the training outcomes can be measured. Evaluation thus compares the training results to the objective expected by both the trainer and trainee. It reveals whether trainees actually learnt new skills, attitudes, and knowledge through the training. If after evaluating training it is realised that the training need is not achieved, then it is possible that one of the initial three processes was not correctly undertaken. An organisation can then decide to start the whole cycle again so as to achieve the desired results.

There are four different evaluation strategies that can be exploited. These include evaluating the reaction of the participant, evaluating their learning, evaluating any change in their behaviour, and evaluating results.

i. Evaluating reaction

This is where the opinions and attitudes that the trainees formulate come to bear. At this stage, some trainers will use either questionnaires or interviews to evaluate the reaction of trainees. The trainer can find out among other things how well the trainees enjoyed the session(s) or course and how well the trainees liked a particular training session(s) or the course as a whole. The overall response of the trainees could be a good indication of the overall response of reaction to the programme.

ii. Evaluating learning

What the trainee has learnt can be evaluated by testing or examining him or her. This could take a form of written test questions, oral test questions, or skill tests. Sometimes tests are conducted before and after the training, and this give the trainer a general idea of what has been learnt. Also test may be conducted on the training material used. This gives the trainer feedback on whole delivery. If the feedback is poor or not what was expected, it gives the trainer the idea to either redesign or change the style of training. However, a positive feedback generally indicates that the training was successful.

iii. Evaluating behaviour

Evaluating behaviour has to do with finding out whether learning has transformed the participant. Trainees are expected to learn a skill or knowledge that results in a positive change in their job behaviour. This can be assessed by measuring the effect of training on job performance through interviewing of the trainee or their teammates. Behaviour can also be evaluated through appraisal by on-the-job supervisors. It must however be noted that behaviour is more difficult to measure than reaction and learning.

iv. Evaluating results

Results of the training can be measured by evaluating the achievement of the organisational objectives to the effect of the training. Sometimes the results are tangible such as improved job performance. Also some types of practical training results, such as typing, are easily measured. Where attitudes are involved, it is usually difficult to measure results. One difficulty in evaluating results is being able to identify whether changes were actually the result of training or other factors of major impact. The diagram in Figure 12.1 summaries the systems approach.

Figure 12.1: The Systematic Approach to Training

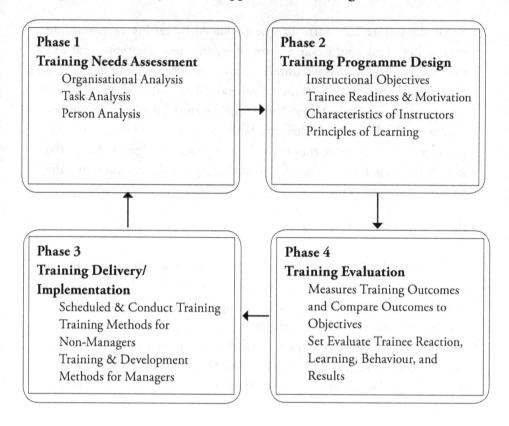

13 CAREER PLANNING, DEVELOPMENT AND MANAGEMENT

Learning Objectives

After reading this chapter, you should be able to:

- Understand the meaning of career

- Differentiate between career planning, development, and management

- Analyse the career planning and development model

- Identify the various people responsible for career development and the various stages in the development process

- Comprehend the meaning of career plateau and strategies for dealing with it

Introduction

Understanding and finding ways to positively influence careers of employees in an organisation is an essential part of HRM. Career management is important to employees because it enables them to satisfy their professional needs. On the other hand, organisations manage and support the career of their employees because it creates and sustains a continuous learning environment. Career planning and management involves two processes, with career planning being employee-centred and career management organisation-centred. Career development, on the other hand, is an employee's responsibility as much as an employer responsibility.

The study of careers and how they develop is one of the most active areas of inquiry in the social sciences. Psychologists, educators, sociologists, economists, and management scholars all seek to understand how a person selects, works within, and makes decisions to change the focus of his or her working life (Werner & DeSimone, 2009). There are also many governmental, legal, and public policy issues that impact career development (DeSimone, Smith, & Ueno, 2006). Decisions relating to careers are very important because most people will spend a greater part of their lives working, and the choices they make regarding their work will influence their success, happiness, and financial well-being of themselves and their families.

13.1 What is a Career?

A career is a pattern of work-related experiences that span the course of one's life. Werner and DeSimone (2009) also define a career as the series of work-related positions a person occupies throughout life. Put differently, a career can be said to be the sum total of paid and unpaid work, learning, and life roles one undertake throughout life.

The term career has often been restricted to suggest an employment commitment to a single trade skill, profession, or business firm for the entire working life of a person. It was traditionally associated with paid employment and referred to a single occupation. The definition of a career has however changed over the years. In today's world of work, a career is seen as a continuous process of learning and development and no longer refers to a single pathway to work. Thus, career covers all types of employment ranging from semi-skilled through skilled and semi-professional to professional. Careers are built through the series of choices people make throughout their lives; hence, it is a life-long process and includes the variety of work roles – paid and unpaid – which one undertakes throughout their lifetime.

13.2 Career Planning Explained

Career planning can be explained as a continuous process of self-assessment and goal setting (Kleinknecht & Hefferin, 1982). Career planning plays a crucial role at every stage of one's career. According to Dawn Rosenberg McKay, a career planning professional, career planning is a lifelong process, which includes choosing an occupation, searching for and getting a job, growing in that job, possibly changing careers, and eventually retiring.

Hall (1976) explains career planning as a deliberate process of (1) becoming aware of self-opportunities, constraints, choices, and consequences; (2) identifying career-related goals, and (3) programming work, education, and related developmental experiences to provide the direction, timing, and sequence of steps to attain a specific career goal.

Sometimes the assistance from career counsellors, supervisors, and others within and outside an organisation can be helpful to the employee; however, the focus of career planning is on the individual. Career planning is not a one-time event, but rather is a process that, over time, becomes part of an employee's range of skills and experiences and enables the individual to develop as a professional and achieve the objectives he or she has set. The planning consists of activities and actions that one takes to achieve his or her personal career goals. It must be noted that each individual has the lead responsibility for planning his or her own career.

For individuals to be successful with the career planning process, they have to know themselves, that is, what they want from work and what you have to offer. It is also important for them to explore as much options as possible. They then need to make decision focusing on the most suitable options, choosing a career goal, and finding ways of making it happen. Thus, career planning is the process whereby an individual explores his or her interests and abilities, strategically plans his or her career goals, and creates his or her future work success by designing learning and action plans to help him or her achieve his or her goals.

13.3 A Career Planning and Development Model

Career planning and development should be important to every employee because the consequences of career success or failure are so closely linked with social influences like each person's self-concept, identity, and satisfaction with life. The process of planning and developing one's career should be an integral part of one's ongoing professional development.

Donner and Wheeler (2001) assert that career development requires individuals to understand the environment in which they live and work.

They need to assess their strengths and weaknesses and validate that assessment so as to articulate their personal career vision. Employees also need to develop a realistic plan for the future and then to market themselves to achieve their career goals. Ideally, it is a focused professional development strategy that helps individuals to take greater responsibility for themselves and their careers and prepare for the ever-work environment.

There are five phases in the carrier planning and development process which are discussed below.

i.   Scan the environment

Scanning the environment involves understanding the current realities in your work environment, as well as future trends at the global, national, and local levels, both within and outside your chosen profession. Through the scanning process, you become better informed and learn to see the world through different perspectives. This can also help you to identify career opportunities, both for the present and future.

ii.   Undertake a self-assessment

Doing a thorough self-assessment is the key to discovering new and previously unconsidered opportunities. It enables one to identify his or her values, experiences, knowledge, strengths, and limitations. This can help the individual to create a career vision and identify the directions to take for the future. Sometime one can even decide to get feedback from colleagues, friends, and family regarding our strengths and limitations.

iii.   Develop a career vision

Once you have undertaken the first two stages, you are ready to think about your career possibilities. Issues that come next are whether you like what you are currently doing and where you see yourself in the next few years. This vision will usually link who you are now to who you want to become. Create a career vision and decide whether you want to develop in your current role or a more challenging role or completely change careers.

iv.   Draw a strategic career plan

According to Barker (1992), vision without action is only a dream; action without vision only passes the time, but vision with action can change the world. Draw a strategic career plan which is a blueprint for action. As part of the process, identify the activities, time span, and resources you need to enable you to achieve your goals and career vision. Write down the specific strategies you will use to take charge of your future. From time to time, re-evaluate your goals and plans.

v.   Marketing yourself

The final stage is to map out a comprehensive self-marketing strategy for your career development. Marketing yourself involves the ability to package your professional and personal qualities, attributes, and expertise and to inform others about what you can offer and why you are the best person to do the job at hand. Use all your resources to present yourself in the most positive way.

13.4 Career Development

Career development is a lifelong process that is unique for each individual. It is the process of managing life, learning, and work. It is a term used to describe the management of work-related activity throughout one's life. It is simply a way of thinking about one's life, particularly in the context of education, training, and employment. It puts an individual at the centre of decision-making about his or her future and enables individuals to continue to build and draw on their experiences and capabilities.

Career development examines your present job situation and features of the job that will enable you to use your aptitudes: values, skills, and competencies. Put differently, career development is an organised planning method used to match the needs of a business with the career goals of employees. Formulating a career development plan can help employees to do their jobs more efficiently and can be beneficial for employees who might want to move up in a company or look for other jobs in the future.

Among other things, the purpose of career development is to

- Enhance each employee's current job performance

- Enable individuals to take advantage of future job opportunities

- Fulfil organisational goals for a dynamic and effective workforce

13.4.1 Who is responsible for career development?

- Managers are responsible for linking the organisation's needs to employee career goals and can assist employees in the career planning process.

- HRM professionals are responsible for designing career paths and employee development programmes that help employees reach their goals.

- Each employee is responsible for planning, developing, and managing his or her own career.

13.5 Stages of Career Development

According to Bohlander et al. (2001), every individual's career development goes through various stages. Planning for one's career starts at very early stage in life, and it is necessary that individuals acquire the necessary level of education and also start the job search as early as possible. The stages in career development and the activities required to achieve them are presented in Table 13.1.

Table 13.1: Stages of Career Development

Stage	Activity Required
Stage 1: Preparation for work (ages 0–25)	Develop occupational self-image, assess alternative occupations, develop initial occupational choice and pursue the necessary education.

Stage 2: Organisational entry (ages 18–25)	Obtain job offer(s) from desired organisation(s), select appropriate job based on complete and accurate information. Additionally, work towards higher qualifications, including professional qualifications.
Stage 3: Early career (ages 25–40)	Learn your job well, acquaint yourself with organisational rules and norms, fit into chosen occupation and organisation, increase competence and pursue goals. Also, continue studying for higher qualifications
Stage 4: Mid-career (ages 40–55)	Re-appraise early career and early adulthood goals, reaffirm or modify goals, make choices appropriate to middle adult years, and remain productive.
Stage 5: Late career (ages 55 to retirement)	Remain productive in work, maintain self-esteem, and prepare for effective retirement.

Source: Adapted from Bohlander et al. (2001).

13.6 Career Management

Career management is defined as an ongoing process of preparing, implementing, and monitoring career plans undertaken by individuals alone or in concert with the organisation's career systems (Hall, 1986). Career management may include activities that help the individual develop and carry out career plans; however, the focus is on taking actions that increase the chances that the organisation's anticipated HR needs will be met. Thus, career management is largely an activity carried out by the organisation; an example is succession planning which is usually carried out by senior management to determine which employee should be prepared to replace people in positions of greater responsibility.

Career management is the combination of structured planning and the active management choice of one's own professional career. The process is based on the establishment of defined goals/objectives whether specific or general. The outcome of successful career management should include personal fulfilment, work-life balance, goal achievement, and financial stability. Career management is the lifelong process of investing resources to achieve your career goals. It is not a singular event but a continuing process that is a necessity for adapting to the changing demands of the twenty-first century.

It is the role of HR managers to ensure that the organisation has programmes and activities that will help the organisation and its employees to achieve their goals. Organisations can focus on the human side of change, be supportive, and assist their employees in being proactive and taking charge of their careers. They can create opportunities for helping their employees to integrate career planning into their professional development and to provide them with the skills they will need if they are to become career-resilient professionals.

13.7 Career Plateau

By definition, a career plateau is a point in the career of an employee where the possibility of vertical promotion within the official hierarchy becomes very low or absent altogether. Employees, especially those who continue to work for the same organisation for a long time and those who belong to the core of an organisation, often reach career plateaus. Sometimes, plateau is reached due to the natural consequences of the way organisations are shaped; it is the highest point in one's career where the probability of, or motivation to progress is low. Most employees find themselves frustrated when they reach a plateau.

Put differently, career plateau is the point where the likelihood of additional hierarchical promotion of employees is very low or impossible. It is not a new phenomenon, but there is a worrying situation about the rate at which it is becoming increasingly widespread in various organisations. Some researchers on organisational careers suggest that plateau is fast becoming a critical managerial and organisational issue which needs to be managed properly to avoid employee's discontentment.

Many employees find themselves in jobs that offer them limited mobility opportunities in terms of upward movement in the organisation. Among other things, career plateau is a major contributing factor to employee turnover in organisations' management, and other stakeholders must develop the best strategies to manage it. In this era of globalisation, however, career plateau in organisation needs to be managed effectively to minimise employee's intention to quit.

There are many drivers that lead to career plateau in organisations, particularly, organisational re-structuring, re-engineering, and downsizing. With regards to the employee, career plateau is caused by many conditions including inappropriate abilities and skills, low need for career mobility, and slow organisation growth. Career plateau affects both management and employees, and HR professionals are in a dilemma on the best interventions to put in place to manage career plateau effectively in order to enhance competitiveness of the organisation.

13.8 Strategies for Dealing with Career Plateau

To deal with career plateau, organisations can adopt the following strategies.

13.8.1 Provide alternative means of recognition

Organisations can give employees special assignments and tasks of special importance, like training new employees, representing the organisation to others, or participating in brainstorming sessions. This will provide an alternative form of recognition, and they will not feel that their career has ended.

13.8.2 Develop ways to make current jobs more satisfying

It is important that HR professionals develop ways of making the employee's current job more satisfying. Things like personal rewards and competition can be created so that instead of being dejected, the employees who are nearing plateau will feel satisfied.

13.8.3 Revitalise through reassignment

Another strategy that can be adopted is to reassign the employee to another position. Organisations can decide to steadily send employee to occupy different positions in the organisation. It is necessary to state that these positions must be the same level of the employee, and they must have the skills and be known to be able to handle it.

13.8.4 Provide career counselling for employees

Organisations can also provide career counselling and guidance for employees. They can introduce them to self-management training and give them developmental feedback. Moreover, mentors can be provided even at this stage of their career. Such supportive environment can help them to boost their career interests and personal abilities.

13.8.5 Change managerial attitudes

Attitude change is another necessary input that can help manage career plateau. Managers and HR professionals should not give up on such employee and start neglecting them. Support from the top-level management is very vital.

PART EIGHT

ENHANCING EMPLOYEE RELATIONS IN ORGANISATIONS

14 INDUSTRIAL RELATIONS IN ORGANISATIONS

Learning Objectives

After reading this chapter, you should be able to

- Understand the meaning of industrial relations and its development in Ghana

- Know some feature of industrial relations

- Comprehend the objectives of industrial relations

- Appreciate some importance of industrial relations

- Know the causes of poor industrial relations

- Appreciate the ways of improving industrial relations

- Understand the approaches to Industrial Relations

Introduction

Industrial relations can be said to be that part of human resource management which studies the formal relationship between employees and employers and ensuring that there is an appropriate mechanisms, systems or procedures to manage all industrial frictions, disputes and conflicts successfully. When employees and their employers are able to relate and work in harmony it will improve productivity and the well-being of both parties. As Henry Ford once said, "Coming together is a beginning. Keeping together is progress. Working together is success."

Industrial Relations (IR) is simply the science and art of togetherness. It is about different entities coming together towards a common interest and mutual growth. It is worthy of note that, these entities in the similitude of employers and leaders must have the competences to implement togetherness. Industrial relations also known as employee relations or labour relations exist wherever employees and employers work together.

There is usually tension, disagreement, conflicts, and dissatisfaction between employers and employees since their interests are by no means the same; one craving to get as much income as possible and the other willing to give as little as possible. In certain situations, employees feel that they are not adequately or sufficiently paid out of the huge gains of the organisation; employers or management also require their employees to give out their maximum best to increase the proceeds of the organisation. It is the cause of and attempts to identify and resolve such conflicts that the field of industrial relations or labour relations continues to be associated with.

In effect, industrial relations focus on striking a bargain or balance between the desires of both management or employers and workers or employees as they try to share the 'fruits of their labour'. The principal aim of industrial relations is to maintain industrial peace and concord or harmony.

14.1 Defining Industrial Relations

According to J.T. Dunlop, "Industrial relations are the complex interrelations among managers, workers and agencies of the government." IR is used to represent the collective relationships between workers and management and it covers various aspects of industrial life such as trade unionism, collective bargaining, discipline and minimizing industrial disputes and maintaining industrial harmony and increasing worker participation.

The field of industrial relations looks at the relationship between management and workers, particularly groups of workers represented by a union. Broadly, it may refer to relations between unions and management, unions themselves, management and government, unions and government, or between employers and unorganised employees. Others describe industrial relations as the contractual framework and sometimes informal settings within which employees and their unions, employers and their representatives or management as well as the state or government and its agencies operate or relate at any workplace with the sole objective of maintaining industrial serenity and unity.

Some of the core elements needed to hold industrial relations together include, leaders and facilitators, systems, norms, ethics, operational procedures, codes of conduct, negotiation, communication networks, standing orders and legal requirements. The focus of industrial relations is on how conflict is contained and controlled rather than how disagreements and disputes are generated. Among other things, the main aim of IR is to maintain industrial peace and harmony, and this can be achieved if motivation is at its best and employee morale is boosted. This conditions can then lead to enhanced performance, increased productivity, and sometimes higher profits in the organisation.

14.2 Features of Industrial Relations

Some of the features of industrial relations include the following;

i.   IR is a product of employment relationships in an industrial enterprise or organisation

ii.   IR can only occur when the two parties namely employers and employees exist

iii.   The IR system creates rules and regulations to maintain harmonious relations between the two parties

iv.   The concept of industrial relations is complex or complicated and multi- dimensional

v. Depending on how it is managed, IR can lead to industrial peace and harmony with undisrupted production activities

vi. When IR is poorly handled, it can lead to numerous distractions or labour unrest in the form of disputes, work stoppages, strikes, lockouts and picketing

vii. The three main parties who interact within the economic and social environment to shape the IR system are the employers and their associations, employees and their unions and the government

viii. In situation where there are disputes between the employer and employee, the government intervenes to help shape the industrial relations through laws, rules, agreements, terms and other mean of settling the impasses

ix. IR is a dynamic and evolving concept and undergoes constant changes based on the structure and development of the diverse industries

x. IR include both individual relations that is, between just a couple of employees and collective relationships between and among all employee and employers

14.3 Objectives of Industrial Relations

There are several aims and objectives of industrial relations and some are as follows;

i. To build a sound and healthy relationship between the employer and the employee as well as between and among the employees themselves

ii. To maintain industrial or organisational democracy based on contribution and participation of labour in the management

iii. To ensure workers' participation in management by giving them a fair say in decision-making and thereby promoting mutual understanding and goodwill

iv. To establish an effective channel of communication within the organisation and resolve disputes amicably

v. To increase the morale as well as maintain discipline and amend conflicting interests in the organisation

vi. To minimize all forms of industrial conflicts so as to ensure industrial peace and provide better working and living standards for all employees

vii. To prevent unhealthy work atmosphere and reduce the incidence of high absenteeism and work stoppages such as, go-slows, gheraos, strikes and lockouts

viii. To regulate and facilitate production and reduce labour turnover in order to increase productivity

ix. To safeguard the rights and interests of both labour and management by enlisting the cooperation of both parties

x. To improve economic conditions of workers in the existing organisational and political milieu so as to achieve a sound, harmonious and mutually beneficial labour management relations

14.4 Importance of Industrial Relations

Industrial relations is very significant in organisations and the nation at large. Some of the major importance are discussed below.

i. A strong industrial relation guarantees protection of employee's interest and the successful attainment of organisational objectives

ii. Another importance of IR is that, it leads to continuous and uninterrupted production which denotes continuous employment for all workers that is, both employers and employees

iii. Good Industrial relations promotes industrial peace and minimizes industrial disputes and reflections of Industrial unrest such as strikes, grievances and lockouts.

iv.   Industrial tranquility and harmony helps in promoting or increasing collaborations and production

v.   IR also boosts the morale of employees and motivate them to be better performers

vi.   IR also reduces organisational wastage and costs and contributes to economic growth and development

vii. Another important of IR is that it also help organisations to uphold discipline, promote orderliness and effectiveness

viii. IR helps management both in the formulation of informed labour relations policies and in their translation into action

ix.   Good industrial relations improve the morale, motivation and satisfaction of employees and drives them to work with enthusiasm and be more devoted.

x.   Peaceful IR is essential because it help organisations to establish and maintain fair practices, strong unions, collective bargaining and negotiation, leading to true industrial democracy

14.5 Causes of Poor Industrial Relations

The causes of poor industrial relations are numerous however five key ones are listed below.

i.   One of the major causes of poor industrial relations is economic reasons. The economic cause is usually translated in poor wages, incentives schemes and working conditions and this breeds unhealthy relations between employers and their employees

ii.   Unfair policies and lack of equity in issues like victimization, undue dismissals, wrong deductions from wages, lack of fringe benefits, and lack of promotion opportunities can all cause poor industrial relations

iii. Other causes of poor IR are inadequate infrastructure, faulty or worn-out plant and machinery, poor layout and unhealthy work environment

iv.   Poor or faulty communications system, non-recognition of trade unions and labour laws are also causes of poor industrial relations

v.   Lack of discipline as well as political causes such as multiple unions and its associated inter union rivalry that weakens the unions can cause poor industrial relations.

14.6 Ways of Improving Industrial Relations

Whenever there are problems with IR one or some of the following solutions can be proffered for solving such situations. Some of the ways of improving IR are;

i.   There should be comprehensive policies in the organisation and this should be communicated and also made available to all employees. These policies should for instance cover issues like compensation, promotion and transfers.

ii.   Trade unions must be responsible and as far as possible remain apolitical. This is because a robust trade union is an asset for both the organisation and its employees.

iii. There should be equity, fairness and transparency in the enterprise and by all the actors in the industrial relations

iv.   The organisation must create a proper communication channel and minimize the excessive use of grapevine and this will reduce grievances and misunderstandings among employers and employees

v.   Both management and trade unions must adopt positive attitude towards one another. Management must recognise the unions and accept employees as partners in production and growth of the organisation

vi.   Employers must make the welfare of employees a priority. They must identify their needs and make efforts to satisfy same. Issues like reasonable compensation and other satisfactory working conditions must be considered and duly met.

vii. Appropriate grievance procedures must be rightly put in place. Thus a well-established and properly administered system committed to the timely and satisfactory addressing and redressal of employee's grievances can be very helpful in improving Industrial relations.

viii. With regards to policy formulation and implementation, management must create an opportunity for employees to have a say in issues that concern their well-being. This in no small way can improve the relationship between the parties.

14.7 Approaches to Industrial Relations

The approaches to industrial relations are numerous and they include unitary approach, pluralist approach, Marxist approach, systems approach, sociological approach, human relations approach, Gandhian approach, psychological approach and human relations approach. However, the most popular ones such as the unitary, pluralist, Marxist and systems approaches will be discussed.

14.7.1 Unitary approach

The unitary approach also known as the paternalistic approach to industrial relations is credited to Alan Fox (1966) and grounded in mutual cooperation, shared goals and team work. With this approach, the organisation is perceived as an integrated and harmonious system - basically one happy family. Unitarianism inclines towards authoritarianism, it is management biased, paternalistic and demands loyalty from all employees. Trade unions are therefore considered as unnecessary and conflict is perceived as bad, an abnormality which is disturbing, distressing and a result of poor management. This approach is based on the strong argument that there is only one source of authority and that is the employer or management. They own and control the organisation and reserve the right to make decisions on issues relating to bargaining and negotiation.

The unitary approach thus frowns on factions and demands total allegiance and absolute respect to authority hence, unions are suppressed and not encouraged. Strikes are not tolerated and striking workers will be sacked rather than have an opportunity to negotiate. The unitary is criticized as manipulative and exploitative, a tool for luring employees away from unionism.

14.7.2 Pluralist approach

Research shows that pluralism was first developed by John R. Commons in the United States and later widely accepted by British industrial relations theorist including Allan Flanders. The pluralist approach sometimes referred to as the conflict approach believes in the existence of more than one ruling principle or a composite of a multitude of interest groups and allows for conflicting interests. This approach accepts that conflict between management and employers is inevitable but containable through various institutional arrangements such as collective bargaining and other forms of reconciliatory methods. Trade unions are perceived as legitimate representative of employee interests and as such, workers are allowed to form and join unions to protect their interests and influence decisions made by management.

The legitimacy and authority of management is not automatically accepted and divergent views or conflict between the management and workers is actually considered essential for innovation, growth and positive change. Unions therefore balance the power between the management and employees and a strong union is not only desirable but necessary.

14.7.3 Marxist approach

The Marxists approach sometimes known as the radical perspective is credited to Karl Marx. This approach is based on the premise that the economic activities of production, manufacturing, and distribution are mainly directed and aimed at profit. Marxists like pluralists also view conflict as inevitable however they take a macro or societal approach and therefore perceive conflict as a product of capitalistic society. Marxism believes that conflict arises not because of rift or disagreement between management and employees in an organisation but because of the division in the society between those who own resources and those who have only labour to offer. Basically conflict arise because of the gap between the "Haves and Have Not's." The approach, thus, focuses on the type of society in which an organisation functions and industrial conflict is therefore equated with political and social unrest.

Trade unions are considered as labour's reaction to exploitation by capitalists, and a weapon to bring about a revolutionary social change. Marxists argue that industrial relation is a relation of clashes of class interest between capital (employer) and labour (employees). The clash will only finish in socialist society only, where capital is controlled by labour class. Some argue that the theory is a general theory of society and of social change with implications for the analysis of IR within capitalist societies.

14.7.4 Systems approach

The systems approach to industrial relations was developed by the labour scholar John T. Dunlop in 1958. According to this approach, every humanbeing belongs to a continuous but independent social system and culture which is accountable for framing his or her actions, behaviour and character. Systems approach stresses on the interrelationship of institutions and behaviours that enables one to understand and explain industrial relation rules. The IR system at any time is comprised of certain actors, certain contexts, and an ideology of the system which binds it together and a body of rules created to govern the actors at the work place and work community. It is all about resolving labour-management problems based on agreement on a common set of facts that affect or are affected by labour, management and government.

This approach is about the structure and development of relationships among the three main actors who are the employers or management, labour unions or employees, and the government. The interaction and relationship between these actors create the set of rules at the workplace that directs the actors in the workplace. The basis of this theory is that group cohesiveness is provided by the common ideology shaped by the societal factors.

14.8 Development of Industrial Relations in Ghana

Industrial relations exist in most countries in the world. Before the eighteenth century, craftsmen such as carpenters, masons, leather workers decided to come together to protect their interest and their working conditions, and this is the predecessor or forerunner of trade union.

Around the 1900s, a growing number of wage or salary workers in Ghana (then the Gold Coast) had been organising themselves into guilds/craft unions. Their objectives had been to argue their collective capacity to acquire a larger share of the resources they help to create and to participate in making decisions that affect their welfare.

The earlier organisations of workers were composed of skilled artisans like carpenters, goldsmiths, and masons. Trades/craft unions like the Motor Drivers' Association mushroomed in 1928, whose members paid a fee of one shilling on joining it and daily dues of six pence when they were employed. There were also the Carpenters' Association in 1929 and the Motor Transport Union of Ashanti in 1931.

These groups of workers were, however, irregularly or haphazardly organised and not structured. They existed mostly as house unions and enjoyed paternalistic relationships with their employers. Their professional aims were 'to regulate wages, to make laws concerning apprentice, to guard against unfair competition and to settle dispute'. They were registered with the then Native Authority.

As labour unrest developed in the late 1930s in many parts of the British Empire, the colonial in 1938 decreed that labour department, union legislation, and industrial dispute procedures should be established. As a colony of the British Empire, a Labour Department had to be created in the then Gold Coast.

On April 1, 1938, the Gold Coast Labour Department was formally established or inaugurated in Kumasi as an agency of government, legally empowered to deal with labour administration generally.

15 TRADE UNIONS, COLLECTIVE BARGAINING AND DISPUTES SETTLEMENT PROCEDURES

Learning Objectives

After reading this chapter, you should be able to

- Evaluate the role and purpose of trade unions

- Learn about some of the major types of trade unions

- Identify the reasons why some employees join labour unions and others do not

- Comprehend the legal provision on trade unions in Ghana

- Understand the tripartite nature of industrial relations and the role of government in the industrial relation system

- Know the meaning, features, advantages, and disadvantages of collective bargaining

- Comprehend labour disputes and their settlement procedure

15.1 Trade Unions

Trade unions or labour unions are associations of workers or employees who have joined together to achieve certain goals. Put differently, trade union can be explained as organisations formed by employees from related fields and they work for the common interest of their members. Simply put, trade unions are usually group of employees who come together to 'fight for their cause'. They can be described as a continuous association of wage earners for the purpose of maintaining or improving the conditions of working lives. Trade unions usually provide a link between employers or management and their employees. They are established for various reasons, including helping employees to achieving better conditions of work, fair pay and conducive work environment.

Generally, trade unions are governed by the laws of their country. They are required to follow specific procedure in their formation and registration. They have specific functions, objectives and duties to perform. Their purpose of existence includes protecting the interest of employees and having the powers of collective bargaining and subsequently reaching collective agreements. Also, trade union have the responsibility to support management and encourage employees to work positively to improve the overall efficiency of organisation.

Their major functions can be categorised under four main headings namely; the Militant function (fighting for what is due employees, e.g. higher wages and better working conditions), Fraternal function (brotherly or friendly function, such as boosting employee morale, promoting discipline, building employee confidence and discouraging discrimination) Social function (welfare activities, education for improved civic life and redressing their grievances), and Political function (getting affiliation from the political party and support during strikes and lockouts).

On April 1, 1938, the Gold Coast labour department was formally established or inaugurated in Kumasi as an agency of government, legally empowered to deal with labour administrations generally. Captain J.R. Dickinson was appointed the first head of department and Mr S. O. Gaisie was appointed his assistant.

15.2 Purposes of Trade Union

Trade union serves many purposes including the following.

i.   Trade unions are formed with the purpose of maintaining or improving the working conditions or working lives of their members.

ii. They exist to primarily promote and protect the interests of its members and usually redress the balance of power between employers and employees.

iii. Trade unions also exist to make management or employers aware that, from time to time, there will be an alternative view on key issues affecting employees.

iv. Broadly, trade unions may be seen as playing the role of participating with management on decisions affecting their members' interest.

v. Trade unions provide workers with a 'collective voice' to make their wishes known to management and thus bring actual and desired conditions closer together.

This applies not only to terms of employment such as pay, working hours, and holidays, but also to the way in which individuals are treated in such aspects of employment such as the redress of grievances, discipline, and redundancy.

15.3 Legal Provision on Trade Unions in Ghana

Sections 79 to 84 of the Ghana Labour Act, 2003 (Act 651) provides for trade unions in Ghana.

Section 79 (1) asserts that 'every worker has the right to form or join a trade union of his or her choice for the promotion and protection of the worker's economic and social interests'.

Section 80 (1) also specifies that two or more workers employed in the same undertaking may form a trade union.

Section 83 (1) states that trade unions shall apply in writing to the Chief Labour Officer to be registered.

Section 83 (2) states that an application for registration under subsection (1) shall be submitted with the constitution, rules, names of officers and office address of the trade union.

Section 83 (3) states that if, after considering the application, the Chief Labour Officer is satisfied that

- there has been compliance with subsection (2),

- the applicant is a trade union or employers' organisation duly established under any enactment for the time being in force as a body corporate,

- the internal organisation of the trade union or employers' organisation conforms to democratic principles,

- the name of the trade union or employers' organisation does not closely resemble that of another registered trade union or employers' organisation, so as to mislead or confuse the public,

- the rules of the trade union or employers' organisation are in conformity with section 85, and

- the constitution or rules of the trade union or employers' organisation do not discriminate on the grounds stated in section 87 against any person,

The Chief Labour Officer shall register the trade union or employers' organisation.

Section 84 of the Act concludes that such union registered shall be issued with a certificate of registration by the Chief Labour Officer.

15.4 Why Employees Join Trade Unions?

Employees join unions for various reasons some of which are discussed below.

15.4.1 Job security

Unions offer job security for their members through labour laws or legislations and collective bargaining agreement. It protects them from unfair dismissals and redundancies from employment. If the minimum notice is not given, employers are compelled to pay compensation to employees.

It must be noted that dismissals for misconduct such as stealing, fighting, SH are, however, not covered under the law.

15.4.2 Means to be heard

Generally, workers complain that they do not have much say in what affects them in the workplace. They believe that by joining unions, employees become more powerful. They have a collective voice to talk about issues that they are dissatisfied with, and this can impact upon management decisions towards them.

15.4.3 Improved pay

Others join with the aim of obtaining equal work for equal or better pay. This factor has been the most attractive for many union members, and trade unions all over the world struggle for higher pay to meet the global ever-increasing cost of living.

15.4.4 Better working conditions

Working conditions (environment, etc.) differs from conditions of service (pay, benefits, etc.). Working conditions refer to the environment and facilities available for the employee to work with and how these affect their health and safety.

15.4.5 Equal opportunity for all

Ghana ratified the International Labour Organisation convention on Discrimination in 1958 and 1961. Labour unions thus through appropriate legislation shun all forms of unfair discrimination and attempt to provide equal opportunity for all their members.

15.4.6 Need to belong

Some employees join unions because of the fact that when they belong to a group it makes them happy and fulfilled. Beside, unions usually bring their members together from time to time for social events and activities, and some will join mainly because of the interaction and the fact that strong bonds could be created.

15.5 Reasons Why Some Employees Do Not Join Labour Unions

Whiles some employees will want to join union others refuse to be associated with unions because of the following reasons.

i. Some employees would want to go alone and would not want to belong to any group.

ii. Others have no faith in union leadership and tend to think that they have poor leadership.

iii. Some employees cite time wasted with regards to union meetings as reasons why they will not join a union.

iv. There are sometimes complaints of mismanagement of resources by union official.

v. Some employees also refuse to join unions for fear that they may be victimised by the employers.

vi. Other people do not join unions because they feel union members have the capacity to be militant, using all forms of industrial action which may not even be effective.

15.6 Parties in the Industrial Relations System

The main forces and institutions that influence the pattern of industrial relations or the parties within the industrial relations (IR) system are as follows:

1. The employees and their unions (Trade Unions)

2. The employers and their associations (Employers Association)

3. The government and its agencies (The Government)

These parties constitute the institutional framework which governs IR system in any country.

15.6.1 Types of trade unions

There are three major types of unions, and they are the craft unions, industrial and occupational unions, and the general workers unions.

i. Craft unions: They are organised workers of a particular trade or skill. Entry is restricted and is usually based on the individual qualification and training. For example, Ghana Railway Enginemen's Union (GREU).

ii. Industrial and occupational unions: These are workers of a particular industry, and it covers numerous grades within the industry. This is less restricted with regards to entry. For example, Health Services Workers Union (HSWU)

iii. General workers' unions: These are organised workers across industries. They are mainly unskilled workforce or groups. Entry is subject to inter-union regulations but is usually not restricted. For example, Ghana Federation of Labour (GFL).

There are numerous trade unions in Ghana including the following:

- UTAG: University Teachers Association of Ghana
- GPRTU: Ghana Private Road Transport Union
- GNAT: Ghana National Association of Teachers
- TEWU: Teachers and Education Workers Union
- NAGRAT: National Association of Graduate Teachers
- CLOGSAG: Civil and Local Government Association of Ghana
- JUSSAG: Judicial Service Staff Association of Ghana
- TUTAG: Technical Universities Teachers Association of Ghana
- ICU: Industrial and Commercial Workers Union

- GMA: Ghana Medical Association

- GRNMA: Ghana Registered Nurses' and Midwives' Association

- GAWU: General Agricultural Workers' Union

- GMWU: Ghana Mine Workers' Union

- PSWU: Public Services Workers' Union

- MDU: Maritime and Dock-workers' Union

It must be noted that in Ghana, the parent union or the umbrella under which all the unions fall is the Trade Union Congress (TUC).

15.6.2 Employers and their associations

Until 1958, apart from the government, there was only one significant employer group in Ghana and that was the Chamber of Mines. The Ghana Employers Association was established in 1959. The aim arose from the fact that employers became aware that it would be beneficial if they consult among themselves and jointly approach matters affecting their business and defend their 'interest against employees'.

Section 80 (2) of the Labour Act states that, two or more employers in the same industry or trade, each of whom employs not less than fifteen workers may form or join an employer's organisation.

Basically, the Ghana Employers Association is a consolidation of employers and organisations of employers into one body. Among other things, they promote good relations and better understanding between employers and employees. In addition, they assist affiliated employers or organisations of employers in negotiations with organised labour.

The aim of the employers association is to provide a means of consultation and exchange of information on questions arising out of the relations between employers and their employees and to promote co-operation, when possible, in this field, between Association of Employers in various industries, trades, and business in Ghana and between individual employers. The full objects of GEA are laid down by the Constitution and Rules of the Association.

15.6.3 The role of government

A government is the organisation, that is the governing authority of a political unit, the ruling power in a political society, and the apparatus through which a governing body functions and exercises authority. Put differently, a government is a body that has the authority and the power to make and enforce rules and laws within a civil, corporate, religious, academic, or other organisation or group. The government usually operates within a political mechanism, and its authority is usually backed by a legal system.

The government plays a twofold or dual role in industrial relations in Ghana. First, the government acts as an employer because the government is the single largest employer in the country. Second, she acts as the third party in the settlement of industrial disputes. Thus, the government is the third actor in the IR system. This role is performed through the labour department.

The government also plays an active role on the National Advisory Committee on Labour and the Tripartite Committee on Salaries and Wages Guidelines. Accordingly, her policies regarding labour relations and disputes are governed by the principle that the parties concerned must use every means to settle their differences mutually and make the workplace closest to how it was before the difference arose.

15.7 The Tripartite Nature of Industrial Relations

The government of Ghana believes in the tripartite nature of industrial relations. This is simply a system whereby the main actors in IR system, that is, the union, employers, and the government, come together to confer, negotiate, or settle disputes when there is a deadlock or impasse.

In this regard, the government has established two committees which provide two forums of consultations among the social partners. They are;

(i)   The National Tripartite Committee, which is in charge of issues relating to wages and salaries; and

(ii)   The National Labour Commission

15.8 Collective Bargaining

Bargaining is the negotiation of the terms of a transaction or agreement. It usually involves two or more parties to an issue. Collective Bargaining (CB) in industrial relations is simply the formal process of negotiations on terms and conditions of service between employers and workers through their respective accredited representatives. It is based on the principle that workers have a right to contract with their employers as to wages and working conditions and that employers recognise this right.

CB can be defined as a voluntary, formalised process by which employers and independent trade unions negotiate, for particular group of employees, terms and conditions of employment and the ways in which certain employment-related issues are to be regulated at national, organisational, and workplace levels.

CB aims to establish by negotiation and discussion, agreed rules and decisions on matters of mutual concern to employers and unions as well as methods of regulating the conditions governing employment. CB gives the conduct of employment relations greater predictability by providing formal channels through which potential conflicts may be aired. The conclusions reached after a collective bargaining is usually referred to as collective agreement (CA).

15.9 Features of Collective Bargaining

There are several essential features of CB, all of which cannot be reflected in a single definition or description of the process. Some are discussed below:

i.   CB is not equivalent to CA because CB refers to the process or means, and CA to the possible result, of bargaining. CB may not always lead to a CA.

ii. CB is a method used by trade unions to improve the terms and conditions of employment of their members.

iii. Where CB leads to an agreement, it modifies, rather than replaces, the individual contract of employment, because it does not create the employer–employee relationship

iv. The process is bipartite, but in some developing countries, the State plays a role in the form of a conciliator where disagreements occur, or where CB impinges or encroaches on government policy.

v.   It seeks to restore the unequal bargaining position between employer and employee.

vi. It is a two-way process. It is a mutual give and take rather than takes it or leaves it method of arriving at the settlement of a dispute. Both parties are involved in it. A rigid position does not make a compromise settlement. CB is a 'civilised' confrontation with a view to arriving at an agreement for the object not 'warfare' but 'compromise'.

vii. CB is not a competitive or aggressive process, but it is essentially complementary and harmonising process.

15.10 Advantages of Collective Bargaining

i.   CB has the advantage of settlement through dialogue and consensus rather than through conflict and confrontation.

ii.   CB has valuable by-products relevant to the relationship between the two parties.

iii. CB is a form of participation. Both parties participate in deciding what proportion of the 'cake' is to be shared by the parties entitled to a share.

iv.   CB usually has the effect of improving industrial relations. This improvement can be at different levels. The continuing dialogue tends to improve relations at the workplace level between workers and the union, on the one hand, and the employer, on the other.

v.   CB can lead to improved working conditions, increased worker motivation, and ultimately increased productivity.

vi.   CB promotes industrial peace and thus avoids costly work stoppages through strikes

15.11 Disadvantages of Collective Bargaining

i.   Usually, the interests of both parties are not fully achieved through bargaining.

ii.   CB is sometimes expensive and time-consuming or even time wasting.

iii. CB may result in conflict such as strike if no compromise is reached.

iv.   The decision-making process in CB is often longer than unilateral decisions management.

v.   Collective interests might be different from individual workers' needs and preferences.

vi.   There is loss of flexibility and increase in bureaucracy.

15.12 Labour Disputes and their Settlement Procedure

Labour disputes prevention and resolution provide all parties in the IR system with an important framework for the future development of employer–employee relations at all levels. However, labour disputes are inevitable in human organisations.

The use of industrial action within industrial relations is an explicit collective expression of concern and power. It is intended to help secure a more favourable outcome to a negotiation or to resist unacceptable management action.

To some individuals or managers, labour dispute is a threat to an established order and it must be controlled; but to others, it is a necessary thing in developing equity in an IR system.

A collective labour dispute is a disagreement between an employer or an association or group of employers and employees or a union or group of employees, which arises upon entry into, or performance of collective agreements or establishment of new working conditions. An example is the recent disagreement and subsequent strike by the Railways Workers.

Collective or group dispute normally emanate from a breach of a CB agreement, except in cases where individual disputes develop into collective dispute. Group disputes may arise from a wrongful interpretation of a CA or failure to implement in whole or parts of the agreement.

In Ghana, the three ways through which disputes are resoled is through negotiation, mediation, and arbitration.

15.12.1 Negotiation

Section 153 of the Ghana Labour Act provides that the parties to an industrial dispute are under an obligation to negotiate in good faith with a view to reaching a settlement of the dispute in accordance with the dispute settlement procedures established in the CA or contract of employment.

15.12.2 Mediation

Section 154 of the Act states that subject to the time limit in respect of essential services, if the parties fail to settle a dispute by negotiation within seven days after the occurrence of the dispute, either party or both parties by agreement may refer the dispute to the Commission and seek assistance of the Commission for the appointment of a mediator.

15.12.3 Arbitration

In cases where negotiation and mediation fail, the dispute is referred to the Commission; the Commission shall with the consent of the parties refer the dispute to an arbitrator or an arbitration panel appointed under section. Thus arbitration is the third stage of settlement. Section 156 provides that, subject to Act, or any general enactment on dispute resolution in force, the parties to an industrial dispute shall agree on the method of appointment of arbitrators or arbitration panel, and in the absence of an agreement by the parties, the Commission shall appoint an arbitrator or an arbitration panel. The decision of the arbitrator at the end of the hearing shall constitute the award and shall be binding on all the parties.

PART NINE

IMPROVING EMPLOYEE HEALTH, SAFETY AND WELL-BEING

16 OCCUPATIONAL HEALTH, SAFETY AND EMPLOYEE WELL-BEING

Learning Objectives

After reading this chapter, you should be able to;

- Comprehend the concept and historical perspectives of occupational health and safety

- Recognise the difference between occupational hazards and risks

- Understand the reasons for promoting and benefits of occupational health and safety

- Know the legislative provisions on occupational health and safety in Ghana

- Explain the roles of human resource managers in occupational health and safety

- Learn about the strategies for promoting workplace health and safety

- Understand the concept of employee well-being at the workplace

- Know how to develop a comprehensive well-being strategy

Introduction

Occupational health, safety and employee well-being is a very important phenomenon in every organisation. Indeed, no organisation can exist without proper health and safety protocols. Like most countries, Ghana is growing by the day and so is its industries and other organisations, hence issues of health, safety and well-being of the employees who work in these setups become a matter of concern. Employees the world over are daily exposed to varied workplace hazards ranging from physical, chemical, biological, ergonomic to psychosocial and the Ghanaian workforce is no exception. Although the right to life is the most crucial right, every year about 2.2 million men and women are deprived of that right through occupational accidents and work related diseases (ILO, 2005).

Today, research shows that several millions of workers still suffer occupational health and safety issues in the form of accidents, diseases and death each year. Accidents, disasters and other occupational maladies are global occurrences which can surface at any time. According to Kofi Annan, former UN Secretary General, "safety and health at work is not only a sound economic policy - it is a basic human right". It is therefore imperative that organisations put proper measures in place to anticipate, recognise, monitor, evaluate, control, forestall or curb health and safety disasters and tragedies.

16.1 Historical Perspectives of Occupational Health and Safety

The history of occupational health and safety and labour related laws dates back to the 19th century. In 1802, the first milestone, which was the British Health and Morals of Apprentices Act also referred to as The Factory Act (1802) was sponsored by the elder Sir Robert Peel, a British politician and industrialist and one of early textile manufacturers of the Industrial Revolution. The introduction of the Act was as a result of the uproar over child labour conditions and it applied to all textile mills and factories who employed three of more apprentices or 20 employees. The Act among other things ensured that the factories observe the following;

- Had adequate windows and entryways for ventilation

- Were properly cleaned with water and quicklime at least two times in a year

- Ensured that working hours for apprentices is limited to no more than 12 hours a day with break times

- Certified that apprentices are stopped from working at night during the hours of 9pm to 6am

- Provided suitable clothing and sleeping place to every apprentice

- Instructed apprentices in reading, writing, arithmetic and also the principles of the Christian religion

Although the Factory Act was limited to a lesser percentage of the total employees and its enforcement was also somehow restricted, it was the foundation of occupational health and safety regulations. Indeed, comparable legislation which were aimed at protecting the young and children was adopted in Zürich and France in 1815 and 1841 respectively. In 1883 and 1884, Germany initiated and established the sickness insurance and workers' compensation, New Zealand then introduced the compulsory arbitration in industrial disputes in 1890s and Ontario introduced the Factory Act of 1884.

In the early part of 1900, a lot of changes took place in the workplace of several countries. In India, adult males in textile mills were limited to 10 hours work per day in 1911, and Japan's elemental regulation on work in the mines which was introduced in 1890 was adopted in 1911. The departments or ministries of labour responsible for the effective management of labour legislation and for supporting its imminent development were established in Canada in 1900, France in 1906, United States in 1913, United Kingdom in 1916, and in Germany in 1918. These administrative machineries and labour legislations became common and significant during the 1930s to the 1940s in other parts of Europe, India and Japan, Latin America, Asia and Africa.

A catastrophic accident that caused the deaths of five workers in 1960, changed the face of safety regulations in Ontario, Canada forever. Safety, then a novel description, was introduced to the Factory Act of 1884 and the name was changed to the Industrial Safety Act of 1964. This Act evolved for some years and some amendments were made, however, in 1978, a comprehensive law covering almost all Ontario workplaces - the Occupational Health and Safety Act (OH&S Act), was passed.

In the United States, it was when the Occupational Safety and Health (OSH) Act was passed into law in 1970, that real occupational health and safety commenced. The Occupational Safety and Health Administration and National Institute for Occupational Safety and Health were also established. History shows that some of the concerns addressed by the Act included health and safety hazards, such as unsanitary conditions, cold and heat stress, as well as environmental pollutants. The key objective of this Act was to enhance safety and assure, maintain or guarantee safer working conditions for all workers, regardless of the kind of work they do or industry they work for.

In the United Kingdom, the Health and Safety at Work Act 1974, is the foundation or the primary piece of legislation that covers occupation health and safety. This law stipulates the general duties of employers to their employees. Among other things, it states that, it is the duty of every employer to ensure that so far as is reasonably practicable, the health, safety and welfare at work of all employees is taken care of. It also guarantees the provision and maintenance of safe, without risks to health, and adequate facilities working environment for employees. The Act in the UK went on to influence other legislations in Europe and other parts of the world.

After the Second World War, workers commonly worked under hostile and negative conditions however, employees reacted to these unfavourable and poor conditions at work and this resulted in the birth of the Factory Act in 1958. In Nigeria, the Factories decree 1987 was a landmark legislation in occupational health and this was a huge modification on the then Factories Act of 1958. The Factory Inspectorate of the Ministry of Labour carries out the enforcement of legislation in Nigeria. The Ministry also produced a National Policy on Safety and Health in 2006 which details the responsibilities of employers, workers, manufacturers and government agencies in the maintenance of the health safety and well-being of employees. In South Africa, the Occupational Health and Safety Act was passed in 1993 and this Act supersedes the earlier Acts.

Previously some of the Acts included the Machinery and Occupational Safety Act, 1983, the Machinery and Occupational Safety Amendment Act, 1989, and the Machinery and Occupational Safety Amendment Act, 1991. Also, in February 2003, South Africa ratified the International Labour Organisation's Occupational Safety and Health Convention 155 of 1981. In August 2004, the Minister of Labour, after consultation with the Advisory Council for Occupational Health and Safety, gazetted the Occupational Health and Safety Act of 1993.

In Ghana the legislative provisions on Occupational Health and Safety, are varied and include the Factories, Offices and Shops Act 1970, (Act 328) and the Mining Regulations 1970 (LI 665). Others laws include the Workmen's Compensation Law 1987 (PNDC 187) which relates to compensation for personal injuries caused by accidents at work, the Environmental Protection Agency Act 1994 (Act 490), and the Ghana Health Service and Teaching Hospital Act 1990 (Act 525). These Acts obligates employers to ensure that every employee in Ghana works under safe and healthy conditions. There is also the Ghana Labour Act, 2003, (Act 651) which aims at protecting the health, safety and well-being of the employee and employers. The provisions in the Labour Act 2003, is in conformity with the section 24 (1) of the 1992 constitution of Ghana which states that (1) "Every person has the right to work under satisfactory, safe and healthy conditions, and shall receive equal pay for equal work without distinction of any kind." Part XV, sections 118 to 120 of the Labour Act also guides and directs employers and employees in their respective roles and responsibilities in managing Occupational Health, Safety issues.

It is important to indicate that, over the years, while the principles in the Acts in the various countries have largely remained the same, it is usually updated and reformed along the development in the workplace and new health and safety challenges that arise from time to time. Indeed, some countries currently have new Occupational Health and Safety Bills going through the legislative process and is yet been passed.

16.2 The Concept of Occupational Health and Safety

Workplace Health and Safety (WHS), or Occupational Health and Safety (OHS) also referred to as Occupational Safety and Health (OSH) is concerned with the safety, health and well-being of employees or people at a workplace. Occupational health and safety is a comprehensive or broad multidisciplinary concept which includes the physical, mental and emotional well-being of employees when attending to their daily duties at the workplace. This presupposes that wherever there is an establishment whether a factory, an industry or office, provided there are workers in such an environment, their health and safety must be considered as a priority. Certainly, it is an important discipline which can hugely contribute to the success or otherwise of any organisation depending on the way it is handled. It must also be noted that, health and safety initiatives or drives are no longer just an issue of organisations having to comply with legislations; rather, it is now part of the overall human resource management strategy of organisations.

Ghana is steadily becoming an industrialized nation, and this transformation is exposing a huge percentage of the personnel or human resource to various health and safety hazards at the workplace. According to the Labour Department of Ghana Annual report (2000) a total of 8,692 work-related accidents were reported to the Department for compensation claims and this is more than double the figure of the previous year. It is important to note that these were accidents that were formally reported and this issues bring to bear the importance of occupational health, safety and well-being. The 2005 Ministry of Employment and Labour Relations statistical report however reported that, the number of accidents declined in 2015 as compared to 2014 and this may perhaps be due to an increase in the number of Occupational Safety and Health talks and training.

In its broadest sense, occupational health and safety is a discipline with an expansive or broad scope and it aims at promoting and maintaining the highest degree of physical, mental and social well-being of workers in all occupations. It is also intended at placing and sustaining workers in an occupational environment adapted to their physical and mental capacities. Also, it aims at preparing and preserving conditions in the workplace that decrease or avert the likelihood of employees being injured while executing their work; and the protection of workers in their places of employment from risks caused by their working conditions and occupational environment.

The International Labour Organisation (ILO) and the World Health Organisation (WHO) have since 1950, shared a common definition of occupational health. This definition was approved and adopted by the Joint ILO/WHO Committee on Occupational Health at its first session in 1950, it was later reviewed or revised at its 12th session in 1995. According to ILO/WHO, "occupational health should aim at: the promotion and maintenance of the highest degree of physical, mental and social well-being of workers in all occupations; the prevention amongst workers of departures from health caused by their working conditions; the protection of workers in their employment from risks resulting from factors adverse to health; the placing and maintenance of the worker in an occupational environment adapted to his physiological and psychological capabilities; and, to summarize, the adaptation of work to man and of each man to his job."

According to Alli (2008), occupational safety and health is generally defined as "the science of the anticipation, recognition, evaluation and control of hazards arising in or from the workplace that could impair the health and well-being of workers, taking into account the possible impact on the surrounding communities and the general environment". Put differently, occupational health and safety has to do with the health, safety, and well-being concerns at the workplace and it covers laws, standards, policies and programmes that are aimed at making the organisation a better place for workers, their co-workers, customers, suppliers and other stakeholders. Occupational health and safety can also be explained as the measures that are taken to ensure that the work environment is safe and the employees are feeling well and healthy.

Health and safety is so important because it is a key element in achieving sustained decent working conditions for all employees. Certainly, workers who have the feeling that their work environment is not safe or that their employers do not care about their health, safety or well-being may be reluctant to give off their best in terms of productivity. Also, when employees witness severe injuries of their colleagues and sometimes have to cover for their jobs it can affect morale and the overall productivity of the organisation they work for. Thus it is only when employees are feeling safe and healthy that they can be more effective, efficient and productive at work. Today, health and safety aims at preventing immense loss of time and money due to accidents, saving the lives of employees as well as retaining talented employees.

16.3 Occupational Hazards and Risks

Most often than not, the term hazard and risk are usually used interchangeably however, though related, there are differences between the two words. Usually the incidence of hazard when not checked leads to actual risks.

16.3.1 Hazard

Broadly, hazard can be said to be the probability or potential source of harm on the health of people, physical injury or damages on property or equipment of organisations, or adverse effect on the environment and in some cases or the combination of all the listed factors. According to the Collins dictionary, an occupational hazard is something unpleasant that you may suffer or experience as a result of doing your job or hobby. In relation to health and safety at the workplace, the term hazard can be explained as any source of potential or possible damage, harm or adverse health effects on someone or something. Hazard can cause harm and can take several forms such as substances or chemicals used for working, energy sources, noisy machinery, moving forklift, climbing a ladder, stress, existing work practice or processes in an organisation.

16.3.2 Risk

Risk unlike hazard, is the chance of the harm being actually caused. In other words, risk is the probability or chance, whether high or low, that an individual may suffer injury or illness due to an existing or prevailing hazard. A risk is the likelihood of something happening that will have a negative effect or the possibility of an unwanted event occurring. It must be noted that, although risk is the probability that a person may be harmed or experience an adverse health effect if exposed to a hazard, risks may also apply to situations with property or equipment loss, or harmful effects on the environment.

The following example gives more meaning to the terms hazard and risk. Let us assume there is a small leakage on a 15 litre water container in an office. The moment this creates a puddle of water on the floor it then becomes a **hazard** (a potential source of harm for anyone in the office). If the container is not removed, a caution sign is not placed there or the water mopped, then there is a significant **risk** (the chance of the harm actually occurring in the office) of someone slipping, falling, injuring themselves or even dying through head injury.

Figure 16.1: The Difference between Hazard and Risk

HAZARD is a potential source of physical injury, damage or harm to an employee, property or environment. It can take several forms such as electricity, noisy machines, falls or chemicals.

RISK is the chance whether great, small, high or low that someone will acutally be harmed or suffer injury or illness due to an existing hazard.

16.4 Forms of Occupations Hazards

An occupational hazard is something unpleasant or distasteful that a person experiences or suffers as a result of doing his or her job. There are varied hazards and potential risks at every workplace or work environment. Falls are one of the most common cause of occupational injuries and fatalities. Employers must thus manage these workplace hazards so as to help reduce to the barest minimum the number of accidents and its associated sickness absence. To safeguard employee health and safety, it is imperative that employers identify, monitor and reduce or curb the risks associated with workplace. There are several types of hazards however, occupational hazards can be classified under the following six categories; biological, chemical, ergonomic, physical, psychosocial and safety.

16.4.1 Biological hazards

Biological hazards also known as biohazards affect workers in many industries. They are biological substances that can threaten the health of employees and other living organisms. This type of hazard may include samples of a toxin of a biological source. Biohazards are harmful to human health and they include, infectious microorganisms or viruses, such as, influenza or corona virus which can affect a large population of employees who work together in the same building. Employees who work outdoors such as construction workers or farmers can equally by exposed to hazards such as insects and animal bites, stings and possible diseases that can be transmitted through animals or poisonous plants.

16.4.2 Chemical hazards

Chemical hazards are also forms of occupational hazards that employees may experience at the workplace whenever they are exposed to chemicals. The harm caused by hazardous chemicals depends on the physical, chemical or toxic properties involved. However, this form of hazard usually possess acute or long term negative health effects to workers. There are several classifications of hazardous chemicals comprising neurotoxins (which destroys the normal function of nerve cells), dermatologic agents (skin effect and diseases), pneumoconiosis agents (diseases caused by inhaled dust), carcinogens (agents that can cause cancer) and sensitizers which are all harmful. Also research shows that, long-term exposure to chemicals such as tobacco smoke, silica dust or quartz and engine exhausts can lead to increased risk of heart disease, stroke, and high blood pressure. It is however important to note that, authorities such as regulatory agencies usually set occupational exposure limits to mitigate the risk of chemical hazards.

16.4.3 Ergonomic hazards

Ergonomic hazards are factors in the work environment that can affect or harm the muscles, bones, and joints or the musculoskeletal system of an employee. This is another form of dangerous occupational hazard because usually, the injuries that are triggered or caused to the body by strain placed on the body from ergonomic hazards are not always immediately obvious or detected. Hence it is not treated till after a long time and sometime the course of the musculoskeletal pain whether chronic or acute is not known. Most often, ergonomic hazards depends on the how many times or level of exposure the employee faces over a period of time. These hazards may emanate from frequent lifting of items, frequent awkward movements, recurrent use of force, improper sitting position or other postures, inappropriate adjustment of workstation, tables, chairs and computers. Ergonomic hazards are sometime the outcomes of the way work spaces are designed in the organisations and it is essential that employers pay attention to that.

16.4.4 Physical hazards

Physical hazards can be described as factors, circumstances or conditions within the work environment that can harm the health of an employee. This type of occupational hazards can cause harm or damage with or without contact. Examples of physical hazard include, radiation, noise, vibration, confined spaces, extreme temperature either hot or cold, height and electricity. Physical hazard affects several employees at the workplace. According to National Institute of Occupational Safety and Health in the United States, occupational hearing loss is the most common work-related injury at the workplace. Research shows that as at 2013, about 22 million US employees were exposed to hazardous noise levels at their work places and a projected amount of $242 million was spent each year on worker's compensation for hearing loss disability. In Ghana, although the Environmental Protection Agency has set a permissible ambient noise, noise level is still a major problem. In industries like construction and mining, noise is expected and unavoidable however, there are some safety protocols to minimize its dangers so that the employee's quality of life is not totally damaged.

16.4.5 Psychosocial hazards

Psychosocial hazards are that characteristics of work which have the potential to cause physical or psychological harm or both. According to Cox and Cox (1993) psychosocial hazards in the workplace can be described as the aspects of work organisation and management that may negatively affect the employee's mental and physical health. Although a person's occupation provides a sense of purpose, identity and enhances ones general well-being, sometimes, there are situations in the work place which can lead to unwelcome effect on the general health and well-being of an employee. These undesirable happenings include, stress, workplace bullying and violence, victimization, long working hours, sexual harassment, customer aggression, poor work-life balance, sudden work place changes and a feelings of job insecurity. It is very crucial that employers check these occurrences so as to create more opportunities for employees to develop their skills, improve confidence and promote self-worth and general well-being.

16.4.6 Safety hazards

Safety hazard is another form of occupational hazard. Basically they are hazards that are unsafe and create dangerous working conditions for employees. These hazards include slipping, tripping and falling and can cause injury, illness, and sometimes death. Also operating dangerous machinery, unguarded machines, electrical cords across the floor, equipment malfunctions or sudden breakdowns, falls from heights, ladders or scaffolds can all be classified as safety hazards. According to a report by the Health and Safety Executive, in the UK between 2018 and 2019, 40 people were killed after falling from height at work and 14 died after they had been in contact with dangerous machinery. Safety hazards are one of the most common workplace risks and potential to harm workers, indeed it exist in every workplace, and it is advisable that employers identify such hazards at their workplace and be better prepared to control or eliminate them so as to prevent accidents and untimely death.

Occupational hazards can emanate from a wide range of sources such as substances, things, materials, processes, or practices that have the ability to cause harm or adverse health effect to a person or property. Below is a table depicting some of such examples.

Table 16.1 Examples of Occupational Hazards and their Potential Harm

No.	Example of Occupational Hazard	Example of Potential Harm
1.	Things such as sharp objects or knife	Cuts
2.	Substances such as benzene	Leukemia, cancer
3.	Energy sources such as electricity	Shock, electrocution
4.	Poor conditions such as wet floor	Slipping, tripping, falling, broken body parts
5.	Processes such as welding	Metal fume fever and other related diseases
6.	Behaviour such as bullying, violence	Anxiety, fear, depression
7.	Conditions like heat, radiation	cardiovascular disease, cancer
8.	Situations such as vibration, high noise levels	Constant headaches, hearing impairment
9.	Inappropriate furniture type and positioning of tables and chairs	Bodily pains, backache, stress
10.	Continuous work overload	Stress, endless pressure and other mental ailments

16.5 Occupational Safety Hazard, Health Hazard, and Accidents

As already explained hazard is a potential source of physical injury, damage or harm to someone or something and it can take several forms such as falls. In organisations, different occupational hazard situations can present themselves however, the three notable ones are safety hazard, health hazards and accidents.

An occupational safety hazard is a situation where something is likely to cause harm or affect the safety of the employee in the process of performing his or her duties. The effect of this hazard is prompt and usually on the spot. Examples are cuts, burns, broken bones, electrical shocks, loss of limb, loss of eyesight, and others which occur instantly on the job.

Occupational health hazards, however, are those situations at the workplace that can impair an employee's physical, mental, or emotional well-being after some time. The adverse effect is usually realised after a period of time or at a later date and not immediately. For example, dust, smoke, loud noise, and vibration emanating from machines, inhaling toxic chemical, lifting of heavy things, and the like.

An occupational accident is an unexpected event that causes damage or harm to employees due to the work they perform and in course of performing their official duties. An accident is a detrimental event that occurs unexpectedly and unintentionally, examples may include unintended collisions or falls, being injured by touching something sharp, hot, or electrical, or ingesting poison. Usually occupational accidents are investigated and preventive or corrective measure adopted.

16.6 Reasons for Promoting Occupational Health and Safety

Workplace safety is very vital for every employee because all workers desire to work in a safe and well protected environment and occupational health and safety is a way of ensuring that the well-being of employees is protected. It is the duty and moral responsibility of employers to know and implement safety and health standards throughout their organisations. These measures ensure that employees are protected from exposures, incidents, or situations that will harm them physically, emotionally, socially, or mentally. Safety measures also help in preventing or minimising accidents and its resultant loss to life and property in organisations. Some major reasons for promoting health and safety at the workplace include legal requirements, economic considerations and humanitarian implications.

16.6.1 Legal requirements

There are laws, acts and other regulations in almost every country that protect both the employer and the employee and Ghana is no exception. These laws provide set of health and safety objectives and ensures that people comply with these legislations and evade prosecutions and convictions. The Ghana labour Act 2003, Act 651 for instance, is one of the laws that ensures that employers do not expose employees to conditions that can lead them to work related injuries or illnesses. The Factories, Offices and Shops Act (328) of 1970 also cover employees in respect of legal provisions. These Acts among others ensures that legally and internationally accepted standards for employee safety, health, and welfare is adhered to, attained and maintained.

It is important to note that, the employer is legally responsible for the health, safety and general welfare of employees at the workplace. Thus, as far as it is reasonably practicable, compliance with safety measures and management which falls squarely under the purview of employers, must be complied with so as to prevent both criminal and/or civil prosecutions and convictions. For instance, BBC News Services report indicated that, the Merlin group, owners of Alton Towers were fined £5million in 2016 for a safety failing in June 2015 that resulted in a crash on a Smiler ride incident with two people suffering amputations and sixteen others injured. Employees must also remain responsible and not negligent so that the workplace will remain continuously safe.

16.6.2 Economic considerations

Economic reasons are very vital considerations for promoting occupational health and safety. This is because, economically, it is always better for the workplace to remain safe and healthy due to the financial and other costs associated with employee or workplace injury. Indeed, maintaining healthy working conditions is even more profitable for organisations, because along with decreasing costs, efficient and effective safety and health management promotes productivity in organisations.

Usually when people get injured at work they stay away from work for a minimum of three days depending on the gravity of the injury and this has economic effects on the organisation and the economy as a whole. Thus ill-health, accidents and diseases related to work can result in several days of absence from work. It is essential to note that the actual cost implications on the potential loss of working hours due to accident, injury or illness is huge and it includes medical expenses, cost of overtime, replacements and/or training employees to replace wounded or sick employee. What is more, issues such as legal costs, loss of goodwill and bad publicity can be shameful or reprehensible. It is therefore more profitable for employers to follow the standards and maintain a safe work environment which can also promote employee job satisfaction, engagement and retention.

16.6.3 Humanitarian implications

It is common knowledge that almost all employers are bread winners in their families. Sadly, some of the people who are injured may never recover fully. Some may be maimed for life while others may even lose their lives, and these situations will affect their ability to take care of their family. Proactive management of health and safety in the workplace helps organisations prevent such injuries and ill-health at work. Also it is ethical and morally right that the life of every employee is well protected from any kind of harm whilst performing his or her duties. The concept of an employer owing a duty of reasonable care to his employees fully applies because employees do not expect to risk a limb, physical health or life as a condition of employment. So when employers make provision for the best care and continuously safeguard a worker's life, the grief and suffering that would have been felt by the employees as well as their family members is avoided.

It is worth noting that when an employee is injured, suffer a terrible disease or is accidentally killed, he is not the only one to suffer but also his or her family, dependents, friends, and colleagues experience the enormous impact. In some situations the accident can affect colleagues and the work they do and this can disrupt the overall performance and productivity of that department. Thus morally it is unacceptable for workers to be exposed to danger when performing their engaged duties to earn some income for their families. Employers must therefore provide some reasonable standard of care and a safe environment for their workers so that they are prevented and protected from pain and sufferings from injuries and ill health.

16.7 Benefits of Occupational Health and Safety in Organisations

Occupational health and the well-being and quality of life of working people are crucial prerequisites for productivity and are of utmost importance for the overall socio-economic and sustainable development (WHO, 1994). This implies that, creating a safe and healthy work environment hold extensive benefit for both the employer and the employee and it is important that employers create and continuously promote such workplaces. Occupational health and safety encompasses physical, emotional, financial health, and legal aspect of the workplace and it can result in the long term success of the organisation.

Some of the benefits of occupational health and safety in organisations are discussed below.

i.   It decreases injury and illness at the workplace

ii.   It reduces medical and insurance expenses, the cost of injury and compensation claims

iii.   Safety work environment boosts or maximises employee performance and organisational productivity

iv.   It ensures that employees take the right actions while performing their jobs and are more responsible

v.   It guarantees that the legal obligations of the employers are undertaken

vi.   The cost of training and re-training workers to replace the injured ones is minimized

vii.   It can lead to improved staff morale, reduced absenteeism and retention of adept staff

viii.   It minimizes litigation and helps the organisation to get a good name or image in the eyes of the general public

ix.   It can lead to good occupational health and safety practices

x.   It can lead to the incorporation of safety culture in the organisation

xi.   Safe workplaces contribute to sustainable development, which is the key to poverty reduction

xii.   It can lead to pollution control and reduction of exposures

xiii.   It can fundamentally improve the public health and prevent major diseases in the work environment

xiv.   It can lead to enhanced self-esteem, reduced stress and decreased turnover

xv.   It can lead to increased job satisfaction and improved sense of well-being

xvi.   The wage costs related to time lost through work stoppage during worker's injury as well as administrative time spent by supervisors, safety personnel and investigators after an injury can be hugely reduced.

16.8 Legislative Provisions on Occupational Health and Safety in Ghana

As with other several countries, nationally, Ghana has some legal occupational health and safety policies or requirements that both employers and employees must adhere to. Enshrined in the Ghana Labour Act 2003, Act 651 for instance is the law that ensures that employers do not expose employees to conditions that would lead them to work related injuries or illnesses. As part of the duties of employers, section 9 (c) enjoins them to take all practicable steps to ensure that the worker or employee is free from risk of personal injury or damage to his or her health during and in the course of the worker's employment or while lawfully on the employer's premises.

Similarly, employees are also obligated to exhibit their duty of care in ensuring that they work as per the employers' standard operating procedures which must incorporate safety and health requirements. For safety and health issues to be properly adhered to, it behooves on employers to ensure that their employees are aware and properly trained in such health and safety rights, responsibilities and obligations. The Ghana Labour Act provides laws regarding the general safety conditions of employees and this can be found in Part XV of Act 651 Occupational Health, Safety, and the Environment.

16.8.1 General health and safety conditions - Part XV (Section 118)

1. It is the duty of an employer to ensure that every worker employed by him or her works under satisfactory, safe, and healthy conditions

2. Without limiting the scope of subsection (1), an employer shall

    i.   provide and maintain at the workplace, plant and system of work that are safe and without risk to health;

    ii. ensure the safety and absence of risks to health in connection with use, handling, storage, and transport of articles and substances;

iii. provide the necessary information, instructions, training, and supervision having regard to the age, literacy level, and other circumstances of the worker to ensure, so far as is reasonably practicable, the health and safety at work of those other workers engaged on the particular work;

iv. take steps to prevent contamination of the workplaces by, and protect the workers from, toxic gases, noxious substances, vapours, dust, fumes, mists, and other substances or materials likely to cause risk to safety or health;

v. supply and maintain at no cost to the worker adequate safety appliances, suitable fire-fighting equipment, personal protective equipment, and instruct the workers in the use of the appliances or equipment;

vi. provide separate, sufficient, and suitable toilet and washing facilities and adequate facilities for the storage, changing, drying, and cleansing from contamination of clothing for male and female workers;

vii. provide adequate supply of clean drinking water at the workplace; and

viii. prevent accidents and injury to health arising out of, connected with, or occurring in the course of, work by minimising the causes of hazards inherent in the working environment.

3. It is the obligation of every worker to use the safety appliances, fire-fighting equipment, and personal protective equipment provided by the employer in compliance with the employer's instructions.

4. An employer shall not be liable for injury suffered by a worker who contravenes subsection (3) where the injury is caused solely by non-compliance by the worker.

5. An employer who, without reasonable excuse, fails to discharge any of the obligations under subsection (1) or (2) commits an offence and is liable on summary conviction to a fine not exceeding 1,000 penalty units or to imprisonment for a term not exceeding three years or to both.

16.8.2 Exposure to imminent hazards - Part XV (Section 119)

The provisions in this section include the following:

1. When a worker finds himself or herself in any situation at the workplace which he or she has reasonable cause to believe presents an imminent and serious danger to his or her life, safety, or health, the worker shall immediately report this fact to his or her immediate supervisor and remove himself or herself from the situation.

2. An employer shall not dismiss or terminate the employment of a worker or withhold any remuneration of a worker who has removed himself or herself from a work situation which the worker has reason to believe presents imminent and serious danger to his or her life, safety, or health.

3. An employer shall not require a worker to return to work in circumstances where there is a continuing imminent and serious danger to the life, safety, or health of the worker.

16.9 Key Principles in Occupational Health and Safety

It is very essential to state that occupational health and safety is aimed at providing comfort, security and safety whilst working or in the work environment. Several key principles underpin the concept of occupational health and safety. These principles and the provisions of both national and international labour standards are all designed and intended to achieve a critical objective of making the workplace a safe and healthy environment. As mentioned previously, occupational health and safety is an extensive multidisciplinary field. However, in spite of this variety of concerns and interests, certain basic principles that cuts across its fields can be identified and ten of such are discussed below.

i. All employees or workers have rights. Workers, their employers and governments, must ensure that these rights are protected and must endeavour to establish and maintain decent working conditions and a decent working environment. More specifically, work should take place in a safe and healthy working environment; conditions of work should be consistent with workers' well-being and human dignity; work should offer real possibilities for personal achievement, self fulfilment and service to society (ILO, 1984).

ii. Occupational health and safety policies must be established in all organisations. It must include mechanisms and elements necessary to build and maintain a health and safety culture. Such policies must be implemented at both the organisational and national or governmental levels. These policies must be efficiently and effectively communicated to all employees and stakeholders concerned.

iii. A national programme on occupational health and safety must be formulated. Once framed, it must be implemented, monitored, evaluated and occasionally reviewed. It is vital that during the formulation, implementation and review of all policies, systems and programmes all stakeholders including workers are consulted.

iv. The workplace and the entire work environments should be deliberately planned and designed to be healthy and safe. Also occupational health and safety programmes and policies must focus on both prevention and protection of life and property at the workplace. Continuous improvement of occupational health and safety must be promoted.

v. Information is vital for the development and implementation of effective programmes and policies. The collection and dissemination of accurate information on hazards and hazardous materials, surveillance of workplaces, monitoring of compliance with policies and good practice, and other related activities are central to the establishment and enforcement of effective policies.

vi. Health promotion is a central element hence efforts must be made to enhance workers' physical, mental and social well-being. This is necessary to ensure that national laws, regulations and technical standards to prevent occupational injuries, diseases and deaths are adapted periodically to social, technical and scientific progress and other changes in the world of work.

vii. It is important that action is duly taken to minimize the consequences of occupational hazards. Compensation, rehabilitation and curative or therapeutic services must be made available to employees who suffer occupational injuries, accidents and work related diseases.

viii. Education and training are vital components of safe and healthy working environments. Employers and employees alike must be made aware of the importance of establishing safe working procedures. There must be training in areas of special relevance to specific industries, so that they can address the specific occupational safety and health concerns when even it arises.

ix. A system of inspection must be in place to secure compliance with occupational health and safety and measures. The policies and all other labour legislation must be enforced ruinously enforced.

x. Workers must follow established safety procedures for their own good; employers must provide safe workplaces and ensure access to first aid; and the national authorities must communicate and periodically review and update occupational health and safety policies.

16.10 Causes and Prevention of Health and Safety Issues at the Workplace

It is in the interest of workers and their representatives to earn a living, and also to reach old age in healthy conditions (WHO, 2007). Generally, there are various health and safety efforts that give rise to right and responsibilities for both the employer and employee and obligates them to keep the workplace safe and healthy. However, in spite of the safety management efforts and the determination of both parties, there are other causes of health and safety related issues that arise mainly due to the increasing pressure to meet the demands of modern day working life. Some of these main causes and how to curb or prevent them are discussed below.

16.10.1 Physical and mental fatigue

Exhaustion, tiredness or fatigue can cause health and safety issues in the organisation. Fatigue can be caused by work-related factors or factors outside of work and/or a combination of both. Some of the factors include, inadequate rest or breaks, length of hours worked, travel time, poor quality of sleep, social life and family problems. When this issues accumulates and linger on over a period of time, it pushes individual – either the employer or employee-over and above their reasonable limits to be accurate and stay on top of the workload. This physical or mental tiredness can translate into problems like slower impulses or reflexes, weakened judgment, inattentiveness, tardy response to urgent situations and lack of paying attention to details. These negative situations can then lead to serious health and safety issues.

To minimize such situations, depending on the actual cause of the fatigue, it is very important for the individual affected, to either cut down on their jobs, take adequate breaks, take some days off or seek expert counselling. This will give them the needed rest or advice and improve their wellness.

16.10.2 Work related stress

Work-related stress is viewed as a global phenomenon affecting workers in various professions. Research shows that stress is deadly and can cause a lot of ailments like hypertension, heart attack, stroke and sometimes death. Work related stress can sometimes emerge due to longer working hours, increased competition among colleagues, higher performance expectations by both the employer and employee, poor workplace relationships and job insecurity. These avoidable expectations can lead to distractions, mistakes, incidents and accidents that can be fatal because the stressed employee is usually focused on the source of stress rather than the work to be performed.

To curb such situations, it is important to discourage unhealthy competition so that employees focus on the core business and as much as possible stay away from their stressors. Also there must be ways of creating cordial relationships in the work environment, workload issues must be discussed with supervisors and supportive teams and teamwork culture must be built, encouraged and sustained.

16.10.3 Workplace violence

It is sad to note that sometime employees face violence at their workplace and this is rather unfortunate. This can occur among co-workers or between a worker and a customer, a supplier, a disgruntled former employee, spouses or ex-spouses or any other individual who have been given legitimate access to the work environment. Some of the causes of such act include common misunderstanding, office politics, gossip and lies or any other sensitive issues. These situations sometimes result in harm, injury, fatal accidents and other serious health and safety problems. On few occasions animal bites and related injuries can also occur.

To manage workplace violence especially among co-workers, the causes of the conflict must be properly investigated, mediated and resolved on time. Where the sources of conflict are external adequate security measures must be adopted. The organisation must be strict on people they give access to their premises and internal security measures must be tightened. It is also necessary that all employees are trained to be emotionally intelligent in their dealings with people from both within and outside their organisation.

16.10.4 Slips, trips and falls

According to the United States Bureau of Labor Statistics, 2017, falls, slips and trips killed 849 workers in 2016. This presupposes that, another major cause of health and safety issues at the workplace is slips, trips and falls, and it can result in serious injuries and sometimes death. Overly smooth or slick tiles or floors are one of the major causes of slips and falls. Other factors may include lack of proper use of signage, wet floors, splashed liquids and spills that are not cleaned up. Improper lighting and improper footwear can also cause slips, trips and falls.

To address these situations, proper tile and carpets must be used at the workplace. There must be vigilance at all levels in an organisation so that the working environment is safe from harmful incidents or happenings. The work environment must be well-lit and visible at all times, spills must be quickly contained and cleaned up and proper signage must be used to avoid potential risks of falls. Safety awareness and education must be constantly promoted.

In summary we can say that no matter how observant, attentive or meticulous that both employers and employees are about observing health and safety rules at the workplace, other potential causes of workplace incidents are ever-present. It is important to prevent such situations because better health and safety outcomes can reduce injuries, workers' compensation claims absenteeism and turnover. When all safety issues are checked it will help workers to become safe and more productive.

16.11 Roles of Human Resource Managers in Occupational Health and Safety

As the World Health Organisation rightly puts it, occupational health is an important strategy not only to ensure the health of workers, but also to contribute positively to productivity, quality of products, work motivation, job satisfaction and thereby to the overall quality of life of individuals and society (WHO, 1994). In several organisations, health and safety duties and responsibilities are housed within the human resources department. Although they are not expected to know the technical aspects of workplace health and safety, human resources professionals know how to use existing resources to respond to employee concerns. They play critical roles in ensuring that employee health and safety needs are fully taken care of so that the workplace is free from risks, accidents and its associated litigation. Some of the responsibilities that human resource managers must take in order to ensure adherence to proper occupational health and safety in the organisations are discussed below.

i.   Understand the health and safety responsibilities of employers or managers, supervisors and employees within the organisation.

ii.   Develop a health and safety policy and enforce same so as to ensure that everyone in the workplace is aware of his/her responsibilities and is adhering to it.

iii. Ensure that the health and safety policies and procedures conform to the nationally accepted health and safety legislation and accepted best practices in other organisation.

iv. Ensure that employees fulfill their health and safety responsibilities as outlined in the organisational policies and programmes.

v. Integrate occupational health and safety in human resources management practices and this should include preventing work related injuries and illnesses.

vi. Develop or nurture safety culture in the workplace so as to create a harmonious, safe and stress free work environment.

vii. Establish administrative procedures that encourage employees to report any unsafe conditions and practices to their superiors without fear of being disliked or wrongly disciplined.

viii. Continue to recruit, train and retain adroit employees who care about their own well-being and the welfare of other co-workers.

ix. Develop ways of helping to reduce costs associated with losses due to accidents, injuries, absenteeism, employee health care and their compensation issues.

x. Provide advice to both employers and employees on matters of occupational health and safety and coordinate first aid training and the provision of first aid to employees.

xi. Ensure that all workers know and implement safety and health protocols expected within the organisation and establish procedures for enforcing such safety rules.

xii. Always improve upon occupational health and safety standards so as to give the organisation a good image, goodwill and increased employee morale.

xiii. Ensure that as much as practicable, employees are protected from exposures, incidents or situations that will harm them physically, emotionally, socially or mentally.

16.12 Strategies for Promoting Workplace Health and Safety

Research have revealed that, there is a huge financial and human costs associated with unhealthy workplace or organisations. Presently, some human resource persons have begun to position healthy workplace activities as a source of competitive advantage to curb increasing health care costs; assist in the attraction, and retention of skillful employees. Promoting health and safety at the workplace is very important to the employee, employer, all other stakeholders and nation as a whole. Hence every effort must be made to build and promote a strong workplace health and safety culture. There are some strategies that encourages and ensures that health and safety thrive in the workplace. They include the following;

16.12.1 Management commitment and employee involvement

The first strategy to adopt in promoting workplace health and safety is to gain management commitment and employee involvement. When managers or employers lead the way by setting up policies, assigning responsibilities and encouraging and promoting employee involvement, it sets a positive tone for health and safety issues to be adhered to and well catered for. The all-round involvement can also make training, understanding, supervision and dealing with potential hazard easy.

16.12.2 Provide basic training on workplace health and safety

Employers must provide basic training on health and safety for their employees. Although certain jobs require first aid and emergency training, and this is done during orientations, it is important that every worker is given a basic training and understanding of first aid. It is crucial that employees also know where the first aid kits containing bandages and other essential items is located at the workplace so that there will be no confusion and panic in emergency situations.

16.12.3 Collaborative health and safety efforts

Another strategy for promoting workplace health and safety is to make the procedures a collaborative effort. Employers must make employees core part of the entire process. This can be done by giving the workers the opportunity to educate their peers on specific topics such as proper use of signage, eyewear, hearing protection and first aid, depending on the hazards that pertain in that particular organisation. This collaborative effort can also make health and safety training easily accessible and interesting.

16.12.4 Create a strong workplace health and safety culture

Organisations must develop a strong workplace culture since it will go a long way to a make a great difference in times of unexpected incidence or emergency. Everyone at the workplace must have a good understanding of what tools and protocols to put in place and adopt to protect them when need be. When the culture of health and safety is encouraged and imbibed, the knowledge will help employees to better avoid injuries and/or address them more efficiently, leading to an overall healthier work environment.

16.12.5 Be an advocate

According to the World Health Organisation, occupational health and safety advocacy, must be encouraged in any organisation that employ people. Advocacy relies on primary prevention of incidents of health and safety. Promoting workplace health and safety relies on making constant efforts to ensure employees are well-prepared for hazardous situations and to mitigate unnecessary risks. This means that by advocating safe and healthy workplaces, organisations can help strengthen public health and help employees lead a more productive and satisfying lives. Advocacy also requires that both managers and employers are diligent and encourage the general wellness of all workers.

16.12.6 Make health and safety part of your business plan

As a key strategy to promote workplace health and safety, organisations must make health and safety an important part of the entire business plan and their day-to-day operations. This will yield much benefit for all employees because as the employer implements the corporate plan, health and safety awareness will become second nature to all employees. This will also give the organisation a positive image in the eyes of both workers and the general public.

16.13 Employee Well-being at the Workplace

Generally, workers represent half of the global population and contribute greatly to the economic and social value of contemporary society (WHO, 2006). Human resource professionals know that employees or human beings are very valuable. They are the heart of any successful enterprise and the success of any business whether big or small, can only thrive and continuously succeed with the help of its employees. It is therefore crucial that employee well-being is rightly catered for by their employers. Most employees devote a significant portion of their lives to their jobs and this bring meaning, structure and financial freedom and stability to their lives. Indeed, full time employees' especially spend several hours each working day on the job, and it is therefore very important that their work environment is safe, healthy and comfortable. Workers well-being is a key factor in determining an organisation's long-term effectiveness and some studies have shown a direct link between productivity levels and the general health and well-being of employees. It is only when the work environment is conducive that the long-term wellness or well-being of the employee and the organisation can be attained.

16.13.1 Well-being explained

The World Health Organisation defines health as not just the absence of disease but as a state of complete physical, mental and social well-being (WHO, 1986). The Oxford dictionary defines well-being as 'the state of being comfortable, healthy, or happy.' The Collins English dictionary also defines it as 'the condition of being contented, healthy, or successful.' Based on these definitions, it can be said that well-being relates to both physical health and a contented, comfortable, happy state of mind. Certainly, this is a state that all employees will like to find themselves in their workplaces. Well-being at the workplace can be explained as a productive work done by skilled employees in a safe and healthy work environment and in a well-managed organisation. These skilled employees find their work meaningful and rewarding. Employee well-being is therefore about enhancing or optimizing the total health of employees, and extends beyond health into happiness and job satisfaction.

16.13.2 Effect of poorly handled employee well-being

Well-being at the workplace relates to all aspects of the working life of the employee, from the sanitation, quality and safety of the physical environment, to how employee feel about their work, their working environment, relationship between colleagues and superiors, the climate and culture at work and the organisation as a whole. Therefore when employee well-being is not taken care of or poorly handled, it can lead to factors such as absenteeism, presenteesim, disputes and grievances, ill health and its associated costs, greater risks of injuries and accidents, loss of time, anxiety, stress and employee turnover. These negative factors have negative effects and do not benefit both the employer and the employee. However, when people experience well-being at work, they have more time for effective work and less time for sickness and are inspired to progress in their work and do more for their organisation.

16.13.3 Factors that increase well-being at the workplace

Research shows that any one percent effort invested in employee well-being can yield a six percent return. Employers must therefore make systematic concerted effort to invest in their employees' well-being so that both performance and organisational productivity will increase. Some of the things that can increase workplace well-being include effective communication, civility and respect shown by co-workers and managers, equality or fairness in the way and manner employees are treated, recognition and appreciation, trust, transparency and honesty exhibited by both management and employee, proactive approach to healthy living for all employees, supportive work-life balance initiatives, and opportunities for growth and development. These vital variables can increase employee morale, creativity, job satisfaction, loyalty, engagement and retention. They can also help the employers to maximize performance and make their organisations great places to work.

16.13.4 How to develop a comprehensive well-being strategy

Some organisations purposefully develop and implement well-being initiatives. Developing a cohesive well-being strategy can help recruit and retain talent; and improve employee engagement and attendance resulting in increased productivity for the company. To be able to institute well-being initiatives in an organisations some important steps such as discussed below can be adopted.

i.   There must be deliberate planning on the exact approach to adopt to achieve high level of wellness in the organisation.

ii.   The second key step to take is to get management to buy into and be wholly involved in the initiative. This will make is easy to secure and actually receive a budget for the programme when need be.

iii.   Next, the strategy to be adopted to achieve total wellness must be drawn. This could be short, medium or long term depending on the programme in mind.

iv.   Also, have a date to actually launch the well-being strategy. This is to outdoor the plan to the employees and where necessary inform them about their individual roles they have to play.

v.   The last step is to review and refresh the plan periodically. This can be done very well when stakeholders are allowed to make input or give feedback on the initiative rolled out.

PART TEN

EMPLOYEE RETENTION STRATEGIES

17 WORK-LIFE BALANCE: A RETENTION STRATEGY

Learning Objectives

After reading this chapter, you should be able to:

- Understand the term work-life balance
- Recognise the various forms of work-life balance arrangements
- Appreciate why work-life balance is important
- Know the positive effects of work-life balance on employees
- Comprehend the consequences of poor work-life balance
- Learn ways to achieve a balanced work-life
- Appreciate work-life balance as employee retention strategy

Introduction

Work-Life Balance (WLB) has become an essential human resource management issue in the life of today's employer and employee. This is due to contemporary challenges that the working world is currently faced with. These constraints include globalization, rapid technological advancement, constant change management efforts, dramatic increases in women labour force participation, diversity in the workforce as well as outsourcing and off-shoring demands on both workers and organisations. Indeed these present-day challenges has brought about a lot of pressure and increasing challenges on employees who needs to successfully reconcile the conflicting demands of their work and their personal or family lives.

In fact, over the past decade, an increasing number of scholarly articles have been upholding the importance of work-life balance. It is worth noting that, the most current addition to research on employee retention is how balancing work and life roles affects an employee's decision to remain with an organisation or otherwise. The demands of work and family are usually not compatible and this leads to conflict between the two domains and this can generate negative effects such as intention to leave or actual turnover. According to Deery (2008) it appears that the conflict between these important dimensions of human activity, that is, work and family, can cause both job dissatisfaction and family conflicts and hence intention to leave an organisation.

17.1 Understanding Work-Life Balance

Historically, the concept of work-life balance dates back to the manufacturing laws of the late 1800s when the working hours of women and children were restricted. In 1938, the Fair Labour Standards Act which allow people to work 44 hours per week was enacted. Research shows that the concept of work-life balance also came up around the 1960s and 1970s, but throughout this period, employers considered WLB largely as an issue for working mothers who struggled with the demands of their jobs and raising children. However, it is the Women's Liberation Movement of the 1980s which brought WLB back to the forefront to accommodate women in the work force, flexible working schedule and maternity leave.

Also, during the 1980s, recognising the value and needs of women contributors in organisations such as Deloitte & Touche and IBM began to change the internal workplace policies, procedures, and benefits. Though issues such as maternity leave, employee assistance programmes, flexitime, and child-care concerns were paramount, men also began to express work-life balance concerns. By the 1990s WLB was recognised as a vital issue affecting everyone be it women, men, parents, non-parents, families, cultures and organisations. Today WLB has become a very important intervention for both professional men and women.

Work-life balance is an important concept in the world of work that recognises that employees have essential family as well as professional responsibilities that compete with each other. Thus, there is opposition between the employee's personal, professional and family roles or commitments hence, individuals who have to work and at the same time play major roles in their homes are likely to experience conflict or face challenges with both duties. Balancing these varied needs is therefore very useful and some benefits that may accrue under work-life balance may allow employees to strike a more meaningful and potentially less stressful balance between commitments at the workplace and obligations at home or for the family.

By way of definition, a definite one is yet to be found. However, WLB can be simply explained as a method of striking a balance between the obligations and responsibilities or duties of professional life and family life. Put differently it can be said to be flexible work options that some organisations implement to help their employees balance their lives both at work and at home. These are work options that enables the employee set clear boundaries and balance family or personal and professional lives effectively. Work-life balance promotes division of time based on priorities and effectively maintaining a balance by developing reasonable time to all useful endeavours – mainly, work, family, health and vacation among others. It is an important aspect of a healthy work environment and when it is well implemented, WLB can reduce stress and motivate employees as well as increase their loyalty towards their organisation. The diagram below thoroughly explains the concept of work-life balance.

Figure 17.1: Diagram Explaining Work-Life Balance

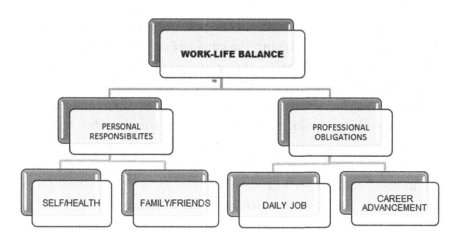

17.2 Forms of Work-Life Balance Arrangements

Usually flexibility is the basic idea behind alternative work arrangements. It is useful because when employees are given some measure of control over their work schedules, it is usually easier for them to manage non-job-related duties or responsibilities and maintain a balanced work and family life. Generally, WLB arrangements are fairly uncommon practice in some Ghanaian organisations. Meanwhile it is a very useful arrangement that can help employers retain experienced workers who are looking for greater work-life balance.

Work-life balance arrangements can take various forms depending on the needs of the employee as well as the employer. Today, jobs are not designed based on only the traditional techniques already discussed. Undoubtedly the exigencies of the times have led to the introduction of contemporary job design leanings which provides flexibility in the working life of the employee. These modern-day trends are aimed at enabling the employee to be more productive as well as balance their work and family life to minimize the associated conflicts. The work-life balance arrangements include flextime, compressed work week, job sharing and telecommuting.

17.2.1 Flexitime or flextime

Flexitime also known as flextime is the most common present-day trend in job design aimed at helping the employee achieve proper work-life balance. Basically, it refers to any arrangement that gives employees options for structuring their work day or week. Christel Kammerer a German management consultant invented the idea of flexitime. It is a system of working in which employees can vary the time they start and finish work provided they work the agreed number of hours required by their employer. Thus, in contrast to traditional work arrangements which require employees to work a standard 9:00 a.m. to 5:00 p.m. or 8:00 am to 4.00 pm daily, flexitime day, offers flexibility in arrival, departure, break times and of course core work time during which all staff members must be present at work.

It must however be noted that flexitime consists of a 'core' period of the day during which employees are required to be at work, a flexible period, and a 'bandwidth'period within which all required hours must be worked (e.g. between 6:00 a.m. and 7:00 p.m.). Core work times or core hours is very useful because it promotes continued connection between staff members and also offer opportunities for group meetings and other forms of communications to take place.

Generally, the total working time required of employees on flextime schedules is the same as that required under traditional work schedules, however, with flexitime the working hours can be adjusted as per the employee's convenience. Research shows that this kind of job design is easy to manage and the most affordable flexible work option. According to the European Commission, "Flexible working provides greater access to a more balanced work-life and improves workplace equality between men and women, giving both more flexibility over their time".

17.2.2 Compressed work week

Compressed work week is another WLB work option. The concept allows employees to do more work in lesser days per week. The work week is condensed or compressed such that the number of working hours per day is increased. It allows employees to work longer hours on some days and accumulate enough time for an additional day off. Put differently, it is an alternative work arrangement where a standard workweek is reduced to fewer than the usual five days, and employees make up the full number of hours per-week by working longer hours. For example, an employee can decide to work 10 hours a day for 4 days in a week or 12 hours a day for three days in a week.

Typically, a compressed work schedule allows an employee to work a traditional 35-40 hours work-week in less than five workdays. It is therefore an alternative schedule that reduces a standard five-day workweek to fewer number of days. It serves as an attractive strategy for employees who want more flexible work schedules and are satisfied building extra hours into their workday for their own benefit.

A small British firm, Roundhay Metal Finishers, at Batley in Yorkshire, first introduced a compressed working week for its 40 employees in 1965. The compressed work week reflects the tendency of contemporary industrial societies or organisations to look for better ways of combining social and economic goals. Many compressed work schedule options may be negotiated by the employer and employee. It provides practical expression to the preference for more extended leisure periods and also give credence for greater variety in work schedules.

17.2.3 Job sharing

Job sharing also known as work sharing is an employment arrangement or flexible work option whereby usually two part-time workers share the work of a full-time employee. The two employees voluntarily sharing the job responsibilities creates regular part-time options such as half day, alternative days or alternative week arrangement for one full time position. Put differently, a job share arrangement is a full-time job split between two individuals, each with responsibility for the success of the total job. Consequently, the two workers employed on part-time basis to perform a job normally undertaken by one person working on full-time basis, receive salary and benefits on pro-rata basis.

It is important to note that, apart from the obvious considerations required of an employee, both workers seeking to share a job need to be qualified for the job. They should also be people who can work together harmoniously in order to make the job share arrangement work. When this is achieved then the employer will have the benefit of two heads thinking about the same problem and solution. Also, creative and innovative schedules should be designed to meet the needs of the job sharers as well as the organisation.

In some situations, there are also opportunities for permanent part-time employment arrangements where an employee constantly works only 20 or 25 hours per week, and is sometimes given the right to decide which days to work and how long they work on such days. This may be rewarding because some organisation may still provide some benefits of full timers to this part timer.

Indeed, job-sharing arrangements can vary and could be 50/50, 60/40 or any comparable combination. It could also be half or split days that is, one person works mornings and the other afternoons or even alternate week that is, each employee works for one week, then takes a week off or three days per week and two days per week arrangement. The salary and benefits are however based on proportion of the job each worker undertakes. There are two basic models of job sharing namely the twin or island model.

17.2.3.1 The Twin model

The twin model also known as 'job share' involves two employees sharing a position and its associated workload. They strive to complete the required tasks but usually work on different days or hours in the day. These job sharers are jointly responsible for all duties and responsibilities of the job and must work as a team to complete the tasks. This model requires a high level of communication and collaboration between the two workers hence the name 'twin'.

17.2.3.2 The Islands model

The islands model also known as 'job split' or independent equally involves two employees sharing a position, but not its workload since they have different specialties and work independently. With this model, duties and responsibilities are split up between the employees based on each person's unique skill set thus the employees work on different tasks separately. The job sharers are then sanctioned and expected to focus on and specialise in dissimilar areas of the position. With this model, job sharers can work in isolation and have little reliance on each other to complete tasks.

Successful job sharing schedules generally place the obligation for a well-designed arrangement on the individuals sharing the job rather than their supervisor. The job sharers will have to determine whether they will be responsible for the position at different times, or if each one will be responsible for different tasks. One important feature of job-sharing is that; it can be attractive to employees who are looking for lighter workload without quitting altogether or those in search of reduced hours of work in order to provide care for their family members at home.

17.2.4 Telecommuting

Telecommuting is another work-life balance intervention. Basically it is a flexible work arrangement in which employees on a regular basis work from home or from another off-site location or non-company site. Sometimes it is even possible to work while travelling, however, in most cases, employees must endeavour to keep in contact with their offices or employers and where possible visit the office once or twice a week when need be.

Telecommuting, has other names such as e-commuting, working from home, teleworking, mobile working, remote working and flexible workplace. This simply means that, instead of travelling or commuting to a central place of work or an office building, the employee 'travels' via telecommunication links, by using a personal computer equipped with modem and communications software as well as keeping in touch with coworkers and employers through telephone and email. It must however be noted that, on a predetermined basis, a worker may occasionally physically visit the office to attend meetings and interact or confer with their employer.

Where equipment and technology are adequate and compatible to support both employer and employee, tele conferencing it is an alternative option to face to face meeting which can be explored to further minimise the need to visit the office or a central work site. It must however be emphasized that, telecommuting may not be appropriate for all employees and jobs. Indeed it is not an organisational-wide benefit that is available to all employees but to some categories of employees. For instance, receptionists in organisations cannot work from home since they are the face of the organisation and must always be on-site. Ideally, in instituting this flexible work option in an organisation, the Ghana Labour Act, or the Fair Labour Standards Act and Occupational Safety and Health Act for other parts of the world must be followed.

Figure 17.2: The Various Forms of Work-Life Balance Arrangements

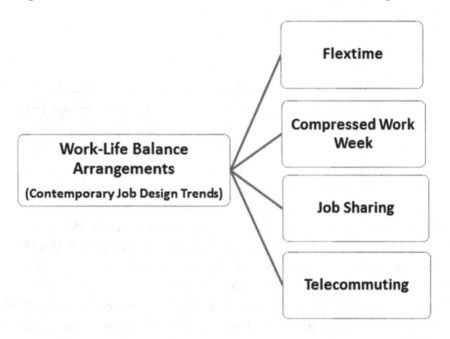

17.3 Importance of Work-Life Balance

Work-life balance can be said to be synonymous to work-family balance and it encompasses a proper prioritizing of one's work-life and family life. Upholding a healthy work-life balance is very essential because it yields a lot of benefits for both the employer and employee. This is why more contemporary employers are trying to make use of best practices to achieve the much needed balance for their employees. Some importance of WLB include the following;

- Decreased health challenges
- Increased motivation and better performance
- Better mental well-being
- Less stress and burnout
- Better engagement
- Increase productivity

17.3.1 Decreased health challenges

When organisations assist their employees to balance their work and family lives effectively, the number of employee health issues are most likely to go down. This is because some of the health issues are caused by work overload, lack of recognition, stress and fatigue, but when there is a balance in this area it can yield positive results. Research shows that, continuous imbalance over work and family issues can lead to lack of sleep, flu and other serious health conditions such as respiratory problems and stroke. According to a research conducted by University College London, over 10,000 participants stated that working overtime puts them at a 60% higher risk of heart-related problems than their other counterparts who do not work overtime. When employers are able to create work-life balance interventions as well as educate their employees to look after themselves well and find the right balance, it will significantly limit employee health problems.

17.3.2 Increased motivation and better performance

Employee motivation is a very critical feature at the workplace to both the employer and the employee. It is beneficial to the organisation because it can lead to increased performance and achievement of other vital goals and objectives. However the achievement of such output and goals is hugely dependent on the employee, in fact, without motivated employees

Rebecca Dei Mensah

organisations will be at a very high risk position. When employees are motivated well, they are generally committed, satisfied, hardworking and better performers. They will rarely waste time and resources and they put in their best effort in any task they are assigned to do making them more productive. Creating work-life opportunities for employees is therefore vital since it assures them that employers are concerned about their general well-being including their family issues and this can indeed motivate workers.

17.3.3 Less stress and burnout and improved mental well-being

Generally, work-related problems can affect either the physical, emotional or mental health of a worker. Like physical well-being, the employee's mental well-being is very crucial and employers must place importance on that aspect too. The issue is really widespread and studies have shown that the dangers and risks of mental pressure could lead to a variety of issues ranging from stress-related illnesses such as high blood pressure to depression. According to the MedlinePlus Medical Encyclopedia, stress is a feeling of emotional or physical tension which occur from any event or thought that makes one feel frustrated, angry or nervous. Put differently, stress can be said to be one's body reaction to a challenge or demand and it is dangerous because when it lasts long it may damage the health of the individual involved.

Burnout on the other hand is a state of emotional, physical, and mental exhaustion caused by excessive and prolonged stress and it occurs when one feels overwhelmed, emotionally drained, and unable to meet constant demands (Helpguide International). It is therefore important that organisations put in place some work-life balance arrangements to minimize stress, work overload and constant pressure to meet deadlines. Burnout is chronic stress it is deadly and can affect the mental well-being of the employee, lead to lack of achievement, pessimism and a feeling of ineffectiveness. Once flexible work options are available and employees are duly supported, there will be less stress and burnout leading to increased mental well-being.

248

17.3.4 Better engagement

Engaged employees are rare but very useful to any organisation. Employees can be better engaged only when their employers acknowledge their hard work, promote their personal development, listen to and act upon their feedback, create a work environment free of fear and most importantly provide work-life balance arrangements for them. Engaged workforce go the extra mile in giving off their best to their organisation and become loyal advocates for products and services. Employee engagement does not mean that an employee is happy or satisfied rather it is the emotional commitment that a worker attaches to his or her organisation, its aims and objectives.

Happy employees may not necessarily be hard working but engaged employees always aim at being productive leading to improved business outcomes. Engaged employees are dedicated, hardworking and always go the extra mile, whether their superior is watching or not. When your employees are engaged, the workplace environment becomes a place of positive attitudes and behaviours. A survey by Towers Watson in 2009 showed that organisations with a higher level of employee engagement had a 9% higher shareholder return. When employers help employees to find the perfect balance between work and home there will be increase in their engagement levels.

17.3.5 Increased productivity

When workers have a balanced family and work-life they are likely to have control over their daily lives, be more focus and concentrate on performing their jobs dutifully. Thus finding and maintaining or sustaining a healthy work-life balance will improve individual health, relationships and performance which will eventually lead to increased employee productivity. Organistions that want their workers to be hardworking and productive must also ensure that they provide the necessary WLB interventions or arrangements for them.

When this flexibility is effectively arranged then instead of worrying about home and family employees will be fully focused whiles at work. Once the employee knows that their employers have their interest at heart, they will be motivated to perform well which will eventually lead to higher productivity or profitability. Thus by encouraging workers to have a healthy work-life balance, employers will end up creating an environment where everyone is dedicated to the task at hand. This will improve retention rates, productivity and ultimately profits.

17.4 Positive Effects of Work-Life Balance to Employees

Generally employees know that they will spend most of their lives working and therefore want to find satisfaction and contentment in their occupation. According to FMP Global an international payroll and HR company, a recent research shows that almost 30% of the working population, some 6.5 million employees in all, are unhappy at work and actually rate job satisfaction higher than higher pay. It is therefore imperative that employers help their workers to attain more satisfaction in their workplaces. One of the ways to achieve satisfaction is creating the opportunity for employees to balance their work and family lives. Some of these benefits include;

- Increased focus and personal growth

- Better time management opportunities

- Higher engagement

- Better health and well-being

- More value and reduced stress

17.4.1 Increased focus and personal growth

A healthy work-life balance promotes the personal growth of the employee. This is because WLB provides autonomy and empowers employees to, choose the days within a week as well as the times when they will report for work without sacrificing productivity or effective performance. Choosing their own schedules gives the employee the power to make decisions regarding their work and personal life and this is beneficial to employees because it can encourage them to become more confident about themselves and more assertive in their daily dealings. A good work-life balance arrangement can help employees to stay focus on what they can do best and provides opportunities for them to become more accountable at the workplace leading to personal growth.

17.4.2 Better time management opportunities

Flexible working hours which is one of the WLB practices provide options for employees and encourage them to manage their time more effectively which in turn become beneficial to both them and their organisation. With WLB arrangements, employees are able to report to work when they are most productive, and are able to increase their performance and complete tasks on time. This can make workers more productive and also allow them to achieve more within a day. Flexible work options also give employees the opportunity to rightly divide their time among different tasks and still make time to attend to personal matters at home without sacrificing efficiency and work.

17.4.3 Higher engagement

For today's organisations to be able to thrive and achieve their purposes, they must appropriately leverage the competencies of adroit employees and be interested in their welfare so as to enjoy benefits such as employee engagement. A balanced work and family life brings about contentment which is also one of the foundations of employee engagement. Employee engagement is the extent to which employees feel passionate about their jobs, show commitment to the organisation, and put in discretionary efforts to help the employer to succeed. Thus, employees who achieve WLB are more likely to be engaged.

17.4.4 Better health and well-being

Successfully balancing work and personal or family life will ultimately lead to better health and well-being. When employers offer flexible work options and benefits, employees will feel more thought about and valued. It is common knowledge that when there is less pressure to meet deadlines as well as reduced work overload due to WLB arrangements, workers feel better and in control of their lives and this can lead to better health and well-being. Certainly, a healthy work-life balance is a foundation of personal well-being because work is principal in the daily lives of many people. When employees feel healthy and have a sense of improved well-being it will obviously reflect in their performance and devotion to work.

17.4.5 Reduced stress

Most of the times, the efforts one need to put in their daily work naturally makes working stressful. Hence combining work with other personal or family issues is even more nerve-racking and can affect employee mental health and performance. However, when employers are able to provide a better WLB arrangement for the employee it can lower their level of stress and help better manage their daily lives. Stress is deadly and a high level of it can lead to even more dangerous health conditions. A well thought out flexible arrangement can lead to reduced stress, minimal medical conditions, healthier and happier employees.

17.5 Positive Results of Work-life Balance to Employers

Employers with healthy work-life balance arrangements will usually end up becoming more profitable and successful. Work-life balance is an effective management of work which is remunerated and the personal or social responsibilities which an individual is expected to perform. Work-life balance presents the following positive results to employers or organisations;

- Improved employee retention
- Higher employee engagement
- Strong brand name or reputation
- Increased morale and reduced absenteeism
- Increased productivity and profitability

17.5.1 Improved employee retention

One of the positive results of WLB to employers is that it can lead to improved employee retention. This is important because turnover is expensive and the cost of replacing workers is high sometimes more than twice an employee's salary, of course, depending on the position being replaced. Employee turnover is costly and can negatively affect organisational effectiveness and employee morale (Kacmar, Andrews, Van Rooy, Steilberg, & Cerrone, 2006; Shaw, Gupta, & Delery, 2005). However, prudent WLB arrangements can lead to satisfied employees who will usually stay with their organisation. Again, an employee who does not want to quit but cannot also work full time due to other pressing family commitments can take advantage of either the job sharing or tele commuting arrangements of WLB, and this can lead to reduction in turnover. By boosting staff retention through promoting healthy work-life balance, organisations become attractive even to potential new employees and talents. Happy and healthy employees have proven to result in better productivity and less turnover. Thus, the end result of providing beneficial WLB arrangements is that employers will boost employee retention levels by retaining talented, adept and well-motivated employees who truly want to be a part of the organisation.

17.5.2 Higher employee engagement

When there is a positive relationship between an organisation and its employees it usually leads to effective employee engagement. Engaged employees are asset to any organisation because they are very dedicated and passionate about their work, take initiative and always try to work for the interest and good reputation of their employers. This presupposes that when WLB interventions which proves to employees that their employers care about them are properly harnessed it can lead to higher levels of engagement. Although engaged employees are committed, trustworthy and willing to go the extra mile for their organisation without necessarily being asked to do so, it is important that they feel thought about and appreciated. Once both the employer and employee understand and assist one another, higher level of engagement will flourish. Higher employee engagement can also lead to higher efficiency, good customer service and improved productivity at the work place.

17.5.3 Strong brand name or reputation

Brand name or reputation is very important and the most beneficial intangible asset that an organisation can possess. It gives rise to noticeable positive outcomes such as employee attraction and retention, higher sales and increased profitability. Although sometimes brand name, position and reputation are built gradually and earned over a long period of time, once it is gained, it can lead to a lasting or permanent employee and customer loyalty and trust. The reputation of an organisation in the eyes of the public have far reaching consequences since it sometimes determine how current and potential job seekers, customers and other stakeholders behave towards it.

Also, a respectable reputation can make employees proud of where they work, and make them true advocates of their organisation's brand and this will continuously boost the organisations standing at the market place. It is therefore imperative that employers who want to carve a niche for themselves as well as maintain their position and reputation introduce viable WLB programmes for their employees. Indeed, promoting a healthy work-life balance in an organisation can make it a more attractive place to work thereby producing a lot of positive results to the employer.

17.5.4 Increased morale and reduced absenteeism

Another positive results that accrues to employers who introduce prudent work-life balance programmes is that they end up increasing the moral of their employees and reducing the level of absenteeism. Employees are more likely to put in extra effort when they experience better balance in their lives both at work and at home. Similarly, the kind of work that does not give employees even minimal time with their family will eventually demoralize them. Generally, high morale leads to high productivity. Morale usually encompasses one's emotions, perspective or opinion towards their organisation and its members. Employees with high morale are usually, self-reliant, disciplined, confident and constantly willing to give off their best for their organisation.

Low morale on the other hand can be lead to factors such as job insecurity and absenteeism and these can negatively affect employee performance. In some situations, when flexible work schedule is introduced it has the ability of decreasing employee absenteeism because it gives them the option to take care of themselves and still get their work done, on their own terms. Proper WLB strategies can make employees happier as well as aid employers to curtail employee stress, mitigate health-related absence and automatically reduce health care costs. It therefore behooves employers to initiate WLB strategies that will help employees balance their lives, love to be at work and boost their morale.

17.5.5 Increased productivity and profitability

The obvious positive results of WLB programmes is that it can lead to increased productivity and its associated profitability. Some theories of human resource management and motivation, suggest that motivated employees tend to be more creative and productive, and it is prudent for any management to utilize these theories in order to increase productivity and competitiveness (Stephen, 2014). Healthy work-life balance arrangements such as flexible working hours and telecommuting can make employees more productive and businesses more profitable. Two-thirds of managers' report that employees who work from home increase their overall productivity (Fundera Inc. 2020). Indeed increased performance, better productivity and improved quality of work can be achieved if the employees are satisfied and have effective WLB arrangements.

Some studies have shown that long working hours have negative effect on employee health and adversely affects cardiovascular and mental health. However, WLB interventions such as flexible working hours give employees more control and have been said to positively influence health, well-being and performance. Flexible work schedules can also boost productivity because employees are allowed to and are able to work when they are most

Rebecca Dei Mensah

productive within the day. Employers must therefore leverage on in such arrangements to achieve positive results.

17.6 Causes and Consequences of Poor Work-Life Balance

Work-life balance has always been a concern for people interested in the quality of working life and its effect on broader quality of life. This section focuses on some reasons why a number of employees experience poor work-life balance and the consequences of such situations.

17.6.1 Causes of poor work-life balance

Some of the reasons for poor work-life balance that can hurt productivity at work as well as balance at home include the under listed.

i.   Increases in cost of goods and services as well as expenses without the associated increase in wages or salaries.

ii. Expanded or increased responsibilities at work or higher demand at work due to either promotion or job redesign.

iii. Longer working hours due to the nature or type of work or due to employee dabbling in excessive workplace competition.

iv. Added responsibilities at home due to childbirth or caring for other older family members.

v.   The age of the employee as well as his or her stage in their career development.

vi. Overly demanding or perfectionist manager who sets very high goals or targets.

vii. When employees set overambitious goals which are not SMART for themselves it can also lead to poor work-life balance.

viii. Lack of structure or non-prioritizing of work and family related issues on the part of the employee can also affect poor work-life balance.

256

ix.   Poor work and general life time management skills with situations where employees have so much work to do and always have to carry work home that is, working even after working hours they never leave work.

x.   Lack or self-discipline or the inability of some employee to politely refuse to take on extra duties especially when they are of no high value thus saying no when non urgent issues come up and at the wrong time.

17.6.2 Consequences of poor work-life balance

Some of the negative or undesirable effects of poor WLB are explained below.

i.   When there is an imbalance between an employee's commitments at the workplace and obligations for their family it can lead to myriad of both physical and emotional health problems.

ii.   Another consequence of poor WLB is higher levels of tension, anxiety, depression and stress.

iii.   Poor sleeping and eating habits do sometime turn worse leading to low level of concentration.

iv.   Working extended hours can distort the balance between the life at work and home and can lead to mental and physical exhaustion.

v.   The increased fatigue due to poor WLB can affect friendship and relationships.

vi.   Research has shown that poor WLB can weaken one's immune system and further lead to leads to hurried or speedy weight gain.

vii.   Work-life imbalance can lead to poor efficiency and effectiveness levels of employees affecting the overall productivity at the workplace.

viii.   Another consequence of poor WLB is the possibility of higher levels of conflict both at home and at work.

17.7 Some Ways to Achieve a Balanced Work and Family Life

According to a Corporate Executive Board (CEB) report, in the year 2006, 53% of employees felt they had good work-life balance. However before mid-2009, CEB reported that only 30% alluded to the same fact. Today, employees are almost always busy working hard to make a living and they thus have little or no time to take care of other life related issues including family and this raises a lot serious concerns on their work-life balance.

Maintaining a healthy work-life balance is usually a challenge in today's competitive work world. Meanwhile, some studies have shown that the most often than not, productive employees are usually the well-rounded professionals with well-balanced lives both at the workplace and at home. This presupposes that work-life balance can be ranked as one of the first three most important attributes at the workplace the other two being compensation and job security.

The following are some ways or conducts that can help people to achieve a balanced work and family life.

i. Thoroughly examine your current situation, that is, how you manage your time, then trace or outline everything you do in a week both at work and personal activities. This will help you to know where you are losing time and need to make adjustments or review to save or use time judiciously.

ii. Earnestly ponder on and make a list of your top priorities, that is, things that are most important to you both at work and at home. Know what you need to continue to do and what you need to stop doing. Also take note of things you have to start doing differently.

iii. Handle and manage your professional and personal life in a sustainable way by paying attention to things that make you happy, promote your general health and well-being, development and relationships.

iv. Make time for yourself, hobbies, rest and recreation and things you are passionate about. Setting aside a day in the week for rest can be very helpful.

v. Pay particular attention to and always make your health a priority. Eat well (balanced diet), regularly exercise or take a walk (minimum three times a week), and sleep well (at least seven hours per night). These practices can among other things reduce stress, give you the needed energy as well as help you to be in good shape physically, mentally and emotionally. Also you are most likely to be more productive when you make your health a priority.

vi. Be proactive with managing your time. Always set aside some time at the beginning of each day to plan your tasks and activities for the day. Prioritize your time taking note of things that are *Urgent and important, Important but not urgent, Urgent but not important, and Neither urgent nor important*. Then set specific and measurable goals. When the goals are Specific, Measurable, Achievable, Relevant and Time bound (SMART) they can easily become reality.

vii. Nurture your personal relationships with family, friends and love ones since this can give you peace of mind and make you more effective and productive at your workplace. This is to say that, by improving your personal relationships, your productivity and effectiveness on the job will actually increase.

viii. Establish boundaries and set fair and realistic limits on what you will and will not do both at home and at the workplace and stick to it. For example, you will not spend time on office work after 11pm unless it is an emergency. Develop the habit of leaving work at work. Once the working day is over try to switch to home, family and other personal issues otherwise, before you know it, you will be working until midnight each day.

ix. If your organisation have a flexible WLB arrangements such as job-sharing, compressed work week and the like, get interested in it, find out which option can be available to you. You may find it more productive, valuable, and less stressful. This can help you enjoy your work as well as make time for family and personal needs.

x. Try to avoid overly pleasing other people. Learn to say "no" especially if there is already too much workload for you to cope with.

xi. Avoid procrastination as the old adage by the English writer Edward Young goes "Procrastination is the thief of time." As we are already aware, procrastination makes you put off very significant tasks till it is almost too late then you start to panic. So break daunting tasks into smaller units, create timelines and deadlines for yourself and make sure you stick to them.

xii. Focus on your strengths and outsource or ask for help when need be. Do not allow things to overwhelm you, keep your stressors in check. Also as much as possible, avoid unhealthy coping mechanisms such as over eating, drinking, smoking and the like.

xiii. If attaining WLB continuously elude you and you are constantly stressed, talk to someone. It can be your superior, a counsellor, mental health worker or any professional you can trust. If there are employee assistance services in your organisation, try to take advantage of such facilities.

xiv. Do not be too hard on yourself. Do not get crushed by assuming that you need to make sudden big leap or changes. Be realistic. Be yourself. At the end of each day, do some reflection and self-assessment. Ask yourself what worked well in the day and what went wrong and find out ways of improving. Sometimes applaud yourself for achieving so much in a day.

Practicing or implementing just a few of the strategies discussed above will yield positive results and benefits in both your work and family life. You need to be resolute put in effort and be determined to make a change and with continuous effort you will achieve much with time. Always remember that it is possible to have a successful professional career and a satisfying personal and family life.

17.8 Work-Life Balance and Employee Retention

Today's employees need to schedule their limited time between their work and personal or family obligations. Work-life balance can be explained as the adequate prioritization between one's work, job responsibilities and career on one hand, and personal life such as leisure, health and family on the other hand and this is a challenge to many employees. In fact, striking a perfect balance between the work which is remunerated and the personal or social responsibilities which an individual is expected to perform on a daily basis it usually difficult. Organisations therefore need to provide a supportive working environment with variety of interventions that give employees a measure of control over and allows them to balance their careers and family lives effectively.

The quality of an employee's personal life to a large extent impacts their quality of work and this makes work-life balance important to both employees and employers. Human Resource professionals are usually responsible to take the initiative for implementing policies and practices that will ensure effective work-life balance. Organisations in general must find positive ways of providing enhanced WLB arrangements in order to retain satisfied and adept employees.

Nowadays, several forward-looking organisations today are crafting policies and programmes that promote employee work-life balance. Similarly, organisation that support employee health, safety and general well-being will be successful because they will find their employee to be better performers and more productive. Indeed, tackling and enhancing employee job satisfaction will lead to retention.

Employee retention can be explained as a phenomenon where employees choose to or are encouraged to stay with their current organisations for a long or maximum period of time and do not keenly seek for other job opportunities. Usually retention is attainable when organisations put in various positive policies and practices not to only to attract employee but also make them stick and stay with the organisation for a longer period of time. Some of the key drivers or strategies of employee retention include work-life balance arrangements such as flexible work arrangements and permanent part time options, attractive compensation packages, job security, training and development as well as opportunity for growth.

Presently, retaining employees is becoming progressively more challenging for both private and public organisations. Keeping skilled and competent employees at work is becoming an increasingly difficult task in the world of work because talented employees in the global job market have the opulence to choose who to work for. Experienced and competent employees can easily be lost to competitors if proper retention policies are not put in place. Hence, most organisations are now recognising the importance of giving maximum attention to employees work and family concerns. This in effect have been shown to improve employee retention, well-being, productivity and engagement.

17.9 Benefits of Retention

Retaining competent employees is very critical for the long term growth and success of any organisation. Therefore, organisations that are determined to create a positive work environment that will support and encourage employees who want to stay with them for a long period of time, need the ability to come up with creative policies and programmes aimed at addressing employee work-life balance needs. Most often an organisation that shows that it cares for its employee's physical health, and general well-being will earn their loyalty and devotion for a long period of time. Some of the several benefits of retaining employees are listed below.

i.   Turnover and its associated substantial costs will be reduced.

ii.   There will be uninterrupted productivity which is financially beneficial for an organisation.

iii. The organisation will benefit from professionals who understand the vision of the organisation and are willing to make significant contribution to its growth.

iv.   Long term skilled employees are often reliable and are able to add substantial value to the company.

v. Retained employees know what is expected of them and how to fulfil such expectations with no training expense or constant supervision.

vi. There is usually reduced or no training need for employees who have stayed with the organisation for a long time.

vii. Unlike new hires, long term employees are mostly confident to carry out their day-to-day tasks or responsibilities and are able to meet deadlines.

17.10 Key Drivers of Employee Retention

Research shows that almost 90% of HR leaders know the importance of employee retention and consider it a major concern. Different organisations may have different things that drive retention. It is therefore imperative for organisation to craft their retention strategies based on their unique strategy and needs. However, the following are some major drivers of employee retention that organisations can focus on.

17.10.1 Work-life balance arrangements

Give employees some level of flexibility and control over their work schedules so that they can also manage their non-work related pressures and responsibilities

17.10.2 Attractive compensation packages

Offer competitive salary, benefits and other incentives. These packages may include health insurance, wellness programmes, paid holidays and bonuses. Once they are well paid for their performance and their efforts are duly acknowledged most employees will stick around or remain for a long time.

17.10.3 Job security

Most employees would not want to work with organisations that have a history of constantly laying people off. Job security is thus a very important consideration and a vital driver of retention. Indeed employees with immediate family obligations will be particular about the security of their job.

17.10.4 Training and career development

Giving employees opportunities for training and career enhancement is a great motivator and a key retention drive. Employees could further develop in their roles through workshops, seminars and other professional or academic training. This can help employees to broaden their current skills, abilities and scope.

17.10.5 Opportunity for growth

According to Francis Bacon "A wise man will make more opportunities than he finds." Ordinarily, every employee will want to grow or climb up higher in their jobs. Therefore, if an organisation is not able to provide such an opportunity it is very likely that the employee will leave to another organisation where that need will be provided. It is thus important that employers make the growth of their employees a priority since it can boost retention.

17.10.6 Good working environment and clear channels of communication

Nice working environment and clear channels of communication are other retention strategies that can be considered. Most employees will want to have a nice working environment since they spend several hours each day in these offices. Also employees are happy when they know who to channel their grievance to as well as where to get vital information or polices that pertain to their work without ambiguity.

Figure 17.3: Key Drivers of Employee Retention

IMPORTANCE OF LEADERSHIP, TEAMWORK, AND COMMUNICATION IN CONTEMPORARY ORGANISATIONS

18 LEADERSHIP IN ORGANISATIONS

Learning Objectives

After reading this chapter, you should be able to

- Understand the concept of leadership and approaches to leadership
- Analyse the various leadership styles in organisations
- Identify some factors influencing leadership effectiveness
- Know the satisfaction and frustration of leaders
- Describe the main sources of power in organisations
- Identify some influence tactics that leadership use in organisations

Introduction

Leadership is a vital element in the social relationships of people at the workplace. The concept of leadership can be said to have emerged within the context of management of human resource. Effective leadership has the potential and is the key ingredient that brings about high-performing organisations. Today, global pressures such as trade liberation and its associated competition call for crucial strategies for catching up. Increasing emergence of sophisticated technology has led to industrial restructuring and major changes as to how work is organised. The rapidly changing world and new technology have created a society yearning for speed, action, and total quality in the provision goods and services. This challenge calls for strong leadership which is able to deal with all these problems. Leaders have the ability to influence people and provide an environment for them to attain team or organisational goals.

18.1 Defining Leadership

Defining leadership, however, has become a problem, and the possible reason is the fact that it involves a complex interaction among the leader, the followers, and the situation. Thus, leadership is dynamic process, influenced by the changing requirements of tasks, the group itself, and the individual members. There is no one best way of leading, and leaders need to be able to exercise a range of behaviour to maintain the role effectively.

Indeed, there are many ways of looking at the term leadership. Simply, leadership might be interpreted as getting people to do things willingly or the use of authority in decision-making. In spite of the immense amount of writing on the subject, it is still difficult to give a precise definition of leadership. However, there is some explanation on the subject.

According to Cole (2002), leadership is a dynamic process at work in a group whereby one individual over a particular period of time and in a particular organisational context influences the other group members to commit themselves to the achievement of organisational goals. Leadership can also be defined as the principal dynamic force that motivates and coordinates the organisation in the accomplishment of its objectives (DuBrin, 1995). Jones, George, and Hill (2000) also define leadership as the process by which an individual exerts influence over other people and inspires, motivates, and directs their activities to help achieve group or organisational goals.

Leadership is exercised and influenced by the particular set of circumstances which form the organisational context. The leader's principal role is to influence the group towards the achievement of group or organisational goals. Due to the importance of leadership, winning organisation actively seek out employees with leadership potential and expose them to career experiences designed to develop them for the continuous success of the organisation. In summary, leadership is;

- Influencing the action and behaviour of other

- Persuading people, not forcing them

- Getting people to work willingly, not getting things done grudgingly

- Achieving organisational goals, not just wielding power

- Building teams, creating cohesion, and resolving conflict, not just getting others to follow

- Mentoring, coaching, inspiring, and motivating, not just relating with people

- Helping group of people define their goals and find ways to achieve them

18.2 Approaches to Leadership

The three major approaches to leadership are the qualities, functional, and contingency approach.

18.2.1 Qualities or trait approach

This approach assumes that leaders are born and not made. It asserts that leadership consist of certain inherited characteristics or personality traits such as intelligence, height, articulacy, or eloquence, which distinguish leaders from their followers. It suggests that attention should be given to the selection of leaders rather than training for leadership.

18.2.2 Functional or group approach

The functional approach, on the other hand, focuses attention on the functions of leadership. It states that leadership is always present in any group engaged in a task. It views leadership in terms of how the leader's behaviour affects and is affected by the group or followers. The functional approach believes that the skills of leadership can be learnt, developed, and perfected. Greater attention is thus given to the successful training of leaders and concentrating on the functions which will lead to effective performance by the work group.

18.2.3 Contingency or situational leadership approach

This is a model of leadership that describes the relationship between leadership styles and specific organisational situation. This approach emphasises that a leader should match his or her style with situations most favourable for his or her success. When the situation is very favourable, the leader will be more effective. A variety of people with differing personalities and backgrounds have emerged as effective leaders in different situations. A favourable leadership situation is considered the most dominant factor in determining effective leadership.

18.3 Leadership Styles

There are three major leadership styles or behaviour, namely autocratic, democratic, and laissez-faire.

18.3.1 Authoritarian or autocratic leadership style

With this kind of leadership, the focus of power is with the leader, and all interactions within the group move towards the leader. It is when someone tends to centralise authority and rely on legitimate rewards and coercive power to manage subordinates. This sort of leader dictates work methods, makes unilateral decisions, limit employee participation, and controls rewards or punishment.

18.3.2 Democratic leadership style

This is type of leader involves employees in decision-making, delegates authority, and uses feedback as an opportunity to coach employees. The leader who uses this style encourages participation and relies on expert knowledge and referent power to manage subordinates. The democratic style can be further divided into two: democratic-consultative leader and democratic-participative leader. A democratic-consultative leader seeks input and listens to the concerns and issues of employees, but makes the final decision. A democratic-participative leader, on the other hand, often allows employees to have a 'say' in what is decided. Decisions are usually made by the group.

18.3.3 Genuine laissez-faire leadership style

The leader who adopts this style observes the members of his group and allows them to work on their own. There is a conscious choice or decision to pass the focus of power to members and to give them the freedom to act. He or she does not interfere but is readily available if the members need suggestions or help on any matter.

18.4 Contemporary Leadership Styles

The contemporary leadership styles include transactional leadership, transformational leadership and charismatic leadership.

18.4.1 Transactional leadership

A transactional leader is the one who clarifies subordinates' role and task requirements, initiates structure, provides rewards, and displays consideration for subordinates. His or her ability to consider the social needs of subordinates may improve productivity. This kind of leader takes pride in keeping things running smoothly and efficiently. Such leaders are usually hardworking, tolerant, and fair-minded and excel at management level.

18.4.2 Transformational leadership

A transformational leader is one who is able to get the workforce to transform the performance or fortunes of an organisation. This is the process of promoting motivation and commitment, creating a vision for transforming the performance of the organisation, and appealing to the higher ideals and values of followers. This type of leader is distinguished by a special ability to bring about innovation and change.

18.4.3 Charismatic leadership

This is a leader who has the ability to motivate subordinates to transcend their expected performance. He or she possesses an attractive, ideal future which is credible even though not readily attainable. They have remarkable ability to distil complex ideas into simple messages. Charismatic leaders possess 'a fire' that ignites followers' energy and commitment, producing results above and far beyond the call of duty. They speak to the heart of the employees, convince them, and make them part of something bigger than themselves.

18.5 Factors Influencing Leadership Effectiveness

Certain factors can influence the effectiveness of leaders, and they include the following factors:

18.5.1 Perceptual accuracy

Perception plays an important role in leadership. Leaders who wrongly perceive their employees may miss the opportunity to achieve optimal results. Usually, if they believe their employees are lazy and tend to treat them as such, they may end up not bringing out the good potential in the employees and may even end up killing any drive they may have. This situation will then have an effect on their overall performance; hence, managerial perception is extremely important.

18.5.2 Background, experience, and personality

The leader's background and experience affect the choice of leadership style. A leader who does not trust his or her followers and who has structured tasks for years will use an autocratic style. Similarly, leader who trusts their employees will give them some level of autonomy and will tend to use democratic style.

18.5.3 Expectations and style

Another factor that influences leadership effectiveness is the leader's expectations and style. A leader who prefers an autocratic approach tends to encourage followers to adopt a similar approach. Imitating the superior's example is a powerful force in shaping leadership styles.

18.5.4 Task understanding

For leaders to be effective, they must understand the task they have asked their subordinates to perform. In an unstructured task situation, autocratic leadership may be very inappropriate since the employees may need guidelines and freedom to act and accomplish the task.

18.5.5 Peer expectations

Leaders form relationships with colleagues who are also leaders. These peer relationships are used to exchange ideas, opinions, experiences, and suggestions. A leader's peers can provide support and encouragement for various leadership behaviours, thus influencing the leader in the future. The expectations of a leader's peers can also affect the leader negatively, for instance, when peers inform a leader that he is being too easy on his employees, the leader may respond by becoming very harsh and restrictive.

18.6 Satisfaction and Frustration of Leaders

The term leader has a positive connotation for most people; indeed, leaders have a lot of satisfaction in their job, but they equally face some frustrations too. Some of the satisfaction and frustrations are listed below.

18.6.1 Satisfactions of leaders

i.   Leaders experience a feeling of power and prestige; they have status and are respected even with reference to how they are addressed.

ii. They have a chance to help others by way of teaching them on the job skills, serving as a mentor, listening to personal problems, and counselling.

iii. Leaders in general receive higher income than their team members.

iv. They have the privilege or first-hand knowledge of all the important information that gets into the organisation.

v.   Leaders have the opportunity to control money and other resources in the organisation.

vi. Leaders have good opportunities for career advancement.

18.6.2 Frustrations of leaders

i.   Leaders have too many issues to deal with in the organisations.

ii. They are sometimes lonely because their position requires that they spend a lot of time on their own.

iii. Leaders have too many problems to solve, and this involves dealing with different people.

iv. There is usually too much paperwork and electronic mail to attend to.

v.   Leaders face incredible pressures to deliver immediate results.

vi.   They are expected to manage an ever-increasing personal workload.

18.7 Sources of Power in Organisations

Power is the capacity to exert influence on others. It is the potential or ability to influence decisions and control resources. Five main sources of power have been identified, and they are the reward power, coercive power, legitimate power, referent power, and expert power.

18.7.1 Reward power

Reward power is the leader's ability to reward those who comply with directives. It is power based on rewards such as pay, promotions, recognition, time off, vacation schedules, and increased responsibility.

18.7.2 Coercive power

This kind of power stems out from the fact that leaders have the authority to punish for non-compliance. Coercive power is based on the fear that the leader can reprimand, demote, withhold pay increases, suspend, or dismiss the employees.

18.7.3 Legitimate power

This is the kind of power a leader has because of his or her position in an organisation. Leaders have a lawful right to expect compliance. It is based on the position the individual occupies.

18.7.4 Referent power

Referent power also known as charisma is when a leader's personality becomes the reason for compliance. Leaders who possess this kind of power are admired and respected because of some personal characteristic. Role models have referent power over those who identify closely with them.

18.7.5 Expert power

A leader with expert power is the one with special knowledge or expertise. Such leaders have credibility and clear evidence of skill or talent. The expertise in this case could be special knowledge in technology or sometime meta-abilities.

The five sources of power can exert compliance, commitment, or resistance. This is depicted in figure 18.1.

- Compliance is the situation where employees obey orders and carry out instructions, although they may personally disagree with them and so may not be enthusiastic.

- Commitment is achieved when employees share the leader's point of view and enthusiastically carry out instructions.

- Resistance is the state where employees will deliberately try to avoid carrying out instructions or will attempt to disobey orders.

Figure 18.1: Sources of Power and What They Emit

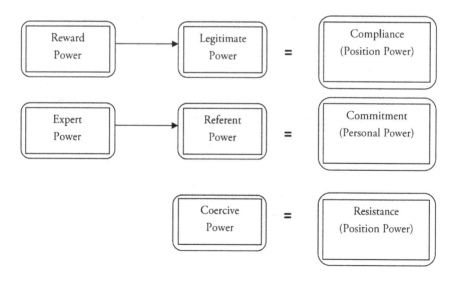

18.8 Leadership Influence Tactics

Leadership tactics has to do with how they get other employees to carry out the leader's wishes. Whiles some of the tactics are quite friendly or soft, others are hard tactics and involve overt pressure. The following are nine influence tactics:

1. **Rational persuasion:** This is where leaders try to convince others with reason, logic, or facts.

2. **Inspirational appeals:** It is the situation where leaders try to build enthusiasm by appealing to the emotions and values of others.

3. **Consultation:** It is a tactics used when leaders try to get others to participate in planning and making decisions and changes in the organisation.

4. **Integration:** It has to do with occasions where leaders try to get others in a good mood prior to making a request. They try to be friendly and helpful making it difficult for the other party to refuse to help.

5. **Personal appeals:** This is where leaders refer to friendship and loyalty when making a request.

6. **Exchange:** It is a tactics used where leaders make express or implied promises and trade favours.

7. **Coalition:** It is an influence tactics of getting others to support a leader's effort to persuade someone.

8. **Pressure means:** It is demanding compliance or using intimidation or threats.

9. **Legitimating:** It is an influence tactics based on request on one's authority or right, organisational rules, or expressing or implying support from superiors.

19 TEAM DYNAMICS AND ORGANISATIONAL EFFECTIVENESS

Learning Objectives

After reading this chapter, you should be able to

- Differentiate between teams and groups

- Identify the various types of teams in organisations

- Understand the features to consider in designing a team

- Describe the various stages in team development

- Know the advantages and disadvantages of teamwork

- Comprehend how to develop teamwork in organisations

Introduction

Developing teamwork is a very important leadership role, and team building is said to differentiate successful from unsuccessful leaders. Teams play very important roles in organisational effectiveness. Most modern-day organisations the world over are discovering that teams have the capability to make more creative and informed decisions. Teams are able to manage and coordinate work without constant or close supervision; hence, the superiors have enough time to manage other critical and strategic issues in the organisation. The keynote activity of teams is collaboration and working together. Teams are thus replacing individuals as the basic building blocks of organisations. Teams have regular interactions, shared vision, collective responsibility, and share performance goals. Leaders have major roles to play in team development; sometimes, a leader's inspiring personality alone can foster teamwork.

19.1 Defining Teams

A team is a unit of two or more people who interact and coordinate their work to accomplish a specific goal. Put differently, teams are groups of two or more people who interact and influence each other and are mutually accountable for achieving common objectives and perceive themselves as a social entity within an organisation. They are a work group that relies on collaboration of each member to experience the optimum success and achievement of a goal. Members of a team work intensely with each other to achieve a specific common goal or objective. Thus, a team is not just a group with a common aim but a group in which the contributions of individuals are seen as complementary.

It is possible for team members work effectively whiles apart, and it is said that the test of and a good and effective team is whether its members can work as a team while they are apart, contributing to a sequence of activities rather than to a common task, which requires their presence in one place and at one time.

19.2 Differences between Teams and Groups

It must be noted that there is a difference between teams and groups. All teams are groups, but not all groups are teams. Whiles a group is two or more people who interact with each other to accomplish certain goals or meet certain needs, a team is a group whose members work intensely and have regular interactions with each other to achieve a specific or common objective. The number of people who make up a team can be quite large; however, they must be fewer than fifteen. Table 14.1 depicts some differences between teams and groups.

Table 19.1: Differences between Teams and Groups

	Teams	Groups
1.	Shares or rotates leadership roles	Has a designated strong leader
2.	Have both individual and mutual accountability, thus members are accountable to each other	Have individual accountability
3.	Have specific team vision or purpose	Have identical purpose for group and organisation
4.	Accomplishes collective work products	Accomplishes individual work products
5.	Meetings encourage open-ended discussion and problem-solving	Groups run efficient meetings
6.	Effectiveness is measured directly by assessing collective work	Effectiveness is measured indirectly by influence on business such as financial performance
7.	Discusses, decides, and shares work among them	Discusses, decides, delegates work to individuals

19.3 Types of Teams in the Organisation

Many types of teams can be found or developed in organisations. The formation, however, depends on the kind of organisation involved. Teams can be permanent work teams or temporary teams. Some teams include the following:

19.3.1 Formal teams

These are teams created by the organisation as part of the formal organisational structure.

19.3.2 Committees

These are long-lasting, sometimes permanent, team in the organisational structure created to deal with tasks that recur regularly, for instance, an advisory committee.

19.3.3 Special purpose or project team

These kinds of teams are created outside the formal organisation to undertake a project of special importance or creativity. Sometimes, this kind of team could also be research and development teams. For instance, if an organisation intends to introduce a new product, a special purpose team can be formed to undertake that project.

19.3.4 Problem-solving team or quality circles

These are small teams of employees typically five to twelve within the same department who meet for a few hours each week to discuss ways of improving quality, efficiency, and the work environment. They propose solutions to management and monitor the implementation and consequences of these solutions in their workplace.

19.3.5 Virtual team

This is part of the new approaches to teamwork via information technology. They are teams that rarely meet face to face but use advanced information and telecommunications technologies so that geographically distant members can collaborate on projects and reach common goals.

19.3.6 Global team

Global team are a work team made up of members of different nationalities whose activities span multiple countries; they may operate as a virtual team or meet face to face. They also form part of the new approaches to team work.

19.4 Features to Consider in Designing a Team

There are several essentials to consider when putting a team together. This is crucial because a wrong combination will result in a dysfunctional rather than an effective team. The three main structure elements to consider when designing teams are task characteristics, team size, and team composition.

19.4.1 Task characteristics

This has to do with the characteristics of the team with reference to the particular task they have to undertake. The tasks must be clearly defined and interdependent.

Teams are generally more effective when tasks are clearly defined. It also makes it easy to implement because team members can learn their roles more quickly. Teams with ill-defined tasks require more time to agree on the best division of labour and the correct way to accomplish the goal, and this can sometimes be time-consuming and confusing.

Interdependent tasks also make a further important characteristic of a team. High task interdependence exists when team members share common inputs to their individual tasks, need to interact in the process of executing their work, or receive incomes or rewards that are partly determined by the performance of others. Moreover, highly interdependent tasks enable teams to coordinate better when working, and they work together than separately to achieve the needed results. Tasks interdependence also creates an additional sense of responsibility among team members which motivates them to work together rather than alone and to some extent unite the team.

19.4.2 Team size

The general rule is that teams should be large enough to provide the necessary competencies and perspectives to perform the work. However, teams must also be small enough to maintain efficient coordination and meaningful involvement of each member.

The optimal size will, however, depend on the amount of coordination needed for work and the organisational style. It is believed that larger teams are typically less effective because members consume more time and effort coordinating their roles and resolving differences. Moreover, individuals have less opportunity to participate and consequently, are less likely to feel they are making meaningful contribution to the success of the team. Ideally teams should be made up of a minimum of three to a maximum of twelve people and not more than fifteen for a large team.

19.4.3 Team composition

When forming teams, organisations require employees with the necessary motivation and competencies to work together. Every member must have the drive to perform the task in a team environment. Specifically, team members must be motivated to agree on the goal, work together as a team or be team players rather than being alone, and also abide by the team's rules of conduct. Thus employees must possess the skills and knowledge necessary to accomplish the team's objectives.

In putting people together to work as teams, it is important for managers to note that each person needs to possess only some necessary skills and not every skill; however, the entire team must have full set of competencies. Additionally, it is significant that the competencies of each member are made known to other team members so that they can be used effectively.

Another dimension of team composition is the diversity of the team members, that is, whether the members are homogeneous or heterogeneous. Homogeneous or identical teams include members with common technical expertise, ethnicity, experiences, or values. Heterogeneous or diverse teams, on the other hand, have members with different personal characteristics and background. Generally, heterogeneous teams experience more conflict, and it takes longer to develop such a team; however, they are more effective than homogeneous teams on complex projects and problems requiring innovative solution.

19.5 Stages in Team Development

Usually, it takes some time for members of a team to be familiar with each other and work together to achieve specific goals. Research has identified five major stages in team development. They are forming, storming, norming, performing, and adjourning. The diagram in figure 14.1 summaries the five stages of team development.

19.5.1 Forming

Forming is the first stage of team development, and it is characterised by orientation and acquaintance. Usually people tend to be polite with each other. There is a high level of uncertainty, and people are concerned with issues like what is expected of them and whether they will fit in the team.

19.5.2 Storming

This stage of team development is when individual personalities and roles and its resultant conflicts emerge. People are more assertive or sometimes rude in clarifying their roles. At the same time, members try to establish norms of appropriate behaviour and performance standards. It is the stage where the grand rules are set.

19.5.3 Norming

This is the stage of team development where conflicts which develop during the storming stage are resolved and team harmony and unity emerge. Consensus is built, and decisions on who leads the team and the roles of members are clearly set.

19.5.4 Performing

Performing is the stage where team members focus on problem-solving and accomplishing the task assigned to the team. Team members interact frequently and direct discussions and influence towards achieving team goals. The leader at this stage is usually concerned with managing high-task performance.

19.5.5 Adjourning

This is the last stage of the team development. It is where members prepare for the team's disbandment or discharge. Task performance is no longer a top priority. The reasons for adjournment may vary for situation to situation. Some may be as a result of accomplishment of the task, layoffs, or plant shutdowns. During this period, some team members may feel happy about the mission accomplished and other sad about the loss of friendship and association.

Figure 19.1: The Five Stages of Team Development

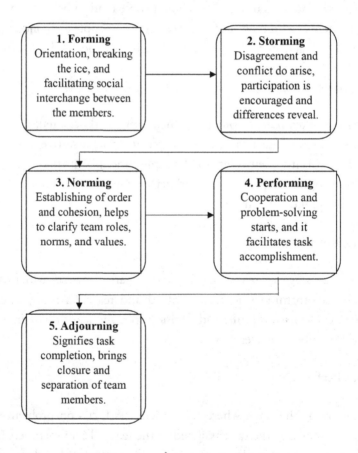

19.6 Advantages of Teamwork

i.   If several knowledgeable people are brought into the decision-making process, a number of useful possibilities may be uncovered.

ii.   It is possible to achieve synergy whereby the group's total outcome exceeds the sum of the individual's contribution.

iii.   Team decision-making is helpful in gaining acceptance and commitment since a number of people are involved in the decision-making.

iv.   Team members evaluate each other's thinking, so the team is likely to avoid major errors.

v.   Working in team also enhances many members' job satisfaction. Being a member of a team makes it possible to satisfy more needs than if one works alone.

vi.   Teamwork increases personal interactions and builds long-lasting friendship and thus meets both task and socio-emotional needs.

19.7 Disadvantages of Teamwork

i.   Usually some members face pressure to conform to team standards of performance and conduct.

ii.   Shirking or dodging of individual responsibility is another problem associated with teams. Unless work is carefully assigned to each team member, some members may not contribute their fair share to a team effort.

iii.   At worst, teams foster conflict on the job. People within the work team often squabble or quarrel about such matters as doing a fair share of the undesirable tasks within the team.

iv.   A well-publicised disadvantage of group decision making is 'group-think', a deterioration of mental efficiency, reality testing, and moral judgment in the interest of group solidarity.

v. The team atmosphere values getting along more than getting things done. They also believe they are solid and cannot be criticised by outsiders, as a result, the team loses its own power of critical analysis.

vi. Some team tend to have disagreement and differences in opinion leading to less friendliness and absenteeism.

19.8 How to Develop Teamwork in Organisations

Modern organisations require leaders to build effective teams. Strong teamwork is required for such activities as group problem-solving and achieving total quality. Unless group members work together smoothly and share information about mistakes and areas of improvement, quality targets are unlikely to be met. Leaders' behaviour and attitude that promote teamwork are discussed below.

19.8.1 Defining the team's mission

A starting point in developing teamwork is to specify the team's mission. The mission should contain a specific goal, purpose, and philosophical tone. For example, 'to plan and implement new total quality approaches to enhance our quality image and boost our competitive edge'. This is clear and informs the members about what exactly is expected of them.

19.8.2 Developing a standard for teamwork

A major strategy for teamwork development is to promote certain attitude among team members. It is important for the member to know that working together effectively is an expected standard of conduct. Developing a norm of teamwork becomes difficult if there is a strong culture of individualism in the organisation itself. However, leaders must encourage team members to treat each other as if they were customers, thus encouraging co-operative behaviour and politeness.

19.8.3 Emphasising pride in being outstanding

Building a team spirit is also a very critical element. A standard way to build team spirit is to help the team realise why they should be proud of their accomplishments. The leader should help the group to identify the task they are good at and promote it as key strength for the group.

19.8.4 Serving as a model of teamwork

An influential way for a leader to foster teamwork is to be a positive model of the team. One way to demonstrate teamwork is to reveal important information about ideas and attitudes relevant to the team's work. As a result of this behaviour, team members may follow accordingly. A leader's self-disclosure fosters teamwork because it leads to share perceptions and concerns. Interacting with team members serves as a model of teamwork because it illustrates the mechanism with which team development takes place. Sometimes frequent informal communication or interacting with team members shows that the leader is part of the team.

19.8.5 Using a consensus leadership style

Teamwork is enhanced when a leader practices consensus decision-making. When members contribute to important decisions, they feel that they are important and valuable team members. Consensus decision-making also leads to an exchange of ideas within the team including supporting and refining each other's suggestions. As a result, the feeling of working jointly on problems is enhanced.

19.8.6 Establishing urgency and demanding performance standards

Research shows that team members need to know that the team needs to perform their task urgently. This knowledge affects their behaviour such that they behave like the team have urgent, constructive purposes. Team members also want to have a list of explicit expectations. The more the urgent and relevant the rationale, the more likely the team will achieve its potential.

19.8.7 Emphasising group recognition

Recognition promotes team identity by enabling the team to take pride in its contributions and progress. Giving rewards for team accomplishment reinforce teamwork because people receive reward for what they have achieved collaboratively. The recognition accompanying the reward should emphasise the team's value to the organisation rather than the individual. As the team evolves, some individuals will be outstanding in their effort and contribution. Such individuals should be recognised and honoured for their outstanding performance.

19.8.8 Challenging the group

Another important factor is that a leader can enhance team work by feeding the team with valid facts and information that motivate the team members to work together and modify the status quo. New information prompts the team to redefine and enrich its understanding of the challenge it is facing. As a result, the team is likely to focus on a common purpose, set clearer goals, and work together more smoothly. Feeding the team with facts and information also helps to combat the problem of groupthink.

19.8.9 Reduce micromanagement

Another perspective in promoting teamwork is for the leader to reduce micromanagement or closely monitoring most aspects of the activities of team members. The leader must give the group members ample opportunity to manage their own activities. Minimising micromanagement is a key to employee empowerment, and empowered employees have the chance to manage their own activities. Research has shown that leaders of self-managed teams encourage self-reinforcement, self-goal setting, self-criticism, self-observation and evaluation, and self-expectation.

19.8.10 Soliciting feedback on team effectiveness

Another approach to build teamwork is for the leader to systematically gather feedback on how the team is working together. After rating its performance as a team, the team can discuss areas for improvement. It is important that after every meeting, there is an evaluation of the team and the leader in the area such as balanced participation in discussion, soliciting member's opinion, and member's influence in the final outcome. Feedback must be received from all members of the team and discussed so that constructive change and strong team spirit can be enhanced.

20 DEVELOPING EFFECTIVE COMMUNICATION SYSTEMS AT THE WORKPLACE

Learning Objectives

After reading this chapter, you should be able to

- Understand the concept of communication

- Identify the various stages in the communication cycle

- Describe the context of communication

- Differentiate between the lines and levels of communication

- Know some factors that can influence the choice of media of communication

- Understand communication in the computerised information age

- Analyse the concept, importance, and dangers of the grapevine

Introduction

Communication is a complex but a very important interactive tool, especially in business organisations. To be able to manage employees properly, every manager or leader must know how to communicate effectively and efficiently. Indeed, the relationship between employers and employees thrive mostly on interaction between the two parties. Communication plays a very important role in organisations because every managerial function and activity involves some act of direct and indirect forms of communication. Managerial decisions and organisational policies are ineffective unless they are well understood by those responsible for implementing them. The efficiency with which orders, instructions, and requests is communicated has a great bearing on the efficiency of an organisation and its continued success.

For today's manager to succeed or otherwise, he or she must try to build trust, promote learning, and solve problems through open and honest communication. Research shows that a manager spends at least 80 per cent of every working day in direct communications with others. Thus, forty-eight minutes of every hour is spent in meetings, on the telephone, communicating online, or talking formally or informally to employees or clients. In fact, the remaining 20 per cent of a typical manager's time is spent doing paperwork, most of which is also communication in the form of reading and writing.

Communication is a fundamental part of the major managerial activities, that is, planning, leading, organising, and controlling. With planning, the manager gathers information through writing letters, memos, reports, as well as meeting with other managers to explain the plan. In leading, managers communicate to share a vision of what the organisation can be and motivate employees to help achieve that objective. Organising is another principal function that allows managers to gather and structure information in a way that enables employees to work together to achieve organisational goals. The controlling function is when the manager evaluates performance and takes action to maintain or improve performance and this is communicated to members.

20.1 Communication Explained

Basically, communication is the exchange of information between two or more persons for the purpose of bringing understanding. It is the act of sending meaningful message from one person to another. It can also be said to be a means whereby people in organisations exchange information regarding the operations of an enterprise. Communication can also be explained as a shared meaning created among two or more people through verbal and non-verbal transaction. It may be viewed as the transfer of information from one person to another and involves listening and exchanging vocal, non-verbal, or written messages.

Communication can also be a process by which information is exchanged and understood by two or more persons, usually with the intention to motivate or influence behaviour. Communication is the means of transmitting information from one person to another in a most effective way so that the intended meaning can be readily grasped or understood.

20.2 Communication in Organisation

The ability of individuals to express themselves is perhaps the most important of all skills a person can possess. Communication in the workplace enhances the exchange of messages to facilitate structure, working relations, and creation of shared meaning among members. It boosts the image and promotes the success of an organisation. As individual employees, how well one read, write, listen, and speak affects the quality of one's personal and professional relationships. It is important for employees to know how to convey their thoughts in writing or speaking in a very large organisation.

Communication in organisation is normally through formal and informal channels. Formal channels are the official means of convening official messages within and outside the organisation. Whiles the informal is the normal chitchat we have with colleagues or customers. Normally, the organisational chart depicts the structure of the organisation and determines the communication channels. Organisational communication can also be internal or external.

Internal communication is the kind of communication between people within an organisation such as communication between employers and employees, company's shareholders, departments and other branches. It can be oral, written, or face-to-face communication. It promotes proper coordination and control of staff, employer–employee harmony, and motivation, helps employees to gain understanding, and enables employee to make inputs or suggestions.

External communication is between a company and the outside world. It involves communication between customers or clients, government departments, suppliers, consultants, and general public. It can be oral, written, or face-to-face communication. Without external communication, organisations would be isolated from potential and existing clients and suppliers. This kind of communication enhances good public relations, dealing promptly with customer complaints leading to satisfaction, and creates the needed publicity for the organisation.

20.3 Stages of the Communication Cycle

Effective communication is usually a two-way process and between the sender and receiver. The cycle of communication, however, involves six different stages. Usually, the first three processes are undertaken by the sender, whiles the next three steps are assumed by the receiver. The stages in the communication cycle are discussed below.

i. The first stage is to *conceive* the idea or message to be sent. This has to do with putting your thoughts together and thinking of the kind of message to send to the receiver. The sender who is usually the person initiating the communication does conceive the message.

ii. The second stage is *encoding* the message, and this is basically formulating your thoughts into spoken or written words, figures, or diagrams.

iii. Selecting the right *medium or channel* to communicate through is also very important because that will help you to obtain the right response. The channels could be letter, text message, phone, or face-to-face conversation. In selecting the medium, factors such as cost, nature of message, confidentiality, time, and distance are considered.

iv. *Decoding* is the stage where the receiver tries to demystify the message received. Basically, it has to do with the receiver translating the message received into understandable language or vocabulary.

v. *Interpretation* is where the receiver tries to get the actual or genuine meaning of the message which has been sent. It can be termed 'reading between the lines'. This is sometimes necessary because sometimes what the sender actually means may be different from what is spoken or written word.

vi. *Feedback* is a very important aspect of the whole cycle. It is the response or communication from the recipient to the sender. It is important to note that communication is not complete until there is some feedback.

20.3.1 Noise

Sometimes *noise* can affect the free flow of the communication cycle. Noise can affect the sending, receiving, and feedback processes of communication or message delivery. Any factor that obstructs, hinders, or interferes with the smooth exchange of information, that is, the transmission and the reception of the intended meaning of the message or the feedback, is known as noise. Noise can take different forms depending on the medium used; hence, it can take the form of poor handwriting, power cuts leading to loss of unsaved document, poor telephone reception, loud and disruptive mobile phone ring tones, facial expressions, and many more.

20.4 Context of Communication

The milieu within which communication takes place determines how formal or otherwise it can be. The environment, time, and setting where communication takes place are very vital. The four contexts are physical, social, cultural, and chronological.

20.4.1 Physical context

Physical context has to do with the location where the communication takes place. The more formal the location, the more formal the conversation and behaviour of communicators will be. The location can include the conference room, the individual's office, superior's office, canteen, or boardroom.

20.4.2 Social context

This has to do with the nature of relationship between the communicators and who is present at the time of communication. The age or position of the person being communicated to plays a very important role and determines how the sender communicates.

20.4.3 Cultural context

The cultural context can also affect communication. It has to do with the national and ethnic backgrounds of communicators. Sometimes some questions can be freely asked depending on the sender or receiver's ethnic background. However, that same question can be unwelcome or even offensive to another due to his or her background.

20.4.4 Chronological context

This context is the effect or influence of timing in effective communication. It is important for the sender to know the preferred or likely to be preferred time by recipient since this enhances the chances of success. Communicating at a time which the either other communicators deem inappropriate can affect the success of the communication.

20.5 Levels of Communication

Communication can occur in several levels notably:

i. Intrapersonal communication is one level of communication. It is really a private interaction within an individual who is initiating the communication no one else is involved at the intrapersonal stage.

ii. Interpersonal communication involves two or more persons. Other people apart from the initiator of the communication are actively involved. Examples of this in the work environment could be communication between management and union, meetings, interviews, conferences, and seminars.

iii. Group communication also engages more than two people. As the name suggest, a number of people are involved. It can be an association or committee meeting.

iv. Organisational communication is the formal groups banded together communicating with the aim of achieving their goals. It could be government agencies or non-governmental organisation.

v. Mass communication is the situation when an organisation communicates to a large group of people at the same time, for instance, through advertisements or corporate websites, intranet, or internet.

20.6 Media of Communication

The four major ways of communication can be classified as follows:

i. Written communication is any communication that is written. It is not face to face. Examples may include articles, notice, posters, reports, letters, memos, or emails.

ii. Oral communication is any communication involving spoken words. It may or may not be face to face. For instance, telephone calls, interviews, lectures, or presentations.

iii. Non-verbal communication is a type of communication that does not involve the use of words. For example, body language, gestures, facial expression, or grooming.

iv. Visual communication has to do with the eyes. This means that words are not involved in this kind of communication. For example, photographs, diagrams, charts, slides, and graphs.

These four media of communication can be classified as synchronous and asynchronous communication. Synchronous communication is where feedback in communication is instant and immediate, for example, telephone, face-to-face meetings, and presentations. Asynchronous communication is the kind of communication where response or feedback is delayed, and this mostly has to do with written communication and sometimes TV and radio.

20.7 Factors that Influence the Choice of Media

There are factors that can influence the choice of media. These include urgency, distance, time, accuracy, and cost.

i.   Urgency has to do with how fast you want your message to reach its destination; how urgent the message is will lead to choose the fastest method available.

ii.   The distance between the sender and the receiver also affect the choice of media. Whether the communicators are within the same country or abroad can dictate which means to use.

iii. Time is of particular relevance if the communicators are in local and foreign countries respectively. This is because sometimes time zones in the different countries may not be the same, for instance, when it is morning in Ghana, it is evening in Australia. It is therefore important that communicators are familiar with the right time to communicate.

iv.   Accuracy has to do with how critical is it for the message to reach the receiver in the exact state it was sent.

v.   The cost is how much money the sender or receiver has available for sending the message. Sometimes using the telephone may be more expensive than using the email.

20.8 Lines of Communication

These are formally structured ways of communicating within an organisation. The lines of communication also depend on the size of the organisation as well as the structure of the organisation. Organisational structure, chart, or organogram depicts chain of command, line of authority, and reporting systems in an organisation. The lines of communication can be vertical, horizontal, or diagonal.

20.8.1 Vertical communication

This is usually an up to down communication, which starts from superiors to subordinates and sometimes vice versa. This kind of communication follows an organisational hierarchy or chain of command. It could be a request or complaint to a superior. Vertical communication can be downward or upward.

Downward communication flows from individuals at higher levels of the hierarchy to those at lower levels. The most common downward communications are job instructions, official memos, policy statements, procedures, manuals, and company publications. Upward communication, on the other hand, provides employees with opportunities to have a say in the organisation. Here, the flow of communication is from individuals at lower levels to those at the higher levels. Widely used communication procedure includes suggestion boxes, group meetings, reports to supervisors, and appeal or grievances procedures.

20.8.2 Horizontal or lateral communication

This is communication or exchange of information between people of same or similar level in an organisation, for instance, sales and marketing managers. The success of horizontal communication depends on the cooperation of the people and departments involved. This kind of communication can suffer if rivalry and jealousy are highly prevalent. It can be distorted because it is mainly oral and the problem of technical language and jargons may arise.

20.8.3 Diagonal or network communication

With this kind of communication, information flow does not follow any hierarchy. It flows from various levels diagonally. This type of communication depends heavily on the relationships and cooperation among members of staff. In theory, network communicators are viewed as equals, but in reality, positions, authority and personality influence the way they communicate with each other.

20.9 The Grapevine

Communication is very crucial in any situation. Among other things, it builds relationships and establishes trust between people. In organisations, an extensive amount of information is transmitted and received through informal means of communication which is known as the grapevine or the rumour mill. It is unofficial information and spreads very fast through employees talking to others at canteens, to and from work, during tea breaks, and the like.

According to Pamela Angell, gossip, false stories, and malicious rumours that travel on the grapevine have about 75 to 90 percent of the information flowing as accurate. Grapevine is prevalent in organisations where communication channels are more closed than open and people are denied easy access to information, so they end up doing guess work, speculation, and gossiping.

Grapevine is usually a product of the situation than persons involved. Issues that lead to or initiate gossip include job insecurity, some benefit given to one employee over another, or uncertainty over promotion. One way to minimise the undesirable aspects of the grapevine is to improve other forms of communication. Moreover, information should be made available for employees.

20.9.1 Importance of grapevine

Though destructive, grapevine constitutes an important part of communication in every organisation. Among other things grapevine

- Serves as emotional relief to employees because they vent built-up emotions through grapevine.

- Provides opportunity for employees to talk to each other and show they care.

- Supplements official channel when they are inadequate.

- Provides feedback for management to enable them to know employees' thoughts.

20.9.2 Dangers of the grapevine

Apart from its varied importance, grapevine comes with the following dangers:

- It is damaging, and its effects are sometimes beyond repair.

- It carries incomplete information leading to misunderstanding and false impression.

- It can adversely affect management and staff relationship.

- Information circulated through grapevine is distorted and baseless and sometimes injurious to the reputation of noble people.

20.10 Communication in the Computerised Information Age

Organisations are increasingly using information technology as a means to improve productivity and customer and employee satisfaction. Consequently, communication patterns at work are rapidly changing. Some key components of information technology that influence communication patterns and management in computerised workplaces includes the internet, intranet, extranet, electronic mail, facsimile, and video-conferencing. The primary benefit of the internet, intranet, and extranet is that they can enhance the ability of employees to find, create, manage, and distribute information.

20.10.1 The Internet

The internet is a network of computer networks. It is a worldwide or global, publicly accessible series of interconnected computer networks that transmit data by packet switching using the standard internet protocol. Today, most organisations use the internet for the benefit of their employees and customers.

20.10.2 An Intranet

An intranet is an organisation's private internet. It is a private computer network that uses internet protocols and network connectivity to securely share part of an organisation's information or operations with its employees. This is usually accessible only to employees within the organisation and not outsiders.

20.10.3 The Extranet

The extranet is an extended form of the intranet. An extranet is a private network that uses internet protocols, network connectivity, and possibly the public telecommunication system to securely share part of an organisation's information or operations with suppliers, wholesaler, partners, customers, or other businesses.

20.10.4 The Electronic mail

The electronic mail is often abbreviated as email and is a store-and-forward method of writing, sending, receiving, and saving messages over electronic communication system. Both the internet and intranet can be used in this form of communication. Email is becoming a major communication medium because it has certain advantages. The email reduces the cost of distributing information to a large number of employees; messages can be sent and received almost instantaneously; and it is a tool for increasing teamwork. In addition, emails enable employees to quickly send messages to colleagues on the work floor, in another building, or in another country. It also reduces the cost and time associated with print duplication and paper distribution.

20.10.5 Facsimile (Fax)

Facsimile is a Latin word *fac simile*, which means 'to make similar' or 'to make a copy'. This is a telecommunications technology used to transfer copies of documents, especially using affordable devices operating over the telephone network. It used to be very common some years back.

20.10.6 Video-conferencing

Video-conferencing also known as teleconferencing uses video and audio links together with computers to enable people located at different

301

settings to see, hear, and talk with one another. This enables people from many locations to conduct a meeting without having to travel, thereby reducing significantly an organisation's travel expenses and time spent on decision-making.

BIBLIOGRAPHY

Aggarwal, A.P. (1992). *Sexual Harassment: A Guide for Understanding and Prevention*. Vancouver, BC: Butterworth.

Alli, B. O. (2008) *Fundamental principles of occupational health and safety* (Second edition) International Labour Office - Geneva: ILO

Armstrong, M. (2006). *A Handbook of Human Resource Management Practice* (10th edition). London: Kogan Page.

Armstrong, M., & Baron, A. (2004). *Performance Management: Action and Impact*. London: CIPD.

Armstrong, M., & Murlis, H. (2007). *Reward Management: A Handbook of Remuneration Strategy and Practice* (5th edition). London: Kogan Page.

Barker, J. (1992). *Paradigms: The Business of Discovering the Future*. New York: HarperCollins.

Bird, J. (2006). *Work-life balance doing it right and avoiding the pitfalls*. Employment Relations Today, vol. 33, no. 3, Wiley Periodicals, Inc.

Bohlander, G., Snell, S., & Sherman, A. (2001). *Managing Human Resources* (12th edition). Mason, OH: South-Western College Publishing.

Boone, L. E. & Kurtz, D. L. (1996). *Contemporary business* (8th edition). Fort Worth Dryden Press

Canadian Centre for Occupational Health and Safety

Cascio, W.F. (2006). *Managing Human Resources: Productivity, Quality of Work-Life, Profits* (7th edition). Burr Ridge, IL: Irwin/McGraw-Hill.

Cole, G.A. (2002). *Personnel and Human Resource Management* (5th edition). London: Thomson Learning.

Cox, T., and Cox, S. (1993). *Psychosocial and Organisational Hazards: Monitoring 299 and Control in Occupational Health.* Copenhagen: World Health Organisation.

DeSimone, L.M., Smith, T.M., & Ueno, K. (2006). *Are teachers who need sustained, content-focused professional development getting it? An administrator's dilemma.* Educational Administration Quarterly, 42 (2), 179–214.

Dessler, G. (2003). *Human Resource Management.* Delhi: Pearson Education Asia.

Dessler, G. (2005). *Employee Safety and Health*, Human Resource Management (10th edition) Prentice Hall Inc.

Döckel, A., Basson, J.S., & Coetzee, M. (2006). The effect of retention factors on organisational commitment: an investigation of high technology employees. *South African Journal of Human Resource Management*, 4 (2), 20-28.

Donner, G.J., & Wheeler, M.M. (2001). Career planning and development for nurses: the time has come. *International Nursing Review*, 48 (2), 79–85.

Donston-Miller, D. (2020). Workforce 2020: What You Need To Know Now Workday, BRANDVOICE.

DuBrin, A.J. (1995). *Leadership: Research Findings, Practice, and Skills.* Boston: Houghton Mifflin.

EHS Insight Resources October 17, 2019 A Brief History of Occupational Health and Safety

Encyclopædia Britannica, (2020). Britannica Digital Learning, Britannica Knowledge Systems, Merriam-Webster,

FMP Global (2018). 7 Benefits of a Work-Life Balance for Employers & Employees.

Gobler, P.A., Warnich, S., Carrell, M.R., Elbert, N.F., & Hatfield, R.D. (2002). *Human Resource Management in South Africa* (2nd edition). London: Thompson Learning.

Hackman JR, Oldham GR. (1976). Motivation through the design of work: Test of a theory. Organisational Behavior and Human Performance, 16, 250-279.

Hall, D.T. (1976). *Careers in Organisations.* Pacific Palisades, CA: Goodyear.

Hall, D.T. (1986). An overview of current career development theory, research, and practice. In D.T. Hall & Associates (Eds.), *Career Development in Organisation.* San Francisco: Jossey-Bass, pp. 1-20.

Harris, M. (2007). Careless hiring can be disastrous, *Sunday/Business Times,* November 18. p.2.

Hewitt, J. (2017). Head of Client Services Europe, Absence Management and Mental Health, LifeWorks.

HR News (2017). Why business must tackle workplace mental health.

Hulin, C. L., & Blood, M. R. (1968). Job enlargement, individual differences, and worker responses. *Psychological Bulletin, 69*(1), 41–55

Ivancevich, J.M. (1998). *Human Resource Management* (7th edition). Boston: McGraw-Hill.

Jones, G.R., George, J.M., & Hill, C.W.L. (2000). *Contemporary Management* (2nd edition). New York: McGraw-Hill.

Kacmar, K.M., Andrews, M.C., Van Rooy, D.L., Steilberg, R.C., & Cerrone, S. (2006). Sure everyone can be replaced but at what cost? Turnover as a predictor of unit-level performance. *Academy of Management Journal*, 49 (1), 133-144.

Kehl, T. (2012). 12 Key Strategies to Achieving a Work-Life Balance. IndustryWeek Library.

Kleinknecht, M.K., & Hefferin, E.A. (1982). Assisting nurses toward professional growth: a career development model. *Journal of Nursing Administration*, 12 (5), 30-36.

Lochhead, C., & Stephens, A. (2004). *Employee Retention, Labour Turnover and Knowledge Transfer: Case Studies from Canadian Plastics Sector*. Canadian Labour and Business Centre (Centre syndical et patronal du Canada).

Lowry, D. (2002). Performance Management. In J. Leopold (Ed.), *Human Resource in Organisations*. London: Prentice Hall.

Lumley, E.J., Coetzee, M., Tladinyane, R., & Ferreira, N. (2011). Exploring the job satisfaction and organisational commitment of employees in the information technology environment. *Southern African Business Review*, 15 (1), 100-118.

Marchington, M., & Wilkinson, A. (2005). *Human Resource Management at Work: People Management and Development* (3rd edition.). London: Chartered Institute of Personnel and Development.

Mathis, R.L., & Jackson, J.H. (2004). *Human Resource Management* (10th edition). Singapore: Thomson Asia.

Michael Armstrong, A handbook of Human resource management practice, (10th edition). Kogan Page Limited

Milkovich, G.T., & Newman, J.M. (1999). *Compensation* (6th edition). New York: Irwin/McGraw-Hill.

Ministry of Employment and Labour Relations Statistical Report 2005 by Rsim Directorate

National Institutes of Health (2020). U.S. Department of Health & Human Services.

Noe, R.A. (2005). *Employee Training and Development* (3rd edition). New York: McGraw-Hill.

Noise and hearing loss prevention, the National Institute of Occupational Safety and Health, Centers for Disease Control and Prevention, U.S. Department of Health & Human Services 2013

Obeng-Ofosu, P. (1999). *Industrial Relations in Ghana* (2nd edition) Accra: Ghana University Press.

Pfeffer, J. (2005). Changing mental models: HR's most important task. *Human Resource Management*, 44 (2), 123–128.

PPC Canada's Employee Webinar (2012). "Live and work well: Strategies to Achieve Balance" Root Causes of Work-Life Imbalance.

Raja, S. & Stein, S. L. (2014). Work-Life Balance: History, Costs, and Budgeting for Balance. Clinics in Colon and Rectal Surgery 27(2): 71-74. doi: 10.1055/s-0034-1376172.

Robinson, I. (2006). *Human Resource Management in Organisations*. London: CIPD.

Samuel, M.O., & Chipunza, C. (2009). Employee retention and turnover: using motivational variables as a panacea. *African Journal of Business Management*, 3 (8), 410–415.

Shaw, J. D., Gupta, N., & Delery, J. E. (2005). Alternative conceptualizations of the relationship between voluntary turnover and organisational performance. Academy of Management Journal, 84: 50-68.

Smith, M., Segal, J., & Robinson, L. (2019). Burnout Prevention and Treatment.

Snell, S., & Bohlander, G. (2007). *Training and Development: Managing Human Resources* (14th edition). Manson, OH: South-Western Cengage Learning.

Stephen, I. D. (2014). Using Motivating Theories to Enhance Productivity in Cement Manufacturing Companies in Nigeria: An Overview. The International Journal of Social Sciences, 20(1) (12) [Accessed Apr 17 2020].

The 1992 Constitution of the Republic of Ghana

The Centre for Occupational Safety, Helsinki, Finland

The Ghana Labour Act, 2003 (Act 651).

The History of the Occupational Health and Safety Act, The Windsor Occupational Health Information Service (WOHIS), Windsor, Ontario

Truss, K., Baron, A., Crawford, D., Debenham, T., Emmott, M., Harding, S., Longman, M., Murray, E., Totterdill, P. Job Design and Employee Engage Engagement. Engage for Success, 2014 Peer-Reviewed White Paper.

Wall, T.D., Clegg, C.W., Jackson, P.R. An evaluation of the Job Characteristics Model Journal of Occupational Psychology. First published: June 1978

Werner, J.M., & DeSimone, L.R. (2009). *Human Resource Development* (5th edition) Mason, OH: South-Western Cengage Learning.

World Health Organisation (1986, 1994)

Young, E. Night-(2010). Thoughts, With Life, Critical Dissertation and Explanatory Notes. [EBook #33156].

INDEX

control 4, 6, 70, 74, 85-86, 136, 188, 207, 212, 218, 223, 241, 249, 252, 255, 261, 263, 273, 274, 292

cooperation 185, 188, 298

cooperative training 162

counselling 11, 13, 142-144, 151, 180, 229, 273

cover letters 117, 121

crafts system 1, 3

cultures 17-18, 240

customers 14-15, 17-18, 36, 51, 75, 132, 148, 150, 212, 254, 286, 292, 300-301,

CV (curriculum vitae) 102, 109, 118-122, 128,

D

Delphi technique 94

demotions 11, 96

development 1, 3-6, 11, 13, 16, 18, 21-25, 27-29, 44, 50, 58, 62, 64, 75, 78-79, 90-92, 95-96, 115, 133, 140-141, 144, 153-158, 164, 168, 170-176, 178, 181, 184, 186, 190-191, 203, 208, 210, 222-223, 227, 236, 249, 256, 258, 262, 264, 277, 280, 283-284, 286-287

dignity 48-51, 227

disability 28, 31, 33-35, 37, 39, 41-42, 45, 217

discipline 9, 11, 14, 26, 44, 153, 182, 185-187, 193-194, 211-212, 257

discrimination 25-26, 28, 30-31, 33, 36-42, 44-46, 49, 108, 124, 193, 196

dismissals 11, 186, 195-196

disputes 3, 14, 136, 181-185, 192, 200, 203-204, 208, 236

downsizing 7, 17, 21-22, 156, 179

E

education 31, 33, 60, 95, 119, 126, 134, 163, 173, 175-176, 193, 198, 228, 231

EEO (equal employment opportunity) 11, 18, 25-31, 42-45, 48, 90-91, 112, 128

EEOC (Equal Employment Opportunity Commission) 30, 48-50, 55

Ergonomics 80-81

electronic mail 102, 273, 300-301

employee relations 24, 140, 181-182, 202, 204

enhancing 65, 79, 141, 181, 236, 261

employees 2-3, 5-19, 21-24, 28, 31, 33, 37-40, 43, 47-48, 51, 54-57, 62, 64-66, 68-70, 72-88, 90-96, 98-105, 107, 109-110, 113, 115-116, 128-132, 134, 136-162, 164, 171, 174-176, 178-190, 192-197, 199, 201, 204, 207-213, 215-217, 219-224, 226-258, 261-264, 268, 270-272, 274-276, 280, 282, 288, 290-292, 298-301

employers 7-8, 10, 19, 23, 28, 30-31, 36, 40-41, 45, 47-48, 55, 66, 72, 76-79, 98-100, 102-104, 108, 128-131, 133, 137, 140-141, 149-150, 162, 181-187, 189-195, 197, 199-201, 204, 209-210, 213, 215-224, 226, 228, 231-236, 239, 241, 245, 247-256, 261, 264, 290, 292

employment 10-11, 13, 18, 25-31, 33-35, 37-38, 40-45, 48-50, 58, 61, 93-95, 102-103, 107-108, 111, 114, 116, 124-125, 131, 146, 158, 172, 175, 183, 185, 194-195, 201-202, 204, 211-212, 222, 224, 226, 243-244 empowerment 22, 24, 69, 288

environment 22-23, 25, 41, 47, 49-51, 53, 56-57, 59, 73-74, 76, 78, 81, 83, 87, 132, 158-159, 165, 171, 173-174, 180, 184, 186, 192, 196, 209, 211-216, 219, 221-227, 229-230, 232, 234-236, 240, 249-250, 261, 262, 264, 267, 280, 282, 294-295

environmental scanning 91-92

Equal Employment Opportunity Act of 1972 31

Equal Pay Acts of 1963 28

equity 43-44, 132-133, 135, 137, 186-187, 204

ethnicity 33, 34, 37, 282

evaluations 150

executive search firms 102-103,

external employee recruitment 98, 105

extranet 300-301

F

facsimile 300-301

feedback 22, 69-71, 73, 75, 78, 81, 141, 144, 147, 150, 153, 160, 169, 174, 180, 237, 249, 270, 288-289, 294 296, 299

freedom 56, 74, 124, 235, 270, 272

G

GEA (Ghana Employers Association) 199-200

GFL (Ghana Federation of Labour) 198

Ghana 18, 22, 25, 27-28, 30, 32, 40-41, 48, 50, 103, 181, 191-192, 194, 196, 198-200, 204, 206-207, 210-211, 217, 220, 224, 246, 297

Ghana Labour Act 40-41, 50, 194, 204, 210-211, 217, 220, 224, 246,

global team 280

globalisation 3, 15, 17-18, 24, 156, 179

Gold Coast 191, 193

gossip 230, 299

government 14, 27-28, 31, 39, 41, 93, 95, 103, 133, 136, 183-184, 192, 197-198, 200-202, 210.292, 296

grapevine 187, 290, 299, 300

graphic rating scales 149

GREU (Ghana Railway Enginemen's Union) 198

H

halo effect error 151-152

harassment 26, 35, 40, 47-51, 53-54, 56, 76, 217,

Hawthorne Works 5

hierarchy 85, 178, 298,

HR (human resource) 2-3, 5, 8-11, 13-15, 17-23, 28-29, 42-44, 56-57, 58-59, 62, 71, 89-91, 93-94, 96-97, 99, 105-106, 108-109, 123, 125, 130, 140-141, 145, 165, 177-180, 206, 211, 231, 233, 235, 238, 255, 261, 267

HR professionals 106, 179-180,

HRIS (Human Resource Information System) 19, 97,

HRM (Human Resource Management) 1-3, 6-10, 12-19, 24-26, 28, 38, 45, 47, 55, 58, 67, 109, 130, 140, 144, 152, 171, 176, 181, 211, 238, 255,

HRM practices 18

HRP (Human Resource Planning) 10, 19, 43, 89-92, 94, 97, 145

HSWU (Health Services Workers Union) 198

human capital 17, 20-21

human relations approach 6, 188

Printed in the United States
By Bookmasters